KT-583-340

ROYA

WITHDRAWN

Chd
.04
9 J

30
24 A
22 A

R0003390

Rugby Site

WITHDRAWN

| WARWICKSHIRE COLLEGE |
| LIBRARY |
| Class No: 658 · 787 |
| Acc. No: 3390 R000 |
| Date: 4/5/05 |

Storage and Supply of Materials

Inbound logistics for commerce, industry and public undertakings

SIXTH EDITION

David Jessop BA, FCIPS

Alex Morrison CBE, FCMA, FCIPS, FCIT

WARWICKSHIRE COLLEGE LIBRARY

THE
CHARTERED INSTITUTE OF
PURCHASING & SUPPLY

 Prentice Hall

FINANCIAL TIMES

An imprint of **Pearson Education**

Harlow, England • London • New York • Boston • San Francisco • Toronto
Sydney • Tokyo • Singapore • Hong Kong • Seoul • Taipei • New Delhi
Cape Town • Madrid • Mexico City • Amsterdam • Munich • Paris • Milan

Pearson Education Limited
Edinburgh Gate
Harlow
Essex CM20 2JE
England

and Associated Companies throughout the world

Visit us on the World Wide Web at:
http://www.pearsoned.co.uk

First published in Great Britain as *Storage and Control of Stock* in 1962
Fifth edition published as *Storage and Supply of Materials* in 1991
Sixth edition 1994

© A Morrison 1962, 1967, 1974, 1981
© A Morrison and D Jessop 1986, 1991, 1994

ISBN 0 273 60323 X

British Library Cataloguing-in-Publication Data
A CIP catalogue record for this book can be obtained from the British Library.

Library of Congress Cataloging-in-Publication Data
A catalog record for this book is available from the Library of Congress.

All rights reserved; no part of this publication may be reproduced, stored
in a retrieval system, or transmitted in any form or by any means, electronic,
mechanical, photocopying, recording, or otherwise without either the prior
written permission of the Publishers or a licence permitting restricted copying
in the United Kingdom issued by the Copyright Licensing Agency Ltd,
90 Tottenham Court Road, London W1T 4LP. This book may not be lent,
resold, hired out or otherwise disposed of by way of trade in any form
of binding or cover other than that in which it is published, without the
prior consent of the Publishers.

15 14 13
07 06 05 04 03

Printed and bound in Great Britain by Bell & Bain, Glasgow

CONTENTS

LIST OF PHOTOGRAPHS

PREFACE

This text, now in its sixth edition, seems to be firmly established as the standard book for practitioners and students interested in the themes suggested by the title. It is pleasing to note that reviews are generally favourable, and it is reassuring to receive the occasional letter from individuals working in the field suggesting this or that amendment or alteration.

With the advent of 'logistics' and other approaches which view supply as an integrated process – which begins with the discovery of a customer requirement and includes all the activities associated with meeting that need – much consideration was given to the idea that the themes covered in the previous edition might be expanded to cover more fully the distribution aspects of supply. In the end, the decision was made not to do this, as the area already covered is quite wide, and there are a number of 'distribution' texts already on the market. So, although one reviewer kindly suggested that there was probably 'no better introduction to the logistics process available today' this edition is not offered as a *complete* treatment of logistics.

The contents have generally been brought up to date, with greater attention being paid to health and safety and to relevant EC directives, and the target readership is, as before, the increasing number of students pursuing logistics, supplies, materials management and related subjects, as well as those employed in the field.

Thanks are due to a number of manufacturers for permission to use their photographs or diagrams; the individual concerns are acknowledged in the captions. I am also grateful to the many colleagues and readers who have offered helpful ideas and comment – in particular, Mr Brian Wright of Plessey and Mr Terry McNamara of the University of Glamorgan.

Extracts from British Standards are reproduced by permission of the British Standards Institution. Complete copies can be obtained from them at Linford Wood, Milton Keynes, MK14 6LE, England.

David Jessop
1994

CHAPTER 1

The supply function

The control of inventories and the management of supplies have, in common with the other major branches of commercial and industrial work, become specialist activities.

The supply function has the responsibility for the receipt, custody and distribution of very large sums of money in the form of goods, and for the determination of appropriate quantities of material to be held in order that operational needs may be met in as economic a manner as is possible. The supply function must be managed and operated in a highly efficient way. The contribution that a good supply function can make to the success of an organisation is today almost universally recognised.

The stores should be considered as a *temporary* location for materials needed for operational purposes, and should be planned, organised and operated in such a way that the period of residence of each item is as short as possible consistent with economic operation. The only reasons for carrying operating stocks is that the material is needed, and that supply can not be exactly matched with demand. Figure 1.1 shows that a single transaction in direct supply replaces the three operations, receive – store – issue. One activity replaces three. Obsolete, redundant or surplus material is simply money sitting on a shelf, requiring more money to be spent on its custody. It should be pointed out that as short a time as possible may range from the hour or two that deliveries of bulk milk may remain in the receiving tanks at a processing plant, through to the several years that emergency equipment, for example a blow-out preventer in an oilfield store, can justifiably be kept. In general, if demand is steady or highly predictable, then we should store for very short periods if at all. The rapid adoption of Just-in-Time (JIT) approaches in recent years reflects the general awareness that stocks are expensive to hold, and that opportunities should be sought to make better use of the money they represent. When demand is highly unpredictable then storage for longer periods may be necessitated.

There is no standard system of management and control which can be universally recommended or applied but, in the course of time,

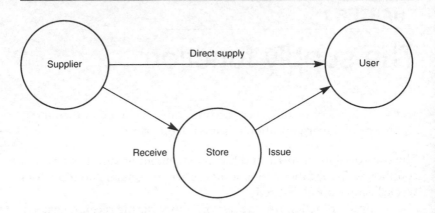

Fig. 1.1 Direct and indirect transactions

certain principles and practices of more or less general application have been evolved. This book examines at length some of these principles and practices but it must always be borne in mind that the conditions of operation are very diverse.

In a mass production unit, such as a car plant, vast quantities of materials and component parts have to be provided every day. Large sums of money are involved and it is essential to organise the materials function so that the investment is kept to the minimum. A big plant can use hundreds of thousands of pounds' worth of material each week. From the supplies point of view the most important thing is to keep the quantities of incoming goods as near as possible to the amounts the assembly lines will use daily. Shortages must be avoided or production lines will have to stop. At the same time too much must not be delivered or it will clog up the marshalling and production areas, apart from the fact that excess deliveries will tie up more capital. So the emphasis is on the manufacturing schedule and everything is governed by that. For bulky or expensive materials or components, the flow will have to be managed hour by hour and this demands a very high degree of cooperation and efficiency.

The Armed Services are different. They need to have enough equipment, ammunition and stores on hand to be able to go into action at short notice. The requirement here is not to keep the amount of stock down as far as possible, but to keep it up to the minimum operational requirement. The obvious example is a warship about to set off on a long spell of sea duty. It must be stocked up with fuel, ammunition, food, clothing and everything else that may be wanted during the voyage.

Between these two extremes there is a great variety of different organisations – wholesale and retail concerns, airlines, petroleum refineries, mining, process industries, sea, air, rail and road transport, electricity, gas and water supply undertakings, hospitals, schools, agricultural enterprises and many others.

It therefore follows that before a system for the provision of materials can sensibly be designed, account must be taken of the nature and needs of the organisation it is intended to serve.

STORES

Purpose

Taking manufacturing as an example, the primary objective of the stores function is to provide a service to the operating departments. All other stores activities, although they have their own relative importance, are subordinate to this main responsibility.

The service given can be analysed into five parts as follows:

1 To make available a balanced flow of raw materials, components, tools, equipment and any other commodities necessary to meet operational requirements.
2 To provide maintenance materials, spare parts and general stores as required.
3 To receive and issue work in progress and finished products.
4 To accept and store scrap and other discarded material as it arises.
5 To account for all receipts, issues and goods in stock.

In the general business context the stores or warehouse function performs roles beyond providing simply a subsidiary service to another function. The storehouse or warehouse can add value in a number of ways, including:

- *Breaking bulk*. Where goods are supplied in large quantities, perhaps because of economies of scale of manufacture or transportation, then it may be the case that the storehouse performs the activity of taking delivery of bulk consignments and issuing in smaller lots to customers or users. The storehouse enables the more efficient matching of demand with supply.
- *Creating bulk*. It may be the case that a good is produced in small quantities in a variety of locations, and needs to be brought together into larger lots for economic shipment to the market or users. The accumulation and aggregation of these smaller supply

quantities is another way in which a warehouse or stockyard can add value. Milk, vegetables, latex and many other natural products are brought together in this way.

- *Smoothing.* In manufacturing, we can think of the storage as an activity which enables production to be certain of having supplies of materials and components as and when needed, or we can store finished goods until the customer needs them. In both cases we are smoothing; that is to say accommodating the fact that the rate of supply and demand, and the associated timings do not exactly match.
- *Combining.* Materials in, say, a retail grocery concern are supplied from a variety of origins, yet we serve our customers best by allowing them to select according to their shopping list from the range of products that we offer. If the store did not provide the value adding function of bringing these materials together into a single location then the customer would find it impossible to enjoy any real choice as shopping would take up an impossible amount of time.

Figure 1.2 illustrates these ideas.

RESPONSIBILITIES

Economy

It has been emphasised that service is the principal objective of the stores function, but it is obviously desirable to provide that service economically. Frequently, but not always, the most important consideration here is to keep the inventory value at the lowest practicable level to economise in the use of working capital and to minimise the costs of storage. It will be readily understood that there is some conflict between the need to give a good service and the need to economise in stockholdings. On the one hand, the more stock held, the easier it is to have items available on demand; on the other hand, the more stock held, the greater the cost, though of course ordering very frequently in order that stockholding costs may be kept low can itself lead to high costs. It is necessary to seek, find and operate a satisfactory compromise between the various opposing forces. In addition, the stores organisation itself should be economically operated and cooperate with other functions to achieve savings in material and other costs wherever practicable.

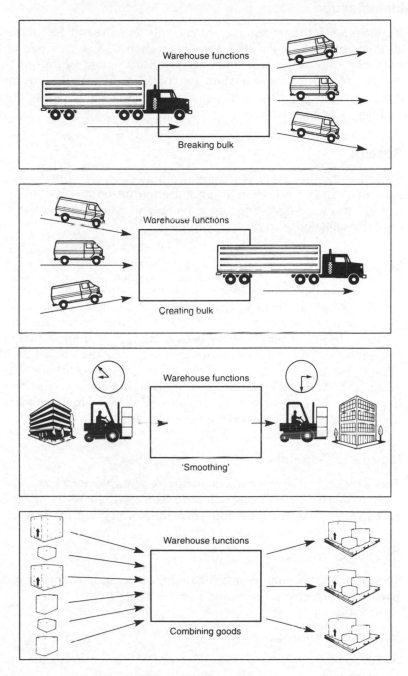

Fig. 1.2 Warehouse added value functions

Identification

Identification is the process of systematically defining and describing all items of stock. It includes the preparation of a stores code or vocabulary, the adoption of materials specifications and the introduction of a degree of standardisation. Part of this work may be done by design, planning or standards departments, and the purchasing department also has an interest.

Receipt

Receipt is the process of accepting, from all sources, all materials, equipment and parts used in the organisation, including supplies for manufacturing or operating processes, plant maintenance, offices, capital installations and finished products.

Inspection

Inspection, in this context, means the examination of incoming consignments for quantity and quality. Very often there is a separate inspection department which does this work, but otherwise goods are inspected by stores personnel. Whatever the system of inspection in force, it is the duty of the stores function to see that the inspection is done before items are accepted into stock. Quality assurance activities, and 'co-maker' relationships between buyers and suppliers have reduced the extent to which the inspection of incoming goods is undertaken, but it remains an important activity.

Issue and dispatch

This is the process of receiving demands, selecting the items required and handing them over to users. It includes also, where necessary, the packaging of issues and the loading of vehicles with goods for delivery.

Stock records

These may be manual, or maintained on a computer, and record particulars of receipts, issues and balances of stock.

Stores accounting

Stores accounting is the process of recording stock movements and balances in value.

A general purpose installation
(Courtesy: Dexion Ltd)

Stock control

Stock control is the operation of continuously arranging flows of materials so that stock balances are adequate to support the current rate of consumption, with due regard to economy. It includes the related process of provisioning, which is the means whereby instructions are given for the placing of orders. In some concerns the production control department may take a large share in provisioning, at least as far as production materials are concerned.

Stocktaking, stock checking and stock audit

Stocktaking is the process of physical verification of the quantities and condition of goods, usually on a periodic basis for the purpose of ensuring that an appropriate figure appears in the organisation's accounts. Stock checking is similar, but may be done on an *ad hoc* basis for operational reasons. Stock audit involves an external agency, and the purpose is verification.

Storage

Storage comprises the management of storehouses and stockyards, the operation of handling and storage equipment, and the safe custody and protection of stock.

ORGANISATION

Policy directive

In any enterprise it is desirable that the board of directors, or other appropriate authority, should issue a written directive covering supplies policy and organisation, clearly defining the limits within which the function operates, and conveying authority to act within these limits.

A directive is usually supplemented by departmental instructions regarding details of systems and operations, and these in turn may be incorporated into a handbook or manual containing all the standing instructions together with specimen forms and lists of duties of the personnel concerned.

Internal organisation

In a small firm the supplies function may be operated from a single office run by one manager but, in a large organisation, it is necessary to apportion the various duties to separate sections, e.g.:

1 Identification or vocabulary section
2 Standardisation section
3 Storehouse section
4 Stockyard section
5 Stock control section
6 Records section
7 Accounts section

Usually, in a large organisation, the person in charge of the stores function occupies a senior supervisory position of managerial status, being described as the stores controller, stores manager, stores superintendent or stores officer. A specimen organisation chart for a large department is shown in Fig. 1.3.

POSITION OF STORES WITHIN THE PURCHASING AND SUPPLY ORGANISATION

In the industrial field particularly, the specialisation of production and the increasing complexity of modern products and machinery requires a very high standard of organisation and performance in

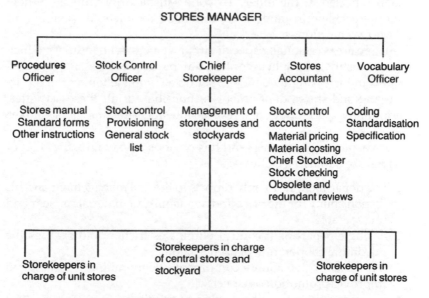

Fig. 1.3 A typical stores organisation

PURCHASING AND SUPPLY FUNCTION

PURCHASING	STOCK CONTROL	STORES
Tendering	Determination of	Storehouse design
Quotations	order quantities	Stock location
Negotiations	Determination of	Storage equipment
Supplier selection	timing of orders	Mechanical handling
Supplier development	Forecasting	equipment
Supplier rating	Analysis of demand	Checking receipts
Contracts	Scheduling	Issuing material
Sales of scrap/surplus	Statistical reports	Maintenance of stock
Expediting	Stores accounting	records
Research	Stock audit	Operation of
Invoice clearance	Review of slow moving	storehouses
etc.	stock	Operation of
	Vocabulary and coding	stockyards
	etc.	Internal distribution
		etc.

Fig. 1.4 The purchasing and supply function

stores work, and the range of materials, components and spares is continually expanding. Stores and purchasing are largely interdependent, and any inefficiency or lack of cooperation on either side is soon reflected in the other. To cope satisfactorily with the whole supply problem in modern conditions, a complete 'dovetailing' of these two functions is essential.

There are occasionally special circumstances in an industry which would justify some split in control, but the more progressive concerns show an increasing tendency to set up a completely integrated purchasing and stores department responsible for all these activities, brining the work under one responsible departmental manager (see Fig. 1.4).

An arrangement of this kind has obvious advantages, the chief of which are outlined as follows:

1 The department head only reports to the line management and his responsibility for the price and availability of materials is clear and unavoidable.
2 A single department control eliminates friction and ensures the maximum cooperation of each section.
3 It is easier to give a more comprehensive training to the staff, and improves promotion prospects.
4 It avoids duplication of records and activities.

RELATIONSHIPS WITH OTHER DEPARTMENTS

To discharge its responsibilities adequately, the stores department must actively cooperate with other departments, not only to provide a service, but to give and receive information so that the service is efficient (see Fig. 1.5). The nature of the other functions involved varies in different organisations, as does the scope and responsibility of the stores function, so that it is difficult to be precise about the relationships unless each case is considered separately. By way of example the following notes indicate the position as it is normally found in production companies.

Production department

This department is the main supplies 'customer' and it is therefore of the first importance that the services to production are satisfactory in all respects. The closest cooperation is essential not only on the

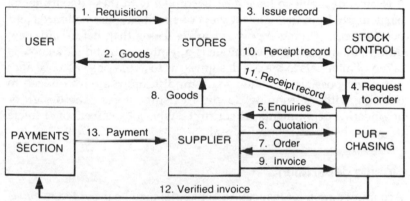

Key
1 User submits requisition to stores.
2 User is handed goods.
3 A record of the issue is transmitted to stock control.
4 Assuming that it is time to do so, a request to order is transmitted to purchasing.
5 Purchasing department sends out enquiries.
6 Quotations submitted by suppliers.
7 Order placed with selected supplier.
8 Goods sent to stores.
9 Invoice sent by supplier to purchasing.
10 Record of receipt sent to stock control.
11 Record of receipt sent to purchasing.
12 Invoice checked, and when verified sent to payment section.
13 Payment made to supplier.

Fig. 1.5 The sequence of operations in a typical purchasing/stores transaction

provision of materials but also on the stock levels to be maintained in accordance with the policy for inventory control.

The stores department provides materials, tools and other shop supplies at the required times and in the required quantities to meet the factory programme, advises anticipated difficulties or failure in supply, and notifies any substitute or surplus materials available from stock. The storehouses are ready to accept work in progress and finished goods at any time and to receive scrap, offcuts, rejected items and salvaged or reclaimed materials as they arise, so that the shop floor may be promptly cleared.

The production department sends in to the appropriate storehouses not only the work in progress and finished goods, but any excess materials, tools, fixtures and equipment not currently required, and notifies as soon as possible any impending changes in the production schedule.

Design and engineering departments

It is most desirable to have a close contact with these departments, particularly from the point of view of specifications, standards and obsolescence. Arrangements are made to see that, before any new design, modification or technique is put into production, due note is taken of materials to the old design, so as to avoid obsolescence and, whenever possible, new items and modifications are introduced to coincide with the running down of existing stocks. The design or engineering departments are consulted when obsolescent or obsolete items are being listed for disposal.

Quality department

Accommodation for inspection personnel may be provided in storehouses, and they are notified of all receipts. The stores department is responsible for holding goods received in 'quarantine' and submitting samples to inspection promptly. In return, the inspection department inspects and tests deliveries without delay, and indicates acceptance or rejection. The supplies function must work closely with the quality department if quality is approached from an 'assurance' viewpoint.

Maintenance department

The supplies service in this case consists in acquiring appropriate materials and machinery spares and being in a position to issue them as and when required. To facilitate this work, the maintenance department advises details of the forward programme on repairs and overhauls as far as possible, particularly where planned maintenance is in operation, and advises on the initial quantities of spares to be provided when any major new plant or machinery is installed.

Finance department

There is a continuous exchange of information covering verification of records and physical stock, clearance of invoices both inwards and outwards, revision of prices, supply of material-cost information, and control of working capital allocated to the financing of stock. Procedures are organised to work together effectively to control the value of inventory and cost of materials. The finance department usually provides regular periodic detailed statements of the cost of operation of the supplies service.

Transport department

The stores department is itself sometimes responsible for transport but, where there is a separate transport department, it is essential that the two work together harmoniously. The supply function reports details of loads, pick-up locations and discharge points, makes facilities available for the speedy, safe loading or discharge of goods, and provides a weighbridge service. The transport department is responsible for the ready availability of vehicles and for advising any circumstances which may delay deliveries or collections, such as breakdowns, strikes or adverse weather.

Sales department

The service provided is normally the acceptance, storage, packing and dispatching of finished products. The sales department cooperates by advising of any appreciable fluctuation in the demand for the finished goods which may affect storage accommodation, and is also responsible for giving instruction on the quantities of spare parts or other materials to be held for servicing sales already made.

MATERIALS MANAGEMENT

Purchasing and supply activities have, in most organisations, long been recognised as warranting departmental status and authority, and the fact that purchasing and supply tasks frequently involve intercourse with other parts of the organisation, as well as with the outside world, is obvious. However, the placing of purchasing and supply in the organisational framework has sometimes led to difficulties in establishing smooth flows of materials and clear channels of communication.

Increasingly, it is being reflected in organisational structures that the involvement of the purchasing and supply function with 'materials' does not begin with the receipt of a detailed specification and request to order, neither does it end when materials are delivered. It has always been the case, for example, that buying activity may involve some contribution to the 'what to buy?' debate, and that the interests of the purchasing executive in bought materials do not end as soon as the material is placed in store.

Many organisations have adopted a broad concept of procurement that goes beyond simply 'buying', and indeed is usually more than 'buying + stock control + stores management.' This concept or approach is known generally as *materials management*, though the approach taken varies greatly from company to company.

M.R. Leenders, H.E. Fearon and W.B. England describe the concept as follows:

> An organisation that has adopted the materials management organisational concept will have a single manager responsible for planning, organising, motivating and controlling all those activities principally concerned with the flow of materials into an organisation. Materials management views material flows as a system.
>
> The specific functions that might be included under the materials manager are material planning and control, production scheduling, material and purchasing research, purchasing, incoming traffic, inventory control, receiving, incoming quality control, stores, in-plant materials movement, and scrap and surplus disposal. Not all functions are necessarily included: the ones often excluded are production scheduling, in-plant materials movements, and incoming quality control.
>
> (*Purchasing and Materials Management*, 9th edn, Irwin, Illinois, 1989, p. 4.)

The main benefit which seems to arise from the adoption of the materials management approach is an improvement in communication and coordination between departments. There is less sub-optimisation, and centralised responsibility and control enables smoother and faster flow of materials. Comprehensive and linked approaches to the acquisition, storage and movement of materials can be devised and employed, thereby reducing the risk of errors at the interface between independent departments.

Materials management is not just a matter of managerial organisation. It is rather a matter of philosophy. It may not matter too much how the components of the materials function in an organisation are organised, provided that a single executive, probably called the materials manager, holds all the appropriate reins.

LOGISTICS

It is generally agreed and recognised that the term logistics has its origins in military usage, where it is used to cover the movement and accommodation of materials and personnel involved in operations. Recent years have seen a wider use of the expression logistics in the business context. However, since business usage of the term is relatively new, there is, as yet, no complete or universal agreement as to the exact meaning of the term.

Definitions of logistics abound; the following are given by way of example:

Logistics is the process of planning, implementing and controlling the efficient, cost-effective flow and storage of raw materials, in-process inventory, finished goods and related information from point of origin to point of consumption for the purpose of conforming to customer requirements. **Council of Logistics Management (CLM)(USA).**

Logistics – The area of support management used throughout the life of the product or system to efficiently utilize resources assuring the adequate consideration of logistics elements during all phases of the life cycle so that timely influence on the system assures an effective approach to resource expenditures. **The Society of Logistics Engineers (SOLE) (USA).**

Logistics – The process of managing the movement and storage of goods and materials from their source to the point of ultimate consumption. **Institute of Logistics (IL) (UK).**

It is interesting to note that the **CLM** and **IL** definitions, along with many others, which lack of space precludes, are concerned with movement and storage of goods in a general sense. The **CLM** imply a manufacturing context and the **IL** definition seems to be more widely applicable. The **SOLE** definition differs markedly, in that it suggests that the focus of logistics is on the long-term, life cycle support of products or systems, for example capital plant and equipment.

The various definitions of logistics often betray their origins by their content. There is a view that logistics is mainly about distribution,

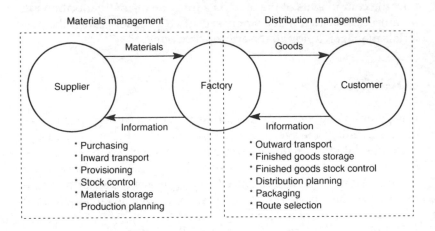

Fig. 1.6   The logistics concept

held, of course, by those bodies mainly concerned with marketing and distribution. It is a way of linking physical distribution management with earlier events in the supply chain.

Another view is that logistics is primarily concerned with acquisition and storage, and the other aspects follow on. It may be suggested that the Chartered Institute of Purchasing and Supply, in including logistics as a final professional level examination subject, views logistics in this way. Their syllabus seems to indicate this view.

The third main school of thought is that logistics is mainly concerned with support operations, and that it is very much a service activity, undertaken to ensure that expensive systems or equipment is maintained continuously through its life cycle.

Figure 1.6 gives a simple interpretation of the general view of 'Logistics'.

THE SUPPLY CHAIN CONCEPT

The Chartered Institute of Purchasing and Supply, in the professional syllabus document, define the supply chain as:

1 Specification of requirements.
2 Sourcing and acquisition of materials and services.
3 Negotiation and management of contracts and projects.
4 Control and movement of materials into and through production and other operational processes.

5 Inspection, quality assurance, handling, storage and distribution to the point of need.
6 Control and disposal of waste and redundant materials.

It may be difficult to view all of the above activities as part of a continuous process, but most of them can be seen as sequential, and dependent on each other, hence 'chain'.

The purely purchasing task is rather easier to depict as a chain, along the following lines:

1 Recognition of need.
2 Requisition prepared.
3 Requisition reviewed by buyer.
4 Specifications developed.
5 Sources located.
6 Source selected.
7 Order placed.
8 Contract formed.
9 Expediting and liaison activities.
10 Receiving and inspection.
11 Approval and payment of invoice.
12 Contract completion.

Clearly, the supply chain does not contain all of the links depicted above in every case, for example specifications will in many cases pre-exist, but the list does show a progression of dependent activities. For stock items it is possible to think of the chain as an endless one, with replenishment enabling issues to take place, and issues eventually triggering the reorder process which in time leads back to replenishment.

The term 'supply chain' is today more widely employed to describe the various organisations and processes through which a product may pass on its way from its origin as raw material(s) to its point of ultimate consumption. This flow of materials or products is sometimes referred to as a downstream flow, and is accompanied in the supply chain by the upstream flow of information from customers to suppliers.

Organisations are investing heavily in concepts, techniques and practices which will increase efficiency by removing waste in the supply chain. The term 'waste' is widely interpreted, and includes delay (of materials or information), inefficient movement (again of materials or information), or indeed any activity which does not enhance or add value to the product supplied.

The term 'supply chain management' is emerging as yet another expression to compete with 'purchasing and supply', 'materials

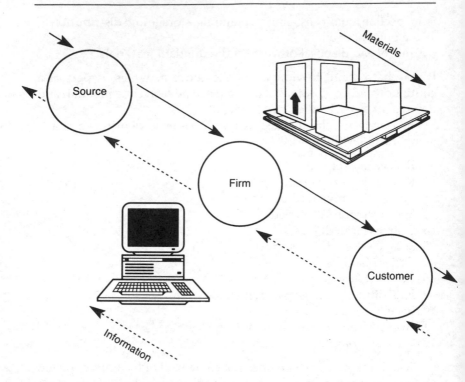

Fig. 1.7   The supply chain flow

management' and 'logistics'. The probability is that the expression will pass into widespread usage, as it encompasses the whole spectrum of materials related activities without the manufacturing connotation of materials management or the transport and distribution emphasis that some place on logistics.

The supply chain is, as has been suggested, also a *demand* chain, the supply of goods being accompanied by the flow of information in the opposite direction.

Figure 1.7 is a simplified representation of a supply chain.

THE BRITISH STANDARD GUIDE TO STOCK CONTROL

BS5729 provides a valuable summary of the basics of stock control and storekeeping and is published in five parts as follows:

Part 1: 1982. Introduction to management of stock control

This part introduces the concepts and objectives of stock control as a part of management strategy and outlines methods of setting target stock levels and their achievement. It summarises the objectives of stock control as the establishment and maintenance of the total investment in stock at the minimum consistent with:

1 adequate customer service
2 operating efficiency
3 physical limitations

taking into account the operating policies of the organisation. Part 1 includes sections on financial considerations, costs of holding stock, how stocks move, stock planning, setting the stock control rules and systems, action to achieve targets and measuring progress.

Part 2: 1981. Demand assessment

Part 2 outlines some basic forecasting procedures suitable for stock control. It is not a complete guide and examines simple methods only. This part is divided into three sections dealing respectively with:

1 Independent demand, where future requirements are uncertain and likely to be irregular, and the demand for one item is largely independent of the demand for any other item.
2 Dependent demand, where future requirements for individual items can be translated from planned production of major items or assemblies. This is basically the Materials Requirement Planning approach (**MRP**).
3 Other methods, where a selection of special problems and methods are described in brief.

Part 3: 1983. Replenishment of stock

This part of BS5729 provides guidance on the determination of a stock replenishment policy using three broad groups of reorder systems. Information is given on which parameters to adopt, both generally and on an item-by-item basis, to take account of the nature of demand, order quantities, safety stocks, replenishment lead times and related costs. Additionally, procedures are provided for selected stock control and the related concept of master scheduling. Sections are included on order quantities, reorder systems, order timing (including safety stocks and lead times), selective stock control and master scheduling. Appendices are included which explain the derivation and use of economic order quantity formulae.

Part 4: 1981. Data processing

Part 4 provides guidance on the application of data processing for use by personnel concerned with stock control. The guide draws attention to both general and initial considerations that need to be taken account of in planning a computer application. This is followed by consideration of system design and development, choice of hardware, implementation and running and evaluating a system.

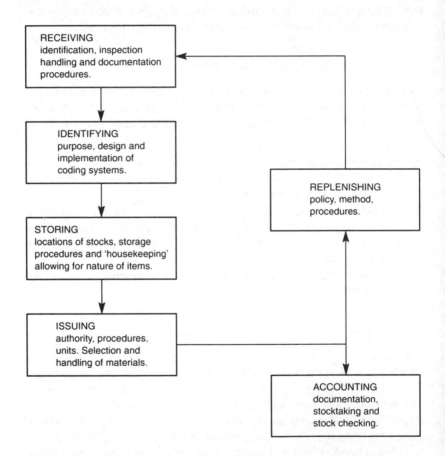

Fig. 1.8   Storekeeping: functions and key tasks (after BS5729)

Part 5: 1980. Storekeeping

This final part of the standard defines storekeeping as: 'Those procedures and means whereby goods are received, identified, stored, issued, accounted for, and replenished in accordance with defined levels of service and with due regard for the statutory requirements for health and safety'. Within this definition six major functions of storekeeping are identified (see Fig. 1.8). Each function is represented as a number of key tasks, and comments are made against each as an aid to those who are setting up a store for who are concerned with storekeeping in an organisation.

At the time of writing the possibility of BS5729 being absorbed and replaced by a more comprehensive standard covering production management is under consideration. Whether this will happen remains to be seen, though a fundamental problem is, of course, the fact that most inventories are nothing to do with production.

CHAPTER 2

Identification of materials

'Materials' is a general term describing goods which are held by organisations. The bulk of these goods is usually intended for use in connection with production or operating activities, but the expression 'materials' also covers finished products awaiting dispatch to customers, goods awaiting point of sale display, scrap and other arisings, and packages held pending return to suppliers.

Some of the terms commonly used to describe various kinds of materials are explained below.

Stock in trade is the material held by a wholesale, retail or other trading concern, usually bought in quantity at a low price to be sold as units at a higher price.

Raw materials. Basic materials which undergo changes through manufacturing processes in the course of being incorporated into the finished product are classed as raw materials – for example, coal, steel, lead, copper, rubber, cotton, wool, timber, limestone. It should be noted that the finished product of one industry may be the raw material of another. Raw materials of the right quality are most important in processing industries.

Piece parts are small components manufactured from raw materials.

Bought parts are finished parts or assemblies purchased from outside suppliers by a manufacturer either to be incorporated into his own finished product or to be resold as spares or accessories. Specialist manufacturers can produce parts in large quantities to supply a number of customers much more cheaply than any one of those customers could make them in the quantities required for his own use only. For example, in the motor industry, most car makers buy most of their major components. Other reasons for buying out may be that the parts concerned are protected by patents, or perhaps that there is not enough plant capacity available in the buyer's own works to produce them.

Equipment and spares include machines, installations and vehicles as well as their associated spare parts. This type of stock is usually most important in extractive industries, agriculture, utility undertakings and the Armed Services.

Tools may be hand tools like hammers and screwdrivers, tools used on machines, such as dies, drills, formers, milling cutters, or portable electric and pneumatic tools.

Gauges are devices for measuring the dimensions of shapes of materials or components. They are of various kinds, including calliper, plug, screw, gap and form gauges.

Jigs and fixtures are pieces of equipment especially designed for holding materials or parts while undergoing machining, fitting, assembly or other processes. They are mainly used in manufacturing industries and particularly in mass-production factories.

Work in progress comprises incomplete items in the course of manufacture, e.g. a bracket for holding the chassis of a television set where only the forming and drilling operations have been completed, but where the tapping and plating operations have still to be done before the bracket is ready for assembly. Most work in progress is to be found actually on the shop floor in the course of undergoing machining, fitting or other processes but, particularly in engineering production factories, there are frequently special work-in-progress storerooms for holding partly machined components between operations. This provides a buffer stock of components at various stages of manufacture, and ensures a balanced flow of production by keeping the machine lines running without interruption. The 'just in time' approach described elsewhere in this text leads to a significant reduction in work-in-progress stocks.

Packaging materials indicates everything used for packing, including wrapping materials such as paper, polystyrene beads, straw, rope, metal binding, containers such as boxes, crates, drums and bottles, and also protective coatings such as grease, wax or plastics.

Scrap and residues are the waste, used or surplus materials or parts arising out of manufacturing processes or other activities; for example, steel and non-ferrous turnings, other scrap metal, rejected components, sawdust, used engine oil, ashes, obsolete machinery.

Free-issue materials are materials or components provided by a customer in connection with some equipment or commodity being manufactured for him. They are delivered to the supplier's factory, but remain the customer's property and are not paid for or charged by the manufacturer concerned. They are usually, but not exclusively, associated with Government contracts, and are sometimes described as 'Embodiment Loan' items.

General materials are all goods which do not fall within any other category. The term covers a large number of items which, although not themselves direct production materials, are required for the day-to-day running of a factory or other undertaking, e.g. cleaning materials, protective clothing, paints, nuts and bolts, emery paper, oils and greases, and so on. These are frequently called Maintenance Repair and Operating (**MRO**) items.

CODING OF MATERIALS

The normal way of identifying an article is by simple description, but this by itself is not entirely satisfactory for stores purposes. Several different names may be used for the same thing, e.g. a 'dustbin', 'refuse container' or 'rubbish receptacle'. Again, in order to identify some articles accurately, a very long and complicated description is required. Everyone knows what a chair is, but there are many kinds of chairs and, to identify only one of them properly, it is necessary to say that it is an armchair, with frame made of beech, polished carved walnut legs, spring seat, back and arms, finished in sage-green leather and fitted with two foam-rubber cushions; even this is not the whole story, for nothing has been said about the quality of the materials or the dimensions of the various parts. It is necessary to have some logical basis of identification which is more precise and less cumbersome. This can be done by using letters or figures or a combination of both in the form of a stores code.

The code is then employed to identify all items exactly – the order mentioned above being indicated by a number such as 70/15/8234, or a letter/numeral combination, e.g. CH8234.

There are many different kinds of codes in use, and most of them are specially designed to suit the needs of the business they serve. They may be based upon the nature of items, the purpose for which items are employed, or on any other basis which is regarded as suitable according to local circumstances.

Materials vocabulary

When the operation of coding is complete, the lists of code numbers, descriptions, size, etc., are published in a document known as the vocabulary. In a large organisation it is not unusual to find that the vocabulary consists of twenty or thirty volumes covering more than 100,000 items.

CD Roms are now widely employed, and have proved to be very suitable for storing the vast amounts of necessary data. See the note under 'Organising a materials vocabulary' later in this chapter.

ADVANTAGES OF A CODING SYSTEM

The principal advantages of a good coding system are listed briefly below, and then examined in detail:

1 Avoids repeated use of long descriptive titles.
2 Accurately identifies all items.
3 Prevents duplication of items.
4 Assists standardisation and the reduction of varieties.
5 Provides a foundation for an efficient purchasing organisation.
6 Forms a convenient basis for the sorting and recording of documents.
7 Simplifies mechanical recording.
8 Is convenient for central analysis of unit storehouse records.
9 Can be employed as a basis for stock control accounts.
10 Simplifies pricing and costing.
11 May be used as a storehouse location system.

Avoidance of long descriptions

It is easy to see that if full and accurate descriptions were used on all stores documents, the clerical labour involved would be immense. Even abbreviated descriptions are cumbersome and soon lead to confusion.

Accurate identification

A separate code symbol is available for every individual type of item in all the different sizes, indicating whether there is an approved specification and any special characteristics. For example, Fig. 2.1 illustrates a page taken from a published vocabulary identifying sixteen different sizes of Fireclay Bends, quoting a British Standard

Main Classification 07, Building Requistes

Section 57. Pipes, bends, junctions, glass, asbestos, concrete, fibre, and stoneware

Vocabulary No.	Description	Vocabulary No.	Description
	UNIT OF ISSUE – SINGLES		UNIT OF ISSUE – SINGLES

BENDS. Fireclay, Glass (Vitreous) Enamelled, Salt-Glazed, to BS65
One-quarter

Medium

Vocabulary No.	Internal diameter in.	Radius r in.	a in.
07/57/1766	3	6	$7\frac{1}{2}$
07/57/1767	4	6	$7\frac{1}{2}$
07/57/1768	5	$7\frac{1}{2}$	9
07/57/1769	6	$7\frac{1}{2}$	9
07/57/1770	7	$8\frac{1}{2}$	$10\frac{1}{2}$
07/57/1771	8	$8\frac{1}{2}$	$10\frac{1}{2}$
07/57/1772	9	$8\frac{1}{2}$	$10\frac{1}{2}$
07/57/1773	10	10	12
07/57/1774	12	10	12

BENDS, Fireclay, Glass (Vitreous) Enamelled. Salt-Glazed, to BS65
One-quarter

Short

Vocabulary No.	Internal diameter in.	Radius r in.	a in.
07/57/1755	3	$3\frac{1}{2}$	$5\frac{1}{2}$
07/57/1756	4	$3\frac{1}{2}$	$5\frac{1}{2}$
07/57/1757	5	6	$7\frac{1}{2}$
07/57/1758	6	6	$7\frac{1}{2}$

Long

Vocabulary No.	Internal diameter in.	Radius r in.	a in.
07/57/1786	4	$8\frac{1}{2}$	10
07/57/1787	5	9	$10\frac{1}{2}$
07/57/1788	6	9	$10\frac{1}{2}$

Fig. 2.1   A page from a stores vocabulary document

specification (BS65), and showing by a diagram the critical dimensions. Different items may share the same name, but they will be given a unique code. See Fig. 2.2.

Prevention of duplication

All items are arranged in some logical order. It therefore follows that similar stores will be grouped together and when an item is coded once it should not be given any alternative code number. For example, if there were no coding, and descriptions alone were being relied upon, there might be a large stock of 'steel brackets' for use in the

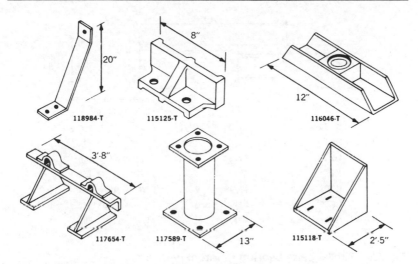

Fig. 2.2   Different items bearing the name 'supports'
(*Courtesy: Brisch, Birn and Partners Ltd*)

assembly shop. If a requisition came from the toolroom for 'angle pieces', which were the same thing, they would very likely be purchased separately and also kept in a different place in the storehouse. The illustration given is a simple one, but the problem is very common and is frequently encountered with expensive items such as roller bearings, electric cable and cutting tools. For example, ball and roller bearing makers have different part numbers of their own for the same size of bearing. If the code for bearings is arranged to tabulate these equivalents, duplication of ordering and stocking can be avoided. Below is an extract from a vocabulary illustrating this point:

Main Classification 66 – Spare Parts for Plant and Equipment
Section 01. Bearing, Ball and Roller

	Roller Journals, Rigid, Single-row, Light Series, Metric Sizes					Unit of Issue Singles		
Vocab. No.	Manufacturer's Reference					Dimensions		
	Maker A	Maker B	Maker C	Maker D	Maker E	Bore mm	O/dia. mm	Width mm
66/01/3724	S 1203	ABC 23	Q 7	T 12	Z 7	20	47	14
66/01/3725	S 1257	ABC 27	Q 9	T 20	Z 9	25	52	15
66/01/3726	S 1301	ABC 32	Q 11	T 25	Z 11	30	62	16
66/01/3727	S 1354	ABC 48	Q 32	T 36	Z 32	35	72	17
66/01/3728	S 1406	ABC 61	Q 47	T 81	Z 47	40	80	18
66/01/3729	S 1452	ABC 73	Q 63	T 94	Z 63	45	85	19

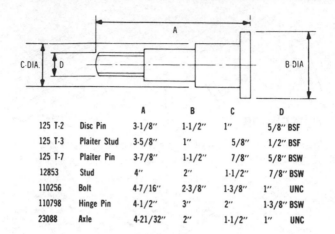

		A	B	C	D
125 T-2	Disc Pin	3-1/8"	1-1/2"	1"	5/8" BSF
125 T-3	Plaiter Stud	3-5/8"	1"	5/8"	1/2" BSF
125 T-7	Plaiter Pin	3-7/8"	1-1/2"	7/8"	5/8" BSW
12853	Stud	4"	2"	1-1/2"	7/8" BSW
110256	Bolt	4-7/16"	2-3/8"	1-3/8"	1" UNC
110798	Hinge Pin	4-1/2"	3"	2"	1-3/8" BSW
23088	Axle	4-21/32"	2"	1-1/2"	1" UNC

Fig. 2.3   Similar parts bearing different names
(*Courtesy: Brisch, Birn and Partners Ltd*)

A suitable coding system will bring similar items together, even though they have different names. See Fig. 2.3.

Assistance in standardisation

This is one of the most important and profitable uses of a code. The grouping of like items together makes it easy to examine the complete range of any given type of items and consider whether the number of varieties used can be reduced and standardisation achieved on the minimum number of the most suitable types. A simple example of this process is the standardisation of nuts and bolts. When all the different types and sizes used have been coded and listed, the list can be examined to see whether the range is too detailed. For instance, it might be found that in 100 mm-long, metric thread, mild steel nuts and bolts there were five different combinations of bolt-head, shank and nut shapes as follows:

Bolt Head	Shank	Nut
hexagon	round	hexagon
hexagon	round	square
square	round	square
square	square	hexagon
square	square	square

An examination of the uses served by these bolts and the quantities consumed could result in standardisation on two types only, say hexagon, round, hexagon, and square, square, square.

Again, if bolts were kept in such lengths as 110 mm, 120 mm, 130 mm, 140 mm, 150 mm and 160 mm, a similar enquiry might establish that the range of 120 mm, 140 mm and 160 mm was adequate.

Use in purchasing

Apart from the fact that a code, by improving stock recording and control, enables buying instructions to be conveyed easily and quickly, grouping of items in the code facilitates the organisation of the purchasing department into commodity sections, each engaged on the buying of a particular range of stores. This is especially important where there is a central buying office serving several dispersed units because demands for materials from the units can be programmed to deal with the same commodity group for all concerned at the same time, thus enabling the buyer to take full advantage of quantity discounts.

Basis for sorting documents

The presence of a code number on receipt notes, issue notes, stocktaking sheets and, in fact, all basic materials documents enables them to be sorted into code number order. Then they are easily posted to the records, which are arranged in the same order.

Simplification of data processing

It would be practically impossible to employ computers for materials recording in the absence of a coding system. The limitations of the equipment prohibit the use of long descriptions, because of the time it would take to input the necessary data.

Central analysis of unit storehouse records

Where there are a number of outlying storehouses, and records are kept at a central point, a code is a necessity to make sure that the same item has the same identification in every unit. The central stock records can therefore be kept in code number order showing how much is in stock and what the movement is for each stockholding point separately, with a total for the organisation as a whole. This not only facilitates economical buying but enables the central office to arrange for the transfer of materials from one unit to another as and when necessary.

Basis for control accounts

The detailed arrangement of control accounts is dealt with in a later chapter. Here it is sufficient to say that they are usually arranged to correspond with the commodity groups laid down in the coding system.

Simplification of pricing and costing materials

Price lists consisting only of descriptions are cumbersome and reference to them is difficult and slow. The use of code numbers automatically provides a reliable index for all items. This feature of coding is emphasised by the use of makers' parts lists by purchasing departments.

Particularly in the case of production materials, code numbers may be arranged so as to correspond with cost headings, thus simplifying material costing.

Use as storehouse location

It is clearly desirable that goods in the storehouse should be kept in some logical order. One way of doing this is to arrange the items in the sequence of the stores coding system, as far as is practicable. Some difficulties may be encountered, especially with vehicle and machinery spares, where the arrangement of the parts list may have little or no relation to the size of the item.

Traceability

The coding systems described are appropriate where identical items need to be identified, but it is not important which item from a number is booked in or out or otherwise moved.

It is sometimes the case that traceability is important. When this is the case a unique single item code needs to be generated. The vehicle identification number attached to a car is possibly the best known example of a unique code. It identifies the model and body style of the vehicle as any code number would do; but it also identifies the actual vehicle. No other car has the same number.

Where individual components such as airframe or engine parts in the aerospace industry need to be uniquely identified it is possible to either combine a 'tracer' or serial number with the generic part code, or to provide a unique number separate from the part code. Whatever the system, the recording of movements must be managed by a system which takes account of the particular item concerned, and enables those concerned to keep track of it.

CODE SYMBOLS

Whatever method of coding is followed, the symbols used are either alphabetical (e.g. ACFG), numerical (e.g. 05/06/1234) or alpha-numerical (e.g. PE.7261). Where letters are included in the code, some attempt may be made to have a mnemonic system whereby the letters themselves are an abbreviation of part of the description of the item – for instance, SMF meaning Steel, Mild, Flat. Such an arrangement can have only a limited application in materials coding; in all but the smallest concerns the variety of items stocked is such that duplicate meanings of letters very soon arise and make any widespread application of mnemonics impracticable. Straight numerical codes may be referred to as 'Decimal Systems', the numbers being segregated into groups of two or three – for example, 12.27.63.51 or 832.617.903. The use of decimal points in this way makes the number easier to read and also tends to reduce errors in transcription.

INTERPRETATION OF CODES

The logical development of a coding system is for every symbol employed to have a significance of its own so that, in theory at least, it should be possible from inspection of the code letters or numbers to say exactly what item is represented, giving sufficient detail in each case to identify the article precisely. This is the ideal arrangement and is particularly effective in the application of standardisation.

Let us consider the coding of copper rod by this system, using numerals only as symbols. To do this, we must begin at the point where the total stock is divided into its main groups and follow the splitting up of these main groups through various subdivisions until we arrive at the individual item.

The first digit indicates the segregation of a total range of materials used by a production engineering factory into the following main classifications:

0	Raw materials	3	Tools
1	Piece parts	4	Gauges
2	Bought-out parts	5	Fixtures

6 Machinery spares	8 General stores
7 Scrap	9 Finished products

The second digit shows the first subdivision of these classifications. Selecting Classification 0 – Raw materials, to illustrate this, the significance of the second digit in the code is:

00 Timber	05 Paper
01 Rubber	06 Glass
02 Metals	07 Leather
03 Textiles	08 Paint
04 Plastics	09 Chemicals

The third digit divides these again as follows, taking 02 Metals, as the example:

02.0 Ferrous metals	02.1 Non-ferrous metals

The other numbers in this sequence, 02.2 to 02.9 are not in use, as all metals are covered by the two categories of ferrous and non-ferrous.

The fourth digit makes another split, in the case of 02.1 Non-ferrous metals, as follows:

02.10 Aluminium	02.14 Copper
02.11 Lead	02.15 Brass
02.12 Zinc	02.16 Bronze
02.13 Nickel	

The fifth digit operates as follows, taking 02.14 Copper, as the example:

02.14.0 Ingot	02.14.3 Wire
02.14.1 Plate	02.14.4 Mesh
02.14.2 Sheet	02.14.5 Rod

The sixth digit continues the process of subdivision, using 02.14.5 Rod, to demonstrate the position:

02.14.50 Squares	02.14.54 Tees
02.14.51 Flats	02.14.55 Hexagon
02.14.52 Angles	02.14.56 Round
02.14.53 Channels	02.14.57 Special sections

The seventh and eighth digits together form the ultimate subdivision. In the case of 02.14.56, Copper, Rod, Round, they indicate the diameter, rising by 1 mm, i.e.:

02.14.56.01–1 mm diameter	02.14.56.03–3 mm diameter
02.14.56.02–2 mm diameter	02.14.56.04–4 mm diameter

and so on.

With a fully significant coding arrangement like this, the code number 02.14.56.08 would represent 8 mm round copper rod, the interpretation of each symbol being given below:

0 Raw material
2 Metal
1 Non-ferrous
4 Copper
5 Rod
6 Round
$\left.\begin{array}{l} 0 \\ 8 \end{array}\right\}$ 8mm diameter

This involves a great deal of detailed work and when applied to a wide range of materials, it tends to become rather complicated. Although all the digits have a definite significance, they cannot easily be 'read' at a glance, and can be interpreted only by an expert, although storekeepers and others may well become familiar with the code numbers of items in common use.

Where the nature of the material justifies the effort, and facilities are available, a fully significant code may be employed but in the majority of enterprises the compilation is thought to be too onerous and, also, there is the consideration that the preparation may take many months, or even years. In practice, therefore, some compromise is often attempted and, while some parts of the symbol are significant, other parts are not.

Random codes may be used which have no 'significance' at all. These are normally all numeric, and are more efficient in that for the same range of items they are shorter in length than a significant code, and hence less prone to error. The main disadvantage is of course that similar items will have totally different code numbers, thus making it difficult for stores personnel to recognise an item from its number.

METHODS OF CODING

Coding by the nature of the item

This involves the consideration of items by reference to their own inherent characteristics. The first stage is to collect similar items into a series of main groups such as raw materials, bought-out parts, tools, machinery spares, etc. Each of these groups is then subdivided into subgroups or sections as far as the circumstances require. This method is illustrated in detail in the previous section entitled 'Interpretation of codes'. It is to be found in many different concerns and is very popular in practice. It must be understood that the groupings employed in any particular organisation will be arranged to suit that organisation, and the subdivisions shown in the example are for the purposes of explanation only.

Coding by the end use

This means arranging the code to correspond with the purposes for which the various items are eventually employed. For example, in an automotive plant the first division of materials would be into Production Items and Non-production Items. Further subdivisions might be arranged somewhat as follows:

Production Items	Engine, body, transmission, steering, suspension, trim.
Engine	Ignition, valve gear, fuel system, cylinder block, cylinder head, etc.
Valve Gear	Individual items, e.g. inlet valves, exhaust valves, valve springs, push rods, tappets, etc.

This method is also very widely used, particularly in concerns producing complex machines or assemblies and for identifying equipment and spares in the Armed Forces.

Other bases of coding

Coding may also be arranged by any other method which seems desirable to suit special circumstances; for example, coding by reference to the location of items in the storehouse, to the source of supply, or to the customer who will eventually purchase the finished product or service.

Colour marking

Code numbers are sometimes supplemented by colour marking on the materials or parts themselves. This can be done with metals, cables, small component parts, drums of oil and various other stores. If the colours are not too complicated, it affords a ready means of identification on sight, and in the case of small electrical components, for instance, it may be that, although there is no satisfactory means of stamping a code number on the item, it is quite satisfactory to use colours instead. For metals, a colour code could be as follows:

Green for Iron
Blue   for Steel
Black for Aluminium
Red   for Copper
White for Zinc

Secondary colours can then be used to give more information, e.g. blue and red to indicate high-speed steel; blue, red and green to identify 18 per cent tungsten high-speed steel, and so on.

Avoidance of change. Whatever coding method is selected, every possible effort should be made to avoid changes in classifications, sections and symbols once they have been put into operation. Code numbers are used on stock files, price lists, location indexes, stocktaking sheets and various other records, and any appreciable change in the coding system may involve extensive clerical or data input work in amending such records.

Technical spares

Where spares for vehicles, machines or equipment are bought, the range can be very extensive and it will be found that the suppliers of these parts usually have already coded them by their own methods. In such circumstances, it is common practice to use the 'Maker's Part Number' as the last part of the code in the user's organisation.

Common user items

It often happens that in a 'Maker's Part' list there are items which are not, in fact, manufactured by that supplier. Such items are nuts and bolts, ball and roller-bearings, oil seals, belts, bulbs, etc., and they may already be included in the customer's own vocabulary in some other classification because they are also in use for other purposes. In these instances, it is advisable to indicate in the vocabulary for equipment spares that these items are 'Common User' because normally they can be bought more cheaply from the actual manufacturer than from the supplier of the main equipment, who has to treat them as bought-out parts. In addition, if they are not so identified, the same item will appear under several vocabulary numbers, will be bought and perhaps stocked separately, and may have the effect of increasing stockholdings unnecessarily as well as involving duplicate locations in the storehouse.

Classification 61 – Production Machinery Spares
Section 12 – Drilling Machine Spares

Maker's Name   Smith, Jones and Robinson – Model XYZ

	Description	Maker's Part No.	*Comments*
61/12/2786	Pinion	ABC 354	
61/12/2787	Pawl	ABD 127	
–	Roller-bearing	ABD 186	Common User Vocab. No. 70/23/7812
61/12/2788	Shaft	ABC 219	
–	Bolt	ABE 720	Common User Vocab. No. 70/03/1262
61/12/2789	Plate	ABF 123	

SELF-VALIDATING CODES

It is now common practice when devising or adopting a coding system to add an extra digit or digits to the item number. These extra digits convey no information whatsoever about the item itself, and are therefore sometimes called redundant digits; their purpose is to provide protection against errors in the transcription or inputting of item numbers. This purpose is reflected in another commonly used name for these digits, 'check digits'.

A simple illustration of the application of a straightforward check digit system follows:

Take a part number, say, 19241 – if an operator were to key in 19341 by mistake, there is a strong possibility that this incorrect number would be accepted by the system and the records would be corrupted. A check digit might be added to the correct number to provide some protection against this, the simplest way being simply to sum the digits, divide the sum by a given number and call the remainder our check digit. In our example, using 7 as the number by which we divide the code number, we get the following result:

$$\frac{1+9+2+4+1}{7} = \frac{17}{7} = 2 \text{ (remainder } 3 \text{)}$$

So, 3 becomes our check digit, and is added to the end of the code number so that the part is now referred to as 192413. The operator keying in 193413 by mistake would be made aware of the fact because the checking procedure would calculate a final digit of 4, not 3

$$\frac{1+9+3+4+1}{7} = \frac{18}{7} = 2 \text{ (remainder } 4 \text{)}$$

The usefulness of the system outlined is rather limited in practice because it will fail to reveal an error of transpositioning of two numbers within the code, a common mistake. The (correct) code 19241 and the erroneous 19421 will not be distinguished between by the checking procedure, as they both have the same sum. This problem can be overcome by multiplying each digit by a different number, like this:

$$(1 \times 1) + (9 \times 2) + (2 \times 3) + (4 \times 4) + (1 \times 5)$$
$$= \ 1 \ + \ 18 \ + \ 6 \ + \ 16 \ + \ 5 \ = 46$$

The number 11 is generally accepted as an appropriate and efficient divisor in this kind of self-validating code, so the check digit for 19241 under this system would be arrived at by dividing 46 by 11 and establishing that the remainder is 2. The full number would then become 192412. The transposition error mentioned earlier (19421) would now be detected, as follows:

$$(1 \times 1) + (9 \times 2) + (4 \times 3) + (2 \times 4) + (1 \times 5)$$
$$= \ 1 \ + \ 18 \ + \ 12 \ + \ 8 \ + \ 5 \ = 44$$

The number 44 is divisible exactly by 11, indicating that the check digit should be 0 as there is no remainder. The checking process will indicate this as an error to be investigated. There are some rather more complicated approaches to the use of check digits in self-validating codes, though the method explained seems to prove adequate for most applications.

Characteristics of an efficient stores code

1 It covers the whole range of stores in use or likely to be used in future. In the first stages of implementation about 70 per cent of the code capacity should be unused.
2 Classifications and sections are designed to meet the needs of the organisation.
3 The number of letters or digits is constant for all items.
4 Numbering is arranged so that there is adequate room for future expansion or amendment, without the risk of duplication or changing existing numbers.
5 There is one place, and one place only, in the vocabulary for each item.
6 Units of issue are given.

7 Descriptions are brief but accurate, and specifications are quoted wherever possible.
8 It is easily understood by those who are to use it.

ORGANISING A MATERIALS VOCABULARY

Up to this point, nothing has been said about the mechanics of preparing, issuing and maintaining a vocabulary. The following paragraphs give a brief outline of a typical procedure.

Catalogue library

If there is not already a catalogue library, one is set up, containing copies of suppliers' catalogues, makers' parts lists, specifications, bills of details of products manufactured by the firm (if any), spares scalings, lists of established standards and any other available information concerning types and varieties of stock.

Present systems

All areas where materials work takes place are visited so that their current systems for identification of stock may be inspected, and full particulars of these systems are recorded. Copies of stocktaking sheets are obtained.

Consultation

Other interested parties, such as production department, design department, finance department, purchasing department, are consulted and with them is agreed:

1 The general content of the vocabulary.
2 Whether the coding system is to be based upon the nature of the materials, the use to which they are put, or any other basis.
3 The classifications and sections to be used.
4 The system of numbering.
5 Whether the vocabulary will be used as a basis for stores accounting, cost allocation and storehouse location.
6 The estimated dates for the preparation and ultimate issue of each classification listed.

Originating sheets

In respect of each classification a list is prepared by the vocabulary office from the information already in their hands showing, in their appropriate sections, all the items it is proposed to include, giving as clear a description as possible and quoting sizes and specifications. No item numbers are allocated at this stage. There is a column on the list for the storekeeper to indicate whether he stocks the item or not, and a space for remarks.

Example:

ORIGINATING SHEET

Classification 40 – Tools
Section 15 – Drills

Item No.	Description	Stock	Remarks
	Drills, twist, straight shank		
	18% tungsten high-speed steel		
	3 mm diameter × 100 mm long	42	
	4 mm diameter × 100 mm long	–	Suggest this should be held
	5 mm diameter × 100 mm long	23	
	5·40 mm diameter × 100 mm long	–	
	6·10 mm diameter × 100 mm long	114	No movement for 12 months
	6·50 mm diameter × 120 mm long	–	
	8·40 mm diameter × 140 mm long	27	Black finish
	etc., etc.		

Storekeepers add to each sheet particulars of similar items which they do stock but which are not listed.

Compilation

When all the originating sheets are returned, the vocabulary office analyses them, removes all items which are apparently not required, adds those which seem necessary, rearranges where desired and finally enters the item number to be used. This sounds quite simple, but it is a very difficult and laborious task. In the course of this process efforts must be made to restrict the number of varieties of items stocked by limiting size ranges, by eliminating alternatives and by omitting items which are used only occasionally. All numbers are allocated in such a way as to provide adequate room for future adjustments or expansion.

Illustrations are frequently helpful and sometimes essential, but they take up a good deal of space, thus making the vocabulary document more bulky. They are also expensive, and tend to delay production of the finished work, and should therefore be used sparingly.

Distribution

Complete copies of the vocabulary are issued only to persons who really have need of them. Individual volumes can be provided as required. Recipients sign for their copies and a permanent record is kept of the distribution list. Special care is taken to ensure that all appropriate officials for user departments are properly supplied with the vocabulary volumes which relate to their duties.

CD Roms.   Compact disc, read only memory has been adopted by some organisations as the medium on which the stores vocabulary is maintained. An enormous amount of information can be stored on a single disc and completely updated editions of the vocabulary can be issued and circulated cheaply. An inexpensive CD-Rom drive (see Fig. 2.4) connected to a PC is all that is needed to retrieve information, with the additional benefit that searches can be made by key words or incomplete descriptions. Users find CD-Rom systems much easier to work with than paper-based vocabularies.

Amendments

Amendments are published at least quarterly, in accordance with the original distribution list. Changes are not made in classifications unless they are absolutely unavoidable.

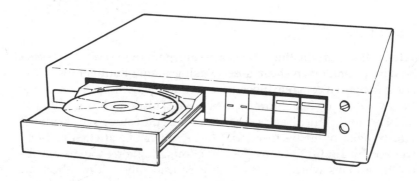

Fig. 2.4   A CD Rom drive

Local coding

Where there are a number of widely dispersed units, some arrangements are necessary to enable local storekeepers to devise their own numbers for new items which occur in their stockholdings. This must be done within the framework of the main vocabulary. One method is to reserve one section (say, Section 99) in each classification for local use only. Section 99 is therefore not quoted or used at all by the central vocabulary office. At the outlying units, when the need arises to allocate a number to an article which is not in the vocabulary, the storekeeper puts the item in its normal classification under Section 99 and gives it an item number on his own list. At regular intervals, the unit storehouses report full details of items locally coded by them in this way. The central office can then examine these and decide if they are to be incorporated in the main vocabulary or not.

Treatment of items not in the vocabulary

For various reasons, it may not be advisable to include in the vocabulary every item of stock, e.g. machine spares which are seldom required and are bought and used straight away, and other articles of a non-repetitive nature. These items are described as 'not in vocabulary' quoting the classification and/or section number, e.g. '19/23/NIV' or simply 'NIV' according to circumstances.

SPECIFICATION

A specification for an item of stores is a description of the item, its dimensions, analysis, performance or other relevant characteristics, in sufficient detail to ensure that it will be suitable in all respects for the purpose for which it is intended.

Dimensions. This implies not only quoting the sizes of the various parts of an article, but also indicating the amount of tolerance which may be permitted in these sizes. Taking a simple illustration, the dimensions of a concrete block:

80 cm long ± 5 mm
40 cm wide ± 5 mm
15 cm deep ± 3 mm

This means that if a block is between the following extreme dimensions, it will meet the specification:

80·5 cm to 79·5 cm

40·5 cm to 39·5 cm
15·3 cm to 14·7 cm

Analysis means a statement of the chemical content of an item, and it is frequently employed in specifications. For example, the analysis of one particular type of steel is as follows:

Carbon	0·12 per cent
Sulphur	0·05 per cent
Phosphorus	0·05 per cent
Manganese	0·50 per cent

The elements quoted above are those which control the properties of the steel. The balance of the material content is, of course, iron.

Performance describes the physical ability of an article to stand up to certain duties; for example, to say that a tyre must be capable of 20,000 kilometres running under a load of 2 tonnes and be able to sustain a specified pressure at a temperature of 70° Centigrade without bursting.

Other characteristics. There are many matters other than dimension, analysis or performance which can be described, and these vary with the goods being specified. Examples are as follows:

Textiles:	colour
Timber:	amount of sapwood or bark permitted
Castings:	freedom from cracks, pitting or porosity
Steel:	condition, i.e. as rolled, normalised, cold-drawn, etc.
Wire ropes:	method of construction.

Combination of requirements

In practice, some specifications give dimensions only, analysis only, or performance only, but it is common to find some element of all three of these requirements and some other characteristic also specified. For example, a particular kind of bar steel might be specified as follows:

Dimensions	50 mm diameter ± 0·05 mm	
	3 metres long ± 20 mm	
Analysis	Carbon	0·50 to 0·70 per cent
	Silicon	0·10 to 0·35
	Sulphur	0·05 maximum
	Phosphorus	0·05 maximum
	Manganese	0·50 to 0·80
	Chromium	0·50 to 0·80

Performance   Yield stress: minimum of 600 MN/m^2
             Ultimate tensile strength: minimum of 700 MN/m^2
Condition   Bright-drawn, hardened and tempered.

Note: MN/m^2= Meganewtons per square metre.

The value of specifications

Specifications will ensure that:

1 All commodities specified will be suitable for their intended purpose when put to use.
2 Material is of a consistent quality at all times. This is most desirable, not only from the point of view of production processes but also for the satisfaction of the customer who buys the finished product.
3 The inspection or testing to be applied to goods purchased is notified in advance to the inspection department, and to suppliers.
4 In respect of the purchase of specified items, all suppliers will have the same data on which to base their quotations. If the specification is adequate, then it can be assumed that the quality being offered by every supplier is adequate and, therefore, the buying decision can be made confidently on price or other considerations not related to quality.

Preparation of specifications

1 Over-specification is to be avoided; i.e. it is only necessary to ask for a quality, performance, etc. which is essential for the job. If the design is too complicated, or the limits of dimensions, analysis or performance are too rigorous, the goods will be more expensive and in extreme cases it may even be difficult to find a manufacturer willing to quote.
2 As far as practicable, pay attention to convenience in handling and storage.
3 If there is to be inspection after delivery, the specification ought to say what tests are to be applied.
4 If any special marking or packing is wanted, include the relevant instructions in the specification.

British Standards specifications

The British Standards Institution is the approved body for the preparation and promulgation of national standards covering, *inter alia*, methods of test; terms, definitions and symbols; standards of quality, of performance or of dimensions; preferred ranges, codes of practice.

The principles observed in the preparation of British Standards are:

1 That they shall be in accordance with the needs of industry and fulfil a generally recognised want.
2 That the interest of both producer and consumer shall be considered.

British Standards are periodically reviewed.

As a general rule it is desirable to use British Standards specifications wherever they are available; they cover a very wide range.

Other specifications

Apart from British Standards there are various other sources of specifications, such as trade associations, consumer organisations, Government departments, technical institutes, etc. In many instances, firms prepare their own specifications to be used in conjunction with their own stores vocabulary.

Trade and brand names

Where there are well-known trade names or brand names for particular items, these can be used in place of a detailed specification. The effect of this is just to make use of the maker's specification.

BAR CODING

Bar code technology has been employed for quite a long time in the retail industry, and most readers will be familiar with the striped panels which appear on many grocery products, and will be aware that this panel contains encoded information which can be automatically scanned at a supermarket checkout by devices which throw a beam of light at the bar code and 'read' the reflections.

More recently this same technology has been adopted for industrial applications, for such purposes as the identification of incoming goods and material, material and document tracking, issue recording and so on.

There are several types of bar code in use, though they have basic characteristics in common, the most fundamental of which is that

**Fig. 2.5   A materials label combining man and machine readable
symbols**
(*Courtesy: Intermec Ltd*)

they consist of a series of dark bars separated by light spaces. The
codes are preceded and determined by 'start' and 'stop' characters
which are special combinations of bars and spaces which make
it possible for the scanning equipment to recognise the beginning
and end of a symbol. It will usually be the case that the bar code will
be accompanied by plain alphanumeric characters so that human
operatives can see and understand a translation of the code (see Fig.
2.5).

Although there are around twelve bar code systems which are
recognised internationally, most industrial applications are based on
one of two standards. These are 'Code 39' and 'interleaved 2 of 5'. A
third standard, UPC/EAN, is the one widely used on retail packs and
read at supermarket checkouts.

Code 39

This system will accommodate alphabetic as well as numeric characters. Each of the characters are represented by a group of five bars and
the four spaces which are included. Not so dense as interleaved 2 of
5, but much more powerful, Code 39 has found wide acceptance in
factories, hospitals and libraries.

Each of the characters of Code 39 is self-checking (self-validating) which means that very high levels of accuracy in reading can be attained.

Code 39 is the most versatile. It can be of any length and can convey both letters and numbers. The system is the most widely used and accepted approach to bar coding.

Interleaved 2 of 5

The interleaved 2 of 5 system has been generally adopted for use in warehousing and industrial applications, and is very widely used in the car industry. It is the standard symbology for use on outer shipping containers for the grocery industry, though not for individual packages.

In this system both bars and spaces are coded. Odd numbered digits are represented by the bars, and the even numbers by the spaces. The interleaved 2 of 5 symbol should contain an even number of digits. If data comprises an odd number of digits a leading zero is added to the date before encoding, so for example, '789' would be encoded as '0789'.

The main advantage of the interleaved 2 of 5 system is that it is 'dense'. That is to say that, because both bars and spaces convey meaning, a lot of information can be encoded in a symbol which occupies a small amount of space. The system can accommodate numeric characters only.

UPC and EAN

The bar codes seen on individual retail packages are of this kind. UPC is an abbreviation of Universal Product Code, and EAN stands for European Article Numbering. The systems are essentially the same, and UPC is in fact a subset of the EAN code.

The UPC symbology was adopted in 1973 by the grocery industry in the USA, and was based on proposals put forward by IBM. The system has been modified on a number of occasions since that time, but the essential features remain the same.

In 1976 the EAN code was adopted, as an extension of the UPC system. UPC was developed for use in supermarkets, to facilitate automatic scanning of code numbers at the checkout, so that prices can be looked up, and stock records amended. It now finds much wider application, on non-food items, liquor, magazines and books (including this one!) UPC/EAN is the ideal symbology for use in EPOS (Electronic Point of Sale) applications. It provides numeric data only, in fixed length fields, and is designed to cope with the fact that the bar code panels may be printed on a variety of materials and not necessarily on flat surfaces. Scanning must be possible in a variety of ways, and will probably not be undertaken with any degree of precision. This type of bar code needs to be printed within exacting tolerances. While ideal in the retail context, this approach is not widely used in other environments.

EPOS technology allows substantial cost savings and gives more 'real time' information on sales of goods, patterns of stores traffic, and the popularity and profitability of every line carried. It enables:

- Stocks to be limited to demand.
- Sales per square metre to be monitored in order to check the best combination of merchandise for sale.
- Sales of any item to be calculated at any time.
- Suppliers' promotional claims to be checked.
- A reduction in theft.
- A reduction in obsolescence and deterioration of stocks.
- Information for buyers to be available to achieve 'best buys' from suppliers.
- Increased customer service.

Bar code readers fall into two main categories: fixed beam readers which do not have any active scanning motion of their own, and line scan readers which actively scan a bar code. Both the widely used pen type reader which the operator manually runs across a bar code, and

A portable data capture unit and scanner
(Courtesy: Intermec Corporation)

a reader across which the code itself is moved fall into the fixed beam category. In a line scan reader it is a moving light beam, rather than simply the relative movement of the bar code and the scanner, which enables the reflections to be read.

VARIETY REDUCTION

Variety reduction in stores is the process of reducing the number of varieties stocked to a controlled workable minimum.

In the course of time, in any organisation, unless active measures are taken to control variety, the number of items stocked and used will gradually increase. When this has been going on over a long period, if the position is examined critically, it will be found that there are many instances where several items of a very similar nature are purchased and held in stock. To quote a simple example: If the stock of paint were to be investigated, the following information is typical of what could be disclosed:

1 No specification is in use.
2 Paint is being supplied by twelve different manufacturers because of individual preferences by users in different parts of the organisation.
3 Paint is purchased in six different sizes of container.
4 It is not clear which paints are to be used for external and internal work.
5 There are ten different shades of green in stock, eight reds, seven blues, and so on.

A proper approach to variety reduction might result in:

1 Issue of specifications for five types of paint only to be used, or a decision to buy from only one manufacturer's range of products.
2 The number of different sizes of container being reduced.
3 Issue of an instruction to the maintenance or other departments concerned, about the type of paint to be applied for various jobs.
4 Colour varieties restricted to 50 per cent of the present range.

The result of such a change would be a drastic reduction of the number of items held in stock in the paint classification, cheaper purchase prices, and better control.

Procedure for variety reduction

The conduct of a programme of variety reduction involves a complete examination of the list of commodities stocked, to determine:

1 The use or users for which each item is intended.
2 Which items have similar characteristics, and can be used as substitutes for each other.
3 What range of sizes is essential.
4 Which items can be eliminated.
5 What specifications are necessary for retained items.

Thereafter, the stores vocabulary requires amendment in accordance with the decisions reached. When a degree of standardisation is introduced, it is necessary to devise some procedure to see that specifications are observed, that new specifications are suitably devised and approved, and that old specifications are reviewed and replaced, amended or eliminated as required.

Prevention of proliferation

Of course variety reduction is a reaction to an existing problem. Most organisations take steps to try to avoid the situation where too many lines are stocked, usually by having some kind of questionnaire to be completed before an item is allowed to be added to inventory. Questions such as 'What is its function?' and 'Are there any substitutes?' are asked, and the answers assessed before an item is put into stock.

SOME WIDELY USED CODING SYSTEMS

The NATO system

In 1958 the US Federal Catalog System was adopted by NATO, with the following objectives in mind:

1 A common supply language for communications and international transactions between NATO armed forces, civil departments and certain non-NATO countries.
2 To encourage each NATO country to use the system for the management and supply of defense (defence) requirements.
3 To build up item information data for easy access by mechanical and manual means.

The main aim of the NATO codification system is to give each item a single name, a single uniform identification, a single uniform classification and a single uniform stock number.

The complete NATO stock number consists of thirteen numeric digits in three separate elements.

1 First four digits – the NATO class code.
2 Fourth and fifth digits – the nation code.
3 Last seven digits – the National Item Identification Number (the IIN).

The nation code usually applies to the producer country. The IIN is a unique but non-significant number which, once assigned, is permanent for the life of the item.

Material and equipment standards and code (MESC)

This coding system was developed and is maintained by Shell Internationale Petroleum MIJ B.V. in The Hague, Netherlands, and is used by Shell companies throughout the world, as well as by a large number of organisations outside the Shell group. Over one hundred and seventy different companies are using the system. First developed in the 1920s, the system has proved remarkably accommodating and flexible, and continues to cope with a proliferation of items and new technologies that were not envisaged at the time of its inception (see Fig. 2.6).

The MESC system has three main elements:

1 A General Index, which contains an alphabetically arranged list of materials and equipment, and the appropriate group numbers.
2 A Coding Schedule, which is the framework within which materials and equipment are coded.
3 The MESC catalogue, which includes information on all the material and equipment recognised as standard. Full specifications and technical details are given in the catalogue, which is now stored and circulated as a CD Rom.

The MESC numbers consist of 10 digits, used as follows:

1 First two digits – 'Group' – the general class of the item.
2 Second two digits – 'Subgroup' – refines the general classification.
3 Third pair of digits – 'Sub-subgroup' – further refines the classification.
4 Next three digits – complete the description, indicating the actual item within the groups.
5 Final digit – completes the MESC number, and is used to categorise the part according to such factors as whether coded centrally or locally, whether the material is salvaged, or whether inspection certificates are required. This last digit does not add any information about the intrinsic nature of the item.

Classification	76 05 39 12 01 76 Fittings and Flanges	(Group)
	05 Screwed API	(Subgroup)
	39 Elbows 90°	(Sub-subgroup)
Identification	12 2 inch, class 3000 lbs	(Item)
	01 Indicates group standard	

Fig. 2.6   An example of an MESC code

European article numbering

European Article Numbers (EAN) are product codes mainly used by organisations producing, distributing and retailing groceries and consumer goods. The code is compatible with the Universal Product Code (USA), and is designed to be used in conjunction with bar coding systems, and hence Electronic Point of Sale (EPOS) technology.

An EAN code consists of thirteen digits, and is ranged vertically as follows:

1 First two digits – indicate country of origin.
2 Next five digits – name of manufacturer, and manufacturer's code.
3 Next five digits – identification of product.
4 Final digit – a check digit.

The NHS national vocabulary coding system

Also known as the national supply vocabulary, this coding system employs a series of seven characters to identify an individual item within the health service. An 'alphanumeric' system, the characters consist of three letters and four numbers, and the codes are configured as follows:

1 First character (letter) – commodity group
2 Second and third characters (letters) – subgroup
3 Next three characters (numbers) – identify individual item
4 Final character – check digit.

An example of an NHS code is AJF 7080:

A = Commodity group – provisions
J = Group – provisions
F = Sub Group – instant mix
708 = Potato, 25 kg.
0 = Check digit.

Brisch classification and coding

The Brisch organisation is a consulting group specialising in the application of classification and coding to all aspects of industrial and commercial activities with the objective of promoting better utilisation of existing resources through variety control and standardisation so that an optimum variety of products can be obtained from the minimum variety of materials and components, with the aid of the minimum variety of tools, machines and methods.

There is no single Brisch coding system; the organisation employs the same principles, rules and general structure to produce 'tailor-made' systems for individual client organisations.

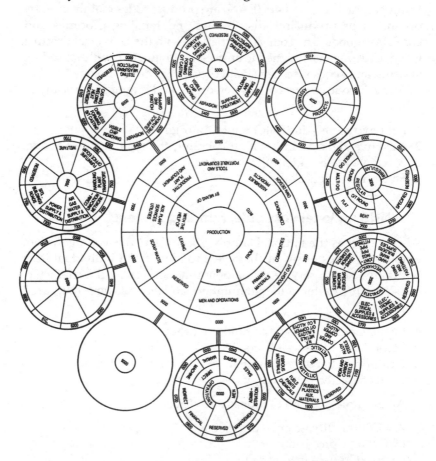

Fig. 2.7   A tailored solution to one firm's classification and coding problem
(*Courtesy: Brisch, Birn and Partners Ltd*)

Brisch coding systems are hierarchical, meaning that each digit is qualified by the preceding one, and the organisation claims that by this means the maximum amount of information is contained in the least number of digits. Brisch numbers (alphabetic characters are not employed) usually consist of a classification of four or five numbers, and a code of three or four numbers, for example:

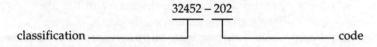

classification ⎯⎯⎯⎯⎯⎯⎯⎯⎯⎯⎯⎯⎯⎯⎯⎯ code

Figure 2.7 is a diagramatic representation of one organisation's Brisch classification and coding system.

CHAPTER 3

Receipt and inspection

Goods may be received from outside suppliers, from production departments or from other stores within the organisation. They may come by hand, by post, by road, rail or air. They must be properly looked after when they arrive. The amount of recording and checking depends greatly on the nature of the goods, and the management techniques of the business. Of course, it is desirable to avoid the expense of a lot of paperwork or data processing if this can be done without undue risk, but the possibility of theft, fraud or mistake is always present.

Similarly, the extent of physical examination, weighing, counting etc., of goods received should be arranged in the most economical way to avoid unnecessary delay or expense.

EXPEDITING

In order to achieve the supplies aim of obtaining delivery on time expediting is frequently undertaken.

A dictionary definition of 'expedite' is 'assist the progress of something'. In manufacturing industry this activity may be undertaken in connection with the progress of a customer's order to the point of dispatch (internal expediting), or liaising with suppliers to ensure that materials are received from them on time (external expediting). In organisations providing a service rather than manufacturing anything, most of the expediting will be external, and in manufacturing it is the external expediting which involves the purchasing function.

The nature of expediting work

Expediting is a planned, proactive task. Expressions such as 'hastening', 'progress chasing' and 'urging' are sometimes used to describe the process of attempting to ensure that delayed supply of materials does not cause problems for the buying organisation. These expressions often indicate that the process is seen as a reactive one, where a problem of lateness arises, and work then begins to try to retrieve the situation.

Ideally, the relationship between the selling and buying organisations is one of mutual trust and respect, and 'liaison' rather than 'expediting' describes the process of ensuring that the contract is executed properly, and that deliveries take place when required.

The need for differentiation

To design and apply a standard set of expediting procedures, and to apply them equally to all orders would have the obvious advantage of being a simple and straightforward approach. Unfortunately though, it would also be a very wasteful approach. Much time and effort would be spent in connection with materials which do not warrant expediting, either because of their low value, or, more usually, because of their low criticality. In other words, we should spend most of our expediting effort on those items where delay would be expensive.

Approaches to differentiation

The 80/20 principle is applicable here. A large proportion of the organisation's orders will together only account for a small proportion of the money spent. There will be a small number of high value orders, and these should be carefully monitored because the buyers will have scheduled receipt in such a way as to avoid the need to carry these items in stock or awaiting use for too long, because of the money which is tied up in them. Due delivery dates will be *needed* dates.

The other main basis for differentiation is the criticality of the item. If a slight delay in delivery will cause only minor inconvenience, then obviously expediting effort should be diverted to other areas. The basic question is 'what will be the consequences for our organisation if delivery failure happens?' The more serious, the greater the expediting effort. Other factors, such as the reliability of the supplier, and how difficult the lead times are will be considered.

RECEIPTS FROM SUPPLIERS

Unloading

The majority of goods will arrive at their final destination by road, despite the fact that they may well have been carried for the major part of their journey by some other method of transport such as rail or air.

It may seem common sense to off-load the goods from the vehicle as promptly as possible, and this will indeed be the case where supplies are routine. Sometimes though, a little thought prior to off-loading can be worthwhile.

The following questions should be asked.

Are we the consignees? It is not that unusual to find that materials are brought to the wrong organisation, particularly if addressing or documentation is unclear, or where the driver is not familiar with the area.

Are the goods for this delivery point? Many large organisations have more than one location where deliveries may take place. The delivery of material to the incorrect location can give rise to substantial delays or additional handling.

Are the materials hazardous in any way? Hazardous materials must be clearly marked as such, and those responsible for receiving them have a duty to ensure that the material is dealt with in the proper manner. Unloading should not take place until the necessary safety and other equipment is in place.

Can we avoid double handling? This can perhaps be done by sending goods direct to point of use.

Are the materials to be given any priority? If goods bear priority markings, or the receiving staff are aware that goods are urgently required, then the news of their arrival should be promptly communicated, perhaps before unloading takes place.

What unloading method is appropriate? A responsible individual should be given the authority to determine the way in which the delivery vehicle is to be unloaded, particularly if the materials are difficult in any way. Many organisations have a variety of handling equipment available in the receiving area, but it is seldom available instantly. It may be tempting to drop cases onto an old tyre, or slide them down makeshift ramps made from planks, and, whilst these and other manual methods are not necessarily inappropriate, the possibility of accidents to personnel, or damage to materials is much more likely than if appropriate mechanical aids (usually in the form of a fork-lift truck) are employed.

Times of deliveries

If storehouses are not to be open for business twenty-four hours a day and seven days a week, then it is advisable to see that all suppliers are informed of the days and times during which facilities will be available to accept deliveries. This information can be on the order form.

Copy orders

When orders are placed, the storekeeper must be informed what he is expected to receive and when it is likely to arrive. This is usually done by sending him a copy of the order form.

Suppliers' advice notes

When a supplier has goods ready for delivery he normally prepares an advice note to be sent through the post to his customer. This document gives a description of the goods, the quantity involved, the method of transport and the date of dispatch, and the intention is that it should be in the hands of the receiving storekeeper before the goods themselves arrive. In some cases, it may not be sent by post, but handed over on arrival by the driver of the vehicle making the delivery. It should be understood that advice notes are not always forthcoming; for articles of small value they are neither necessary nor desirable, and they are frequently not sent for regular routine deliveries from established suppliers who use their own transport.

Carriers' consignment notes

If an independent transport organisation, such as the railway or a road-haulage company, is employed to convey goods to the customer, the supplier still sends an advice note in the usual way, but the carrier may also send a carrier's consignment note by post in advance. This is most important in the case of rail transport. If several wagons are involved, it may be necessary to make special preparations for unloading to avoid demurrage. Demurrage is a charge made by the railway authorities where wagons are held awaiting unloading by a consignee. The charge is at a rate per wagon per day, and the rate increases as time goes on. Undue delay can, therefore, be very expensive. Similar documents are used by road hauliers but, as a rule, they accompany the vehicle. The carrier's consignment note shows the name and address of the consignor, the description of the goods, the number of packages and their identification marks if any, the weight, details of the delivery vehicle, and the name and address of the carrier.

Suppliers' packing notes

Where materials are supplied crated or otherwise packaged, it is usual for the supplier to send a packing note which is either included in, or securely fixed to, the package. This may be a specially prepared document but sometimes a copy of the advice note is used. Where separate packing notes are available, they normally give much more detail about the contents than the corresponding advice notes.

Checking for quantity

From the above it will be seen that the receiver may be informed of deliveries by a variety of methods:

1 The copy order
2 The supplier's advice note
3 The carrier's consignment note
4 The supplier's packing note
5 Electronically, via the computer.

A typical receiving routine is as follows:

1 Before delivery, the receiver marries up the supplier's advice note and the carrier's consignment note with the corresponding copy order to see that there is no disagreement.

2 When the goods arrive the receiver makes sure that the quantity and description correspond with what has been advised. This is done by weighing, counting or measuring, and the appropriate equipment, such as weighbridges, scales, tape-measures, etc., must be provided. Where a consignment consists of one or more full loads in lorries or railway wagons, the check is best done over a weighbridge, taking the gross and tare (or unladen) weight. The gross weight is the weight of the vehicle plus its load, and the tare is the weight of the empty vehicle itself. All railway trucks and load-carrying road vehicles are required by law to have their tare weight painted upon them. Sometimes it is not practicable actually to weigh the vehicle empty at the time of receipt without a lot of trouble, and then the consignee will accept the painted tare. If the net weight or quantity of a delivery corresponds with that stated on the carrier's consignment note, and the goods appear to be undamaged, the storekeeper signs that document to confirm receipt of the goods and returns it to the carrier by post or to his representative (e.g. the lorry driver) by hand if he is available.

3 Where short weight is received, goods are damaged or packages are missing, it is necessary to inform the carrier immediately, irrespec-

tive of whether the delivery is made in the supplier's own transport or not. If a consignment note is available, it is the storekeeper's responsibility to endorse that document with details of the damage or shortage. Where it is not possible, in the time available, to examine a consignment sufficiently to find out whether there is any damage or shortage, the storekeeper signs the consignment note and endorses it 'Unexamined'. Where damage subsequently becomes apparent, the storekeeper should be authorised to notify the carrier direct in order to avoid claims being time-barred.

Goods-inwards records

As far as possible goods ought to be checked completely as soon as they arrive, but it sometimes happens that deliveries cannot be reported in detail on the day of receipt. This may be so where there is a large number of small deliveries or, alternatively, in the case of major consignments where labour is perhaps not readily available. It is important that certain information is promptly recorded at the time of receipt, and that there is a check that all items are finally reported in detail. For this purpose a goods-inwards record should be kept to maintain, every day, brief details of all goods from outside suppliers, showing the following particulars of each consignment:

1 Date
2 Consignor
3 Method of transport
4 Vehicle number
5 Brief description of goods
6 Goods Received Note number (*see* below)

These records are sometimes referred to as log books if kept in manual form, though it is usual today to employ a software system. They are maintained to make certain that no receipt is overlooked, and are particularly useful where materials are taken in at several different locations. The goods-inwards record requires examination at regular intervals to confirm that a transaction has, in fact, been prepared in respect of every entry.

Goods-received information

This may be directly keyed into the computer, or a separate goods-received note may be prepared for each delivery. In either case the following information will be used.

1 Date of receipt (as log sheet)
2 Consignor
3 Consignor's advice note number
4 Order number
5 Vocabulary number
6 Description
7 Quantity received, undamaged
8 Number and type of packages
9 Method of transport
10 Damage/Shortage report number (if applicable)
11 Any delivery in excess of the quantity ordered
12 Storekeeper's identity
13 Inspector's identity.

Information on receipts needs to be passed to various locations. Typically, the accounts payable section, the purchasing department, the using department and the inspection department will need to know. The range of interested parties will vary from one organisation to another of course.

The information may be made available via the computer, or by hard copies of goods received notes.

Damage/shortage report

The storekeeper raises a serially numbered damage/shortage report form or keys in the necessary information on the appropriate computer screen in any of the following circumstances:

1 If goods are delivered damaged.
2 If goods received show a shortage in comparison with the supplier's advice note or packing note.
3 If goods have not arrived within the allowed time for the method of carriage.

If a form is used, it is normally raised in four copies, distributed as follows:

Copy No. 1 to the carrier
Copy No. 2 to the supplier
Copy No. 3 to the office responsible for clearing invoices
Copy No. 4 for retention in the storehouse

Every day the file of suppliers' advice notes is examined to ensure that claims for non-delivery are submitted within the allowed time for road and rail carriage or postal service, as the case may be. This is important because carriers, including the railways and the Post Office, will not accept liability for non-delivery, loss, damage or shortage unless they are notified immediately in writing of the circumstances, and a detailed claim in writing is made within a few days.

As a general rule in cases of non-delivery, damage, shortage or excess deliveries, the storekeeper's duties cease with the preparation of the damage/shortage report. Further correspondence with the carrier or suppliers is normally dealt with by the invoice section after this stage. The storekeeper, however, retains the package in which the goods are received, so that it is available for subsequent inspection if required. In due course, the invoice section will give the storekeeper disposal instructions for the damaged goods.

Packages slips

Packages may be listed in three categories:

1 Non-returnable, e.g. paper wrappings, small cardboard cartons. For these no documentation is necessary.
2 Charged by the supplier and to be paid for immediately, the payment being recoverable when the packages are returned.
3 Those for which no charge is made at the time of delivery but which are chargeable in due course if they are not returned to the supplier.

For the last two categories some record is necessary to ensure either that repayment is obtained or charges are avoided for packages returned. Returnable package data may be entered on the computer at the same time as the receipt of goods is recorded. Alternatively in a manual system, at the same time as the goods received note is made out, a further document giving details of each returnable package is drawn up. This document is usually called a package receipt slip and is normally prepared in two copies, one to be retained in the stores and one to be sent to the invoice section which will enter the invoice number and the amount paid for packages, and use the document to support the clearance of invoices for payment.

It is practice in some organisations not to pay for returnable packages, but simply to return them when empty.

Demurrage

Sometimes called detention, this is the name given to the penalty charges that may be levied by a supplier or shipper if the receiving organisation retains delivery vehicles or equipment beyond the contractual period of 'free' time.

A trailer, container, rail wagon or other item will be required to be turned round and made available to the carrier within an agreed period, typically 48 hours excluding weekends or holidays. If this is not done, a charge will be levied. The charge may be on a sliding scale, with the rate increasing as the period of delay grows longer.

TRANSFERS FROM OTHER STOREHOUSES WITHIN THE ORGANISATION

From time to time goods are moved from one storehouse to another, and the arrangements have to be somewhat different from the practice followed for receipts from outside suppliers. There is no need for quality inspection in respect of materials transferred within the same organisation, but it is still necessary to check quantities and inspect for damage.

Where the storehouses are within the same factory perimeter, the movement of goods from one to another is documented by a transfer note, which is usually prepared by the issuing storekeeper in four copies, distributed as follows:

Copy No. 1 ⎱
Copy No. 2 ⎰ to the receiving storekeeper
Copy No. 3 to the store accounts section
Copy No. 4 to be retained by the issuing storekeeper

When the consignment has been checked on arrival, the receiving storekeeper signs Copy No. 1 to indicate that the goods have been received as advised, and sends the document to the store accounts section to record the transaction in the stock control accounts. He retains Copy No. 2 in his own files. Where any damage or shortage arises, a damage/shortage report should be prepared.

Receipts from a central store can be dealt with in a similar way but, instead of using a transfer note, a demand-on-central-stores form may be employed.

RETURNS FROM PRODUCTION OR OTHER DEPARTMENTS

It may occasionally be necessary for production or other departments to return materials which have been drawn from the storehouse and subsequently found either to be in excess of their needs or unsuitable for the intended purpose.

Return-to-store Notes. Transactions of this nature are normally documented by the use of return-to-store notes prepared by the departments responsible for sending the goods back to the storehouse. The information on the note will, following acceptance by the storekeeper, be input to the computer.

SCRAP ARISING

In many industries, there are regular arisings of scrap in the form of offcuts, turnings, residues, production rejects and waste materials handed over to the stores department. This can be done by using an ordinary return-to-stores note, but in many organisations a special scrap-advice form is used instead.

In some circumstances it may not be practicable for the production department to give details of the weight of scrap or for the storekeeper to weigh it as it arises, and the scrap material is simply accumulated in the storehouse or stockyard until a suitable quantity is available for disposal. When the sale is made, the material is weighed as it is removed, and the appropriate credit can then be given to the department concerned by means of the storekeeper raising a scrap-advice form instead of the document being prepared in the first instance by the user.

INSPECTION

Checking for quality

A part of the procedure associated with the receipt of goods and their placement in storage is a check for quality. A great deal of attention is being paid to quality in industry today; there seems to have been a realisation that getting the product right is a paramount concern for any organisation operating in a competitive environment.

This increased concern for quality, which is reflected in the widespread use of quality assurance schemes, quality circles, 'right first time' initiatives and so on has, paradoxically, led to less rather than more inspection taking place. It has recently been reported that in a typical Western mass-production manufacturing concern it would be expected that around ten per cent of shop floor personnel would be employed as specialist inspectors, whereas in the equivalent Japanese company, where quality assurance activities have been developed to a very sophisticated level, one or two per cent would be the norm. The reason is of course that responsibility for quality is seen as being the concern of all, and checking is built into the actual production or assembly processes.

Notwithstanding this 'quality revolution', it is an obvious fact that defective material lying ready for use in the company store is a kind of time bomb, which will do its damage at, or following, the time of issue.

The possible outcomes range from, at best, the inconvenience and costs of a user returning defective material for replacement, through the range of delays from minor production stoppages to the failure of a product in service, with possible serious damage, loss of customer goodwill or heavy warranty claims.

An obvious means of ensuring that the quality of incoming goods is up to standard is to inspect every item of the incoming delivery. Indeed, in cases where the very highest levels of reliability are essential, 100 per cent inspection, at least, is regarded as necessary. In the majority of cases, however, the cost precludes 100 per cent inspection, which is also out of the question where destructive testing is the only means of assessing product quality, for example if fuses have to be tested, or fail loads determined.

Sampling inspection

The advantages of sampling over 100 per cent inspection have long been recognised, relatively arbitrary and crude 'spot checking' procedures being employed long before the development of statistically based acceptance sampling techniques. With no real foundation at all, it was – and perhaps still is – often recommended that, for instance, 10 per cent of an incoming batch should be inspected as a check on product quality; only those batches represented by samples containing no defects being accepted. Such a plan offers virtually nothing in return for the cost of inspection. To be successful, an acceptance sampling plan must be designed to suit each particular case, seeking an economic balance between the costs of inspection and the increased costs of processing defective items. Or, if the defective parts are dispatched to customers, a balance between the cost of rehandling, replacement and possible loss of goodwill and the cost of increasing the quality control and inspection effort.

In the simplest form, acceptance sampling decisions are based on the testing of a sample size (n), taken at random from a batch size (N). If a rejection condition is indicated, it is usual to carry out a 100 per cent inspection of the batch. In general, acceptance sampling is appropriate where:

1 Inspection involves destructive testing.
2 The costs of accepting a defective item are not prohibitive.
3 Material arrives in large batches.
4 It is possible to take a truly random sample.
5 It is economically feasible consistently to identify material as acceptable or not. Sampling cannot predict the quality of the parent batch if this consistency cannot be achieved.

It is desirable, where possible, to inspect for 'attributes' rather than by 'variables' where sampling inspection is concerned. The distinction, which is an important one, is simply that an attribute is something which is either there or not, for example a lug on a casting, 'light' when a lamp is energised, or a component on a printed circuit board. A variable on the other hand is something which needs to be measured in some way, for example the thickness of a coat of paint, the pitch of a screw thread or the resistance of an electronic component. By far the easiest and most consistent form of inspection is for attributes, and much ingenuity has been employed in attempts to reduce variables, with an infinity of possible measurements, to attributes which simply indicate 'pass' or 'fail'. Many kinds of 'go/no go' gauges are in use, all of them having in common the fact that a part within the permissible tolerance will fit or 'go' when one part of the gauge is applied, and will not fit 'no go' when a different part of the gauge is used. A common type of go/no go gauge takes the form of a double-ended plug gauge used for checking the diameter, of, say, a drilled hole. One end, the 'go' part, will just fit into a hole of the correct size, the 'no go' end will not. If the hole is too small, neither plug will fit; if it is too big then both parts of the gauge will enter; in either case the part fails inspection, as it does not have the attributes for passing the test.

Statistical inspection is based on the practice of taking a sample of a specific size (n) from an incoming delivery, and either rejecting the entire batch, or subjecting it to a 100 per cent inspection if more than a certain number of defectives (c) are found in the sample. The incoming batches will be of a certain size (N). Thus the expression $N = 50, n = 10, c = 5$ defines a 'sampling plan', indicating that material will be arriving in batches of 50, that samples of 10 will be randomly selected from each batch, and if more than 5 defectives are found in the sample then the whole batch will fail inspection.

The design of sampling plans, based on the rules of probability, is a scientific activity best performed by qualified statisticians. The objectives of all sampling plans are to provide economically for inspection which will give rise to a high probability of acceptance of good quality batches and a high probability of rejection if the quality is poor.

Fortunately for those concerned with the inspection of incoming goods, there will be no need to commission the design of sampling plans to suit particular circumstances, as various comprehensive volumes of sampling plans are published such as the Dodge-Roming tables, or those produced by the British Standards Institution (BS 6000 and 6001). It is perhaps unnecessary to point out that the field of statistical quality control is a somewhat complex area, and that in a text of this kind a mention of only the fundamentals must suffice.

Inspection by storekeepers

Where there is no separate inspection department, or where that department deals only with a limited number of commodities, the storekeeper may be required to undertake the examination of goods for quality as well as quantity. He is, therefore, provided not only with a copy of the official order on the supplier, but also with relevant specifications or samples and with suitable equipment necessary for the degree of inspection which he is required to perform. In these circumstances the storekeeper signs the goods-received note not only for the receipt of the goods but also for their inspection.

Inspection by technical staff

In small organisations, inspection arrangements by storekeepers as described above may be supplemented, for items of a technical nature, by some degree of examination carried out by suitable members of the technical staff such as the plant engineer or the works manager. It is essential that appropriate instructions be issued, making clear to all concerned which items are to be inspected by storekeepers and which require also the signature of a technical officer.

Inspection by inspection department

The responsibility of the inspection department staff for goods received from suppliers must be clearly defined and, if they are not to inspect all deliveries, the items with which they are to deal must be listed. Inspectors have authority to accept or reject materials and endorse goods-received notes accordingly, unless separate inspection certificates are prepared. Storekeepers are instructed that goods awaiting inspection are to be segregated in a separate place in the storehouse (preferably enclosed) and that they are not to be made available for issue until cleared by the inspection department.

Inspection at supplier's premises

In large organisations, particularly Government departments, arrangements may be made for material to be inspected on the supplier's premises including, in some cases, examination during the various stages of manufacture. Where this is done an inspection certificate is given before the goods are dispatched and no inspection, or at least only a limited check, is necessary at the point of receipt. In these circumstances, a copy of the inspection certificate is sent to the storekeeper as soon as it is available. This avoids the need for the material to be held in the inspection bay and it can be put away in its appropriate place in the storehouse immediately on receipt, thus avoiding double handling.

Rejection

Where items are rejected, the inspection department representative either signs the appropriate space on the goods-received note as rejected, or alternatively indicates the reason for rejection on the inspection certificate or prepares a separate rejection-report document, or causes the computer record of the transaction to be amended. The accounts payable section is informed, and the goods are held pending negotiations or ultimate return to the supplier, in accordance with instructions to be issued in due course by the purchasing office.

Bonded or quarantine stores

These expressions are used to describe goods which are held in a special storehouse or a separate enclosure within the storehouse, awaiting clearance by the inspection authorities. They are commonly encountered in firms engaged on work where materials are subject to examination by Government inspecting officers before, during, or after manufacture. Nothing should be issued from such a storehouse without the permission of the appropriate inspector.

VENDOR QUALITY RATING

Although not directly concerned with receipt, a note on quality rating is appropriate at this point. It is now generally recognised that inspection is a cost, and adds no value to a product. Emphasis has swung to the prevention of defectives rather than their detection, and vendor quality rating can contribute to this approach.

As has been said, the need for high levels of quality and reliability is accepted, but nothing can be done without considering costs and prices. The buyer's aim is to obtain goods of the required standard of quality and reliability at the most favourable price available and it is often difficult to decide what is the best value for money. Perhaps the most objective approach to this problem has been the introduction of quantitative assessments of quality into the purchasing formula. These arrangements are known by various names such as vendor quality rating schemes, suppliers quality assurance schemes, suppliers incentive schemes and so on. Whatever the title may be, they are procedures based mainly or exclusively on a logical evaluation by the purchaser of 'bought out' articles, in order to produce a quality grading factor for each supplier which can be used to make purchasing decisions based on both quality and price.

Vendor quality rating is most easily devised and applied to subcontracted or 'bought out' supplies in the electrical and mechanical-engineering fields where there are large quantities of repetition work of a relatively light class of components but there are procedures for the assessment of quality in other fields of industry or commerce which are no less significant.

In this connection the term quality is used in the restricted sense of quality of manufacture only, that is, whether an article conforms to the specification provided and whether the standard of workmanship is appropriate to the design. It follows, therefore, that what is said here applies only to items for which the design and specification have been clearly set out or approved by the purchaser.

In the normal competitive business world there has always been some incentive to attain higher standards of quality but often it has presented itself only in an abstract form which is so easily discounted, particularly when short-term views are ruling. Vendor quality rating is a challenge to this less than satisfactory condition. It is valuable both for the purpose of creating a rapid improvement in quality in the first instance and as a permanent discipline. It is a natural development of the inspection procedures which have been going on for many years, such as the approved inspection organisation system of the Ministry of Defence, and similar arrangements operated by other Government Departments, the Air Registration Board and many large-scale purchasers.

Conditions favouring introduction

A quality incentive procedure can only be introduced and successfully worked under certain conditions. First of all the purchaser must have a demand for 'bought out' supplies in sufficient quantities over an extended period of time so that there is enough statistical evidence on which to base a scheme and enough potential business for the suppliers to be interested. Another important condition is that the purchaser should already be running, within his own organisation, a satisfactory quality control system from which he has acquired firsthand experience of the practical problems and results so that he has the knowledge successfully to introduce the principles involved to his outside suppliers and to give them guidance and help where necessary.

Most schemes have been started not only to improve the quality of deliveries but also to make a saving in the inspection costs of the buyer. Good and well controlled vendor quality rating is a first step towards removing duplication of inspection at the supplier's and the purchaser's premises and ultimately leads to giving the supplier a full sense of responsibility for the quality of his work.

Preparatory steps

It is essential that an approach should be made to the top level of the suppliers' managements in the first place. Only at this level can the full implications of the arrangements and the value of the incentive be assessed. Different circumstances may put the emphasis on different aspects of the advantages to both parties, but the two principal arguments to gain a supplier's support are:

1 That to achieve and continue to maintain an acceptable level of consistent quality is a powerful means of attracting more business, particularly long-term business.
2 That by becoming a preferred supplier to a large organisation, access is gained to their resources of technical knowledge, experience and facilities, with consequent advantages.

The Vendor Quality Rating Scheme is normally the responsibility of an established senior executive who knows the purchasing, production, inspection, and economic problems pertaining to the class of work under consideration, in particular those bearing on the reputation of existing suppliers. When seeking fresh suppliers a standard form of questionnaire will be found necessary, incorporating questions of the type shown below:

Numbers, grading, qualifications, experience and responsibilities of inspection staff.

Facilities available, such as laboratory, view room, receiving inspection department, gauge inspection department, tool, gauge and drawing stores, and precision inspection equipment.

What inspection stations are established, are there any 100 per cent stations and is there a patrol inspection?

Are drawings, route cards and gauges available to operators?

What quality-control procedure is used for incoming supplies?

Is the procedure for inspecting tools satisfactory and is the machine-tool maintenance adequate?

What the procedure is for approving the 'first off'.

How corrective action is taken during production.

Are salvaged are re-worked parts re-inspected?

How is defective material segregated and what are the arrangements for disposing of rejections and scrap?

Whether the paper work is adequate and up-to-date.

Assessing and supplementing the responses is a task demanding broad experience; decisions operating against 'the small man' with his limited resources but possibly first-class ability and good intent should be avoided. A personally conducted appraisal is frequently required in the place of, or supplementing, written questions and answers.

The importance of impartiality

The system should be a logical and gradually introduced development of the existing incoming inspection procedures. An initial rating may have nothing more to support it than a necessarily arbitrary assessment deduced from an appraisal of a potential supplier's resources and his methods of controlling quality, and should be reviewed and revised if necessary, immediately more evidence is forthcoming about the quality of deliveries. Established ratings must be based on the facts which emerge from statistical evidence.

Each scheme must be tailored expressly to suit not only the product but also the current needs and past experience of the organisation.

Assessment of quality rating

Adequate records are kept for all incoming consignments, showing full particulars of the methods of inspection, and the numbers accepted, rectified, and rejected outright. It is also most desirable to keep detailed costs for these inspection operations and for any associated expenses such as extra transport, works visits, etc. The results can then be applied by various methods to suit the circumstances of the business, for example:

1   The most elementary form is to place suppliers in two simple categories – acceptable and unacceptable. Any unacceptable firm, therefore, gets no business until they show some evidence of improvement.

This method can be extended to produce a number of broad categories such as excellent, good, fair and unacceptable, with the result that those in the 'excellent' or 'good' range will tend to get more work than those classified as 'fair', unless there are large differences in prices offered.

2   If the quality control records are sufficiently well-developed, it is possible to rate suppliers numerically in relation to the proportion of rejects found, and to express the result as a percentage, e.g. 98, 96, 85 and so on – ratings below a certain figure being of course unacceptable. These percentages may simply be used as a general guide in placing business, but alternatively if there is enough confidence in the scheme they can be applied as a factor to the quoted price, and orders placed on this basis, e.g.:

Supplier A –   price quoted £1,000, rating 85 per cent – effective price £1,176.

Supplier B –   price quoted £1,050, rating 95 per cent – effective price £1,105.

3   If it is possible from the purchaser's records to derive an actual cost of receiving inspection for individual components from each supplier, this amount can be added to the quoted price before the buying decision is made, e.g.:

Supplier A –   price quoted £1,000 – purchaser's inspection cost £120 – effective price £1,120.

Supplier B –   price quoted £1,050 – purchaser's inspection cost £25 – effective price £1,075.

These examples are not the only methods available, nor have they been dealt with in detail. Some of the more sophisticated applications can be very complicated.

When ratings have been calculated, it is normal practice to communicate the results to the suppliers, to inform them from time to time of any changes in their rating, and to help in every way possible to improve the performance of those not in the highest category. The nature of the work affects the method of rating. Some items have closer tolerances than others and are of more consequence functionally, and for these, a higher standard is required. Sometimes suppliers are grouped according to the nature of the business they handle, and different standards are adopted for each group.

Assessment of delivery rating

In a similar way to what is done in respect of quality performance, it is possible to keep delivery records, showing shortages, early or late consignments, or any variation on the contracted delivery programme. These facts can be used to produce a delivery rating, which may be applied either separately or in conjunction with the quality rating. This makes the whole operation more complicated, and is normally attempted only where delivery is of vital importance and where the quality scheme is already well established.

Other assessments

Some firms who have already had quality and delivery rating arrangements working successfully for a period of years are investigating the practicability of bringing in other facts which may be relevant, such as service, packaging, and product improvement by the supplier. These experiments appear at the moment to be tentative and inconclusive and there is little evidence of any significant development.

Conclusion

The quality rating is the most objective and also probably the most important, but the assessment of all the factors presents difficulty, and none of the methods so far devised is ideal. There are also certain practical considerations which may override the theoretical conclusions. For instance, if delivery is required within one month there is no point in accepting the quotation of a contractor who cannot supply until three months hence, however good his rating may be. If a firm has been receiving satisfactory bulk deliveries of an important component from one supplier for a long time it might be thought unwise to switch the whole of the order all at once to somebody else.

MARSHALLING RECEIPTS

In an organisation operating on a large scale, it is not always practicable to pass goods to production or to the stores immediately they are received. At the same time it is necessary to segregate items awaiting inspection and to sort the various articles into groups which are ultimately to be delivered to the same locations. To meet these needs, a marshalling area may be marked out on the floor between the unloading dock and the storage area. This space is subdivided into sections appropriate to the locations of the main categories of goods in the storehouse or user department. Where necessary, inspection benches are also provided and the staff checking receipts operate in conjunction with the inspection department staff. Items accepted and ready to be put away are handed over daily to the personnel in charge of the destination areas.

In some concerns the goods-receiving section is an independent organisation occupying its own separate building and forwarding materials to the storehouses only after the receipt and inspection procedure and documentation have been completed.

RECEIPT OF CAPITAL ITEMS

Where a capital development programme is going on, some special stores arrangements are necessary. Copy orders for the equipment or materials to be treated as capital should indicate that fact to the storekeeper. It may be thought worthwhile to have a special series of goods-received notes but, if not, then the relevant documents ought to be specially marked 'Capital'. As far as possible, all capital goods should be placed in a separate location and items associated with individual projects kept together. It may be inconvenient to have some items sent to the storehouse at all. Especially if bulky materials or heavy machines are involved, it is desirable for delivery to be made to the actual site where the equipment is to be installed. In this event, care must be taken to see that the storekeeper is fully aware of the position and is advised of the date of delivery so that he can make arrangements for such inspection as may be required, and complete the appropriate receipt documents.

CHAPTER 4

Issue and dispatch

The service given by the stores department to other departments becomes effective at the point where a storekeeper makes issues of goods, and users will naturally judge the efficiency of the stores organisation by the standard of service provided to them.

AUTHORISATION OF ISSUES

Stores in stock represent money, and should not be misappropriated, wasted or improperly used. For this reason, issues cannot be made indiscriminately and, before goods can be withdrawn from a storehouse, there must be some authority for the transaction. This may be in the form of a signed document, a verbal instruction or a routine arrangement.

The normal method is to use an issue note signed in the appropriate box by an authorised person. Storekeepers should have full details of the names, designations and specimen signatures of all persons empowered to approve issue notes. In some circumstances it is desirable to restrict the authority of different levels of management within certain financial limits; for example, foremen may be permitted to sign for goods up to a value of £100, shop superintendents up to £1,000, the signature of the works manager being required above that figure. In a similar way, authority may be restricted for certain types of materials to officers in specific departments, e.g. only the chief electrical engineer or the foreman electrician being in a position to demand cable or electrical fittings, and the garage foreman being the sole authority for motor-vehicle spares.

Where there are scheduled issues to production or any other form of regular issues such as spares scalings, the authorisation may be undertaken by the production control department.

In some circumstances it is convenient to hand over stores simply on a spoken request by a known colleague, without the presentation of any written document. This is normally done only for items of comparatively small value.

Whatever method of authorisation is employed, it should be appropriate to the everyday needs of the organisation. If there are too few authorised signatories, a workman requiring material may have to spend an unreasonable time finding a supervisor to approve his demand, and a similar situation is likely to arise if more than one signature is required.

IDENTIFICATION OF REQUIREMENTS

Provision is made on issue documents for the description and stores code number of required items to be quoted, and this information is entered by the user who prepares the document in the first place. In practice, however, it often happens that the details given are inadequate or even inaccurate, and experienced storekeepers will be expected to find out exactly what is wanted and see that it is supplied. They will also check the code number on the issue voucher. Storekeepers must, therefore, be provided with copies of vocabularies, spare-parts lists and catalogues so that they have the means of identifying requirements without relying entirely on memory.

Goods demanded are not always available and, when this happens, the storekeeper may be required to suggest suitable alternatives. To do this effectively, the storekeeper must be thoroughly familiar with the materials and have some general knowledge of the production or operational processes in his firm.

TIMING OF ISSUES

So as to avoid delay in a busy storehouse, there will be a routine to provide for a smooth and even flow of work. Arrangements may be made for issues to some departments to be handled in the morning and some in the afternoon; workmen requiring stores may be instructed to attend at the storehouse only during certain hours, and so on. This should not be overdone, because it must be remembered that the watchword is service. The storekeeper should try to meet the convenience of users, and restricted times of issue should be applied only to avoid uneconomical peak loads of work in the storehouse, and to prevent waiting time on the part of those sent to collect materials.

Issuing documentation

Generally material will be withdrawn from stock and exchanged for a duly authorised document, the name of which will vary depending on the nature of the organisation and the type of issue.

Some of the names used are:

Stores requisition
Requirement voucher
Stores indent
Issue ticket/note/voucher
Stores order
Demand note
Kit marshall list
Picking list/note
Stores schedule

METHODS OF ISSUING STORES FOR INTERNAL USE

Issues must be organised to correspond with the needs of the enterprise and several different methods may be employed in one concern at the same time for various kinds of stores. For example, materials and components for the production shops can be supplied in accordance with prearranged schedules to meet the planned output, tools and gauges can be issued to machine operators on a replacement system, and special equipment used by fitters and electricians on maintenance jobs dealt with on a loan basis.

Some of the methods in common use are described below.

Issues on request

This is the simplest method, and there are three variations:

1 Immediate issues on presentation of an issue note by hand.
2 Issues made after the receipt of an issue note by post.
3 Immediate issues on verbal request only.

Issues on request – Method 1. The orthodox form of issue procedure is where the user comes to the storehouse and presents a properly authorised issue note or similar voucher giving details of what is required. The storekeeper then selects the items wanted, and hands them over in exchange for the document.

Issue notes may be prepared in any number of copies to suit individual needs, but the following is typical:

Copy No. 1. (Original) Handed to storekeeper, then passed to the stock record section for entering the quantity records; then to the store accounts section to credit the stock control accounts and debit the cost code chargeable.

Copy No. 2. Handed to the storekeeper and retained by him as his evidence of having made the issue.

Copy No. 3. Retained by the user department as evidence of the demand

Considering the information shown in the illustration in detail, the following points are worthy of note:

'*Serial number.*' This is for the purpose of controlling the documents. Examination of the numbers, after action in the stores office, will immediately indicate if any are missing from the sequence, thus providing a check on vouchers lost or misplaced. At the same time, if queries arise after the issue has been made, the issue note can easily be traced by its number. The serial number may be inserted by the storekeeper but, alternatively, the notes can be automatically pre-numbered before they are supplied to the using departments. In this latter case it will also be possible to check that users have presented all their vouchers up to date in the proper sequence and, if not, they can be asked to account for any discrepancies. This prevents issue vouchers being transferred from one person to another or otherwise used improperly.

'*Job number or cost code number.*' It is the duty of the user to provide this information. When the issue notes arrive in the stores accounts section, they are sorted into job or cost-code order, and the value of the material is charged to the appropriate job number or cost code. This is the basic mechanics of material costing.

'*Vocabulary number.*' This is the stores code number and is used to identify the goods accurately. The user is normally expected to insert this number but, where he neglects or is unable to do so, it is for the storekeeper to see that it is recorded.

'*Issued by.*' This space is for the signature or initials of the storekeeper making the issue. In the event of any subsequent query it serves to indicate who dealt with the transaction, but it is not always considered necessary, especially if a receipt signature is obtained.

'*Posted to stock records.*' This provides for the initials of the storekeeper or clerk to confirm that he has entered on the stock record or computer file the appropriate details from the issue note, and its purpose is to check that the posting has, in fact, been made.

'*Received.*' Here the recipient of the goods should sign to provide evidence of receipt. As mentioned above, if this space is completed, it may not be necessary for the storekeeper to sign the 'Issued by' section. Conversely, if the storekeeper signs his part, a receipt may not be required.

'*Classification summary.*' The information given here shows the numbers of the stock control accounts to which the values of the items appearing on the document are to be credited.

'*Place.*' If the stock records are kept in quantity and value, this amount is entered by the record section. If the records are in quantity only, the value is normally calculated by the accounts section.

The reader will observe that the issue note illustrated provides space for several items to be entered; this is known as a 'multiple' document. Alternatively, 'unit' or 'single item' documents may be employed; that is to say, a separate issue note for each item required. The choice between multiple and unit documents arises in respect of other stores forms such as goods-received notes and purchase requisitions, but it is usually of particular importance in connection with issue notes, because the number of issue notes to be handled is greater than the number of any of the other vouchers used in the stores organisation.

Issues on request – Method 2. Under this arrangement, the issue note is sent in by hand or post by the demanding department and the physical handing over of stores takes place later, either when the user calls for them at a prearranged time or when they are loaded by the storekeeper for delivery. The storehouse staff have adequate time available for selection and marshalling of the materials, and recipients have the advantage that they do not have to wait while the storekeeper finds and assembles whatever is required. The method is most convenient when the consumer is at some distance from the storehouse. It is also useful where the list of requirements is lengthy or complicated as, for example, with spares for machinery overhauls.

Issues on request – Method 3. In the case of issues on verbal demand, a person requiring stores calls at the issue counter and states his requirements. The storekeeper then selects the items wanted and hands them over. A procedure of this kind is normally employed only for items of comparatively small value which are required at short notice, such as hand tools, nuts and bolts, cleaning materials, lubricants, emery paper and other consumables. The storekeeper would be expected to know all callers by sight and would not, therefore, make any issues to a stranger without some inquiry.

Scheduled issues to production

In mass-production concerns, with the cooperation of the production control department or some other technical planning office, production materials are issued in quantities and at times to correspond with the manufacturing programme. The goods concerned are usually collected into a marshalling area in the first place. Thereafter they may be dealt with in several different ways:

1 Collected from the storehouse by the production department.
2 Delivered by the storehouse staff to the point on the production lines at which the process of manufacture is to commence.
3 Transferred into 'open-access' stores within the production shops. Open-access stores are storage areas on the shop floor which are not enclosed and are fitted with bins or racks containing materials which are taken and used by production personnel without documentation.

The documentation for scheduled issues is usually prepared by the production control or some such similar department, and the storekeeper's authority for issue is conveyed to him by his copy of the schedule.

Assemblies and kits

There are instances where composite issues of a standard nature are required at frequent intervals. This is most commonly encountered in the assembly stores of production factories where balanced sets of parts are required for assemblies or subassemblies included in the manufacturing programme. For example, the piston assembly for a diesel engine might consist of the following list of separate parts:

Number off	Name of Part	Stores Code Number
4	Piston head	25/02/3410
8	Compression ring	25/02/3411
4	Scraper ring	25/02/3412
8	Small-end bush	25/02/3413
4	Small-end pinion	25/02/3414
4	Connecting rod	25/02/3415
4	Big-end bearing	25/02/3416
8	Big-end nut and bolt	25/02/3417
8	Tab washer	25/02/3418

In practice, the document presented to the storehouse by the production department quotes simply the required number of piston assemblies and it is the duty of the storekeeper to see that all the individual parts are forthcoming in the appropriate numbers. In a similar way, tools or gauges for special jobs may be issued as complete kits. Sometimes the translation of complete kits into components is a very complicated operation involving technical interpretation in respect of variable items, e.g. radio equipment for the Armed Services. In these circumstances, the work is normally done by the stock control section instead of the storekeeper.

Imprest issues

An imprest system is one whereby a list of certain types of materials in given quantities is approved to be held either in a substore or on a production line or elsewhere. At the end of a given period, say a week or a month, the user concerned prepares a list of the materials consumed during that time, and presents an appropriate issue document at the main storehouse for replacement goods to bring the imprest stock up to the same level as it was at the beginning of the period. The arrangement is often used for supplying parts and materials to technicians who travel about in vans providing after-sales service or repair facilities to customers.

Replacement issues

For certain items, e.g. tools and gauges, operators may be required to present a used article to the storekeeper before a new one can be issued. This can be done with or without issue notes.

Loan issues

As a general rule, the issue of articles on loan from storehouses should not be encouraged, but it is sometimes unavoidable. For example, in the maintenance department, a number of comparatively expensive tools or pieces of equipment are required for short periods of use at frequent intervals. Such items are ammeters, surveyors' chains, instruments, electric handlamps, tap-and-die sets, special tools, and so on. These may not be on stores charge, but are controlled by the storekeeper and kept in the storehouse when not in use. It is necessary to keep stock records for the equipment concerned and also to maintain a register showing all loans made in date order. Workmen sign the register for everything issued to them and sign again when items are returned to store. The storekeeper inspects the register at regular intervals, makes inquiries about anything which has been out on loan for a protracted period, and reports to the appropriate supervisor any doubtful case. As an alternative to signing the loan register, users are sometimes provided with metal or plastic discs (known usually as 'tallies'). These discs bear the man's name and/or works number and are handed over in exchange for loaned equipment.

Issues to employees on repayment

Sales to employees from stock are often encountered in respect of tools, protective clothing, firewood, etc. Storekeepers concerned with these sales are instructed in writing as to the articles permitted and the persons to whom they may be sold. Payment is made either in cash or by deduction from wages, but storekeepers do not normally handle cash. Lists of sales are kept showing the date of the transaction, the employee's name and number, and the vocabulary number, description and quantity of goods sold. The purchaser signs for the items, and the original list is sent to the cashier to collect the money or to the wages office to arrange deduction from wages, as the case may be. Another copy is used for posting the stock records and subsequently passed to the accounts section. A third copy is retained by the storekeeper.

Allocated issues

In accordance with manufacturing schedules, some materials may be received on a programmed-delivery basis and kept for use only on the production line for which they have been purchased. This is done to make sure that there will be no interruption of production and the storekeeper will check that issues are not made elsewhere. For example, 20 mm diameter bright-steel bar to a given specification may be allocated to the production component 'XYZ'. If the maintenance department wishes to have some of this material to repair a machine, it cannot be issued unless the maintenance manager can obtain special authority from some senior official, such as the works manager.

Another type of allocation is that certain items are reserved for specific jobs or purposes to avoid the unnecessary use of material which is expensive or in very short supply. For instance, good quality deep-drawing steel sheet, although usable for many standard stamping and pressing jobs, may be restricted for issue only to special jobs where deep-drawing quality is essential.

The storekeeper must be informed of all allocations and enter appropriate particulars on his records, and issue notes relating to allocated materials should indicate the purpose for which these items are required.

Capital issues

Where the replacement of capital goods is a normal day-to-day feature, or where a capital development or reconstruction programme is in operation, special attention is usually given to the control and recording of the issues of capital material from storehouses. Instructions are given about the authorisation of such issues, and stock records (including bin cards, if any) are marked to show that the items concerned are reserved for a particular capital project. The storekeeper checks that, when issue documents are presented to him, the capital-project number quoted thereon for cost-allocation purposes corresponds with the project number which appears in his own records, and in some cases it is thought necessary to employ a special form of issue note. The procedure is similar in principle to that described previously for allocated issues.

Delivery and collection

In respect of all internal stores issues, the instructions should make it clear whether goods are to be delivered by the storehouse staff, collected by the user, or handled by some third party such as the transport department. If there are any restrictions about stores' opening hours or particular times for issue, or if any advanced notice is required by storehouses before issues can be made, the circumstances should be made known to all concerned.

Bulk issues

Bulk issues are made in set agreed quantities to designated departments. Material issued in this way is usually of a low-value high-usage category such as industrial fastenings, small electronic components or cleaning materials. Following issue from the stores this material is normally placed in an open access location in the user department so that staff can simply draw their requirements as and when they arise. Sometimes called 'free issue', this arrangement saves clerical work within the stores and helps the user by avoiding frequent completion of issue documents and associated trips to the stores.

Bulk issues do need to be carefully monitored and controlled to make sure that goods are properly located and cared for in the user departments, otherwise waste is likely to occur. The idea of bulk issuing, which is an arrangement designed to give rise to economies, should not be confused with the tendency for private sub-stores to be set up by user departments outside the control of the main stores.

DISPATCH OF GOODS OUTSIDE THE ORGANISATION

Finished products sent to customers

The storekeeper is informed of the issues to be made by means of a sales advice note, issue order or similar document from the sales department giving details of the items, the consignee's name and address, and any special requirements about packing, labelling or method of transport. Thereupon the storekeeper selects, packs and dispatches the goods in accordance with these instructions, and documents the transaction by preparing an advice note, and a packing note.

Items for repair and sales of scrap

When articles are sent out for repair or reconditioning, e.g. an electric motor to be rewound, when scrap is dispatched to a customer, or when goods are returned to suppliers because of excess deliveries or rejections, the procedure followed is similar to that for finished products sent to customers.

Free issues to suppliers

In some industries and in Government departments, materials, parts, tools, fixtures, patterns, etc., are supplied to contractors in connection with products which are being manufactured by them. Issues of this kind are recorded in such a way that the total amount issued to any given supplier may easily be ascertained, and a record kept of the number of free issues which have been returned by the supplier incorporated in finished products or otherwise. In this way the balance of free issues in the hands of any contractor for any particular order at any given time can be established. On dispatch from the storehouse, the documentation for free issues is similar to that for finished products.

Cost allocation

Whenever material is issued, the value has to be charged to the appropriate internal department or activity or to an outside customer. For this reason, all issue documents must show either the cost-allocation code number for internal issues, or the customer's name for external transactions. The appropriate cost or customer's account can then be debited with the value of the goods, and the stock control account concerned credited at the same time. For internal transfers between storehouses, the value of the issue will be simply a debit to the stock control account of the receiving storehouse and a credit to the account of the issuing storehouse. Special accounting arrangements are necessary for goods sent out for repair and for free issues, as neither of these categories is chargeable to the consignee.

Picking

Picking is the term used to describe the process of extracting goods from the bins and racks in a storehouse to collect all the items required to satisfy any particular issue note or other demand. In principle there are two main ways of doing this; sectional picking and travelling picking.

In the first case there is a storekeeper, with appropriate issuing staff, in charge of a particular section of the storage area, e.g. there may be separate sections for nuts and bolts, steel, machinery spares, bought-out parts, etc. When an issue document is received, the items appropriate to each section of the storehouse are segregated and the storekeepers are given lists of the items referring to their section only. Each section head then collects his items and delivers them to the issues-marshalling area. Alternatively, the same end may be achieved by sending the original issue document round from one section head to another until everything has been prepared. This system is only appropriate in very large storehouses and requires a good deal of organisation and coordination.

The second method, i.e. travelling picking, is to make one storekeeper responsible for collecting all the items appearing on the issue document wherever they may be located, and is the method employed in most medium-sized or small stores.

Marshalling

In a large storehouse, especially a central storehouse serving a number of operating units, the process of selection is followed by a further process of collecting together all items which are to be sent out at the same time to the same consignee. This is described as 'marshalling' and is usually done in a special place adjacent to the dispatch dock, described as the 'marshalling area', where there are either large compartments for each unit served, or spaces are marked off with lines on the floor for each unit. When goods have been selected they are deposited in the appropriate compartment or space in the marshalling area and, when the whole of a consignment has been so assembled, it is checked off by the dispatcher before it is loaded on the outgoing transport vehicle.

Dispatch

In a large storehouse there must be a routine for dispatch to the places served, including the following:

1 A routine system for the time of receipt of issue notes, the selection of what is required and marshalling of the needs of each customer.
2 A timed schedule of loading vehicles.
3 A detailed transport plan for journeys to users, timing and routeing each vehicle and providing, as far as practicable, for full loads outwards and return loads.
4 A regular system of checking to ensure that all items due for dispatch are loaded, and that no unauthorised items are put on the vehicles.

CHAPTER 5

Records and systems

The operation of the stores function and the control of stocks cannot be performed in an efficient manner without some means of capturing and storing information, and a facility for the analysis and use of this information.

The system of stock recording and the mechanism for the use of recorded information must be very carefully selected; and it may well be the case that more than one system is employed by a single organisation. Records and techniques should be appropriate to the stores in question, and the fact that any form of control costs money borne in mind. A highly sophisticated, complex and effective system suitable for recording and controlling the movement of main parts in a manufacturing plant would be inappropriate in, say, a stationery store.

Where goods are of low value and are fast moving it may be preferable to dispense with the idea of an orthodox stock record altogether. If the number of movements is several hundred a week, the cost of records entered daily will be very high and the information retained may not be worth the money spent on it. Some other form of control such as periodic physical check might be more appropriate.

Computers are generally employed for the purpose of maintaining and manipulating stock records, indeed stock control is perhaps an ideal area for the application of electronic data processing involving, as it does, the storage of large amounts of information, and the performance of a variety of procedures and processes using this information.

Perpetual inventory

Stock records are expected to maintain particulars of receipts, issues and balances remaining in stock for each individual item held in the storehouse from day to day. Because a system of records of this kind indicates at any time the quantity of goods on hand, it is sometimes described as a 'perpetual inventory'.

PURPOSES OF STOCK RECORDS

The reasons for maintaining records of stock are:

1 To indicate the amount of stock of any item at any time without it being necessary for the stock to be counted physically.

2 To establish a link between the physical stock and the stores accounts. All receipts and issues of stock cause adjustments to the stores accounts. At any time, therefore, if the records and accounts are both up to date, the sum of all the quantity balances on the records, when priced and evaluated, should equal the value balance on the corresponding stock control accounts.

3 To provide a means of provisioning, i.e. determining how much should be ordered to maintain stocks at the required level. To do this, it is necessary for the records to indicate outstanding orders and quantities allocated or reserved for special jobs.

4 To supply information for stocktaking, whereby the quantities of all items in the storehouse ascertained by physical checking are compared with the corresponding quantity balances on the records.

5 To provide a method of informing storehouse staff of the location of goods in the storehouse. If issue documents are passed through the record office before being dealt with in the storehouse, and stock location numbers are available from the system, these numbers can be entered on the documents to tell the storehouse staff where to find the goods.

6 To serve the purpose of a price list. If unit prices are recorded they can be used to price transactions.

In designing a system for any particular application, the extent of the information to be provided will be governed by the number of the above purposes which the system is expected to serve.

MANUAL SYSTEMS

Location of record cards

Stock record cards are usually kept together in one place. It is difficult to generalise on this point, but there is much to be said for holding the records in, or very near to, the storehouse building. If this is done, contact between the clerks keeping the records and the storehouse staff responsible for receipts, issues and stocktaking is easy, and queries or mistakes can be settled quickly without the need for telephone calls or written inquiries and explanations. At the same time, the transit of the various documents used is limited to the minimum and there is, therefore, a better opportunity of keeping the records up to date, less need for registration of incoming and outgoing forms, and less likelihood of documents being mislaid or lost. It is not desirable to have the records in open-storage areas because then it is necessary to allow all persons wishing to consult them to have access to the stores enclosures, and supervision is more difficult.

The best arrangement is to have the records in an office immediately adjacent to the storage area, on the same floor level and with direct access to it. In a large storehouse, with separate receipt and issue bays, it is perhaps best to have the record office near the receipt end because the receipt procedure is usually more complicated than that for issues, and more queries are likely to arise involving references to the records or their associated basic documents such as copy orders, inspection certificates, etc. Except in small storehouses, where the storekeeper has to maintain his own records, staff responsible for the physical processes of receipt and issue should not be allowed to have access to the stores records without supervision. This precaution minimises the risk of fraud or theft.

Quantity, price and value

Stock records can be kept in three ways:

1 Showing quantities only.
2 Showing quantity and unit price.
3 Showing quantity, unit price, the value of each transaction, and the total value of the balance of stock.

The arrangement under (1) above has the merit of simplicity, but limits the uses of the record.

If unit prices are shown as in (2) the following advantages may be obtained:

(a) The record can be used as a price list, and pricing of documents at the actual time of receipt or issue saves time later in the preparation of costing information.
(b) When it is necessary to compare the physical stock with the corresponding stock control accounts, the list of stock balances can be evaluated without reference to any other price records.
(c) When provisioning is being done, it is helpful to know the prices. More attention can then be paid to the more expensive items.

In the case of (3) above, where values are given as well as quantities and prices, there are additional advantages, shown below:

(a) Comparison with stock control accounts can be done by simple addition of the value balances on the records.

(b) The total value being shown for every movement makes it easy for supervisors to investigate major items where desirable.

The use of values has the drawback that additional operations are necessary to post the records, particularly where average prices are in force.

COMPUTERISED SYSTEMS

There are many systems for the maintenance of stock records and the processing of these data in use, many of them proprietary 'off the peg' pieces of software for implementation on standard computers, and others individually designed or adapted to meet an organisation's particular needs.

A computerised system will receive input data, carry out a computation or process on it, and output results. The input may be typed in directly on a keyboard, or read by appropriate devices from printed characters, bar codes, magnetic disc or tape, punched cards and other media. The output will usually either be displayed on a screen or take the form of a printout.

The computer can, in the simplest applications, merely replace a set of stock record cards by maintaining a set of information on stock levels and carrying out adjustment as necessary when directly instructed. A full-scale implementation of a computerised system will make much more than this simple 'record keeping' possible though. For example, the computer might assist in determining requirements by producing 'explosions' from production plans, whereby a detailed list of the necessary materials and components is computed from a simple statement of how many units of which particular products are to be assembled. Future requirements might also be computed, perhaps through the use of forecasting or simulation routines within the system's software. It is naturally commonplace to find that the stores and stock control elements of a computer system are integrated with the purchasing routines as part of a 'materials' system, and there is an increasing tendency for fully integrated suites of business software to be employed, in which all information records and flows are maintained by one set of records.

As has been mentioned, whether a company decides upon a manual or computer system for stores records and control will depend upon its particular circumstances, and whichever method is eventually chosen will depend upon the perceived economics of the alternatives. It is not possible in a text of this kind to deal in any comprehensive way with the vast range of computerised systems in current use, but the following three case histories might suffice to indicate some features and benefits of, respectively, a small, medium and large system. The case histories depict real organisations, though the names have been changed.

Welltill Ltd

Welltill Ltd is a manufacturer of mowing, cultivating and other gardening and horticultural equipment. In the early 1980s, at the time of the adoption of the computerised system, its turnover was £750,000 per year. Like many other companies, many of Welltill's vital paper-work systems had changed little since the company was a one-man-and-a-boy operation. The company invested £8,000 in a microcomputer and appropriate standard software and found the following advantages:

1 Staff devoted to stock records, purchase analysis and materials analysis dropped from 'one and a half men' to 'half a man'.
2 The value of components and sub-assemblies in stock went down by 50 per cent in a short period of time.
3 The ability of the company to respond to urgent orders and unex-pected peaks in demand was considerably improved.

These benefits were achieved by the straightforward purchase of a standard software package which maintained stock records and per-formed various analyses relating to stock movements and value.

Samson Adhesives

Samson Adhesives is a company producing industrial finishes, seal-ants, adhesives and related products for industrial and domestic use. The organisation was formed as a result of the merger of two similar companies, and the subsequent acquisition of a third concern.

Problems were encountered as a result of there being no systematic approach to stock records and control, each plant having at least one system of its own and a rather undisciplined approach to the oper-ation of the systems, with problems associated with shelf-life of materials, unrecorded issues, free issue to other plants and so on. The problems within the group were not confined to the supplies function;

there was also a diversity of approaches to production planning and control and accounting.

A decision was made that the systems in use within the company should be streamlined and standardised and should be dependent upon a central database accessed by visual display units at various locations in each factory. The database consists of a large amount of information which is continually brought up to date by, for example, new orders being received, price changes, materials issues and so on. An important part of this database is complete information on stocks.

The system is 'interactive' and 'on line' meaning that it can be interrogated by the users and that it can be contacted at any time. It also operates in 'real time', enabling transactions to be entered as they take place, and allowing users to see the current situation (rather than a printout of the state of affairs yesterday) at any time.

This system provides a very powerful tool for general management in that it is not dedicated to just one aspect of the firm's operations, but enables the interactions between all kinds of transaction to be viewed.

Inter Oil

Inter Oil is a very large multinational oil company operating on a worldwide basis in all sectors of the oil industry. It has long had a computerised purchasing and stock recording system, and has evolved a standard approach to electronic data processing for purchasing and supply. The system is sufficiently comprehensive and versatile to be used in all the organisation's operating territories. The system is designed to 'optimise' inventories, giving maximum service at minimum cost, rather than simply to record stock levels and movements.

The system is an 'exception reporting' one, meaning that it will indicate the fact that an item is not behaving according to set patterns. Printouts under such headings as 'slow moving items', 'overdue orders' and 'allocated material' can be generated. It is also possible for the system to make decisions based on criteria forming part of the programs, these criteria being adjusted or supplemented if necessary by the individual operating company within the group. Thus it is possible for the system not only to tell the user that it is time to reorder a particular item, but also to recommend an order quantity and a supplier.

The system covers the entire cycle of stock control and related activities including the following:

1 Stock records. Receipts issues and balances.
2 Stock valuation.
3 Stock check records including preparation of stock check lists and analysis of discrepancies.
4 Inventory planning. All active stock items are scanned periodically and action is recommended automatically when 'exceptions' are encountered.
5 Invoice control. The system assists in ensuring that materials are not paid for until safely received.
6 Surplus stock reporting.
7 Management control reporting, for example, actual stock values compared with optimums.
8 Ordering. Orders and other documents can be automatically prepared.
9 Direct to contract items can be entered on to and monitored by the system.

Naturally this large-scale system covering many thousands of part numbers depends upon the support of a large mainframe computer for its operation.

The database

Most computerised supply systems rely upon a database maintained by computer which will, typically, contain details for each stock item (filed by vocabulary or part number) as follows:

1 Description in words.
2 Unit value.
3 History of usage.
4 Outstanding orders.
5 Goods received but not yet available.
6 Unfulfilled demand.
7 Location.
8 Allocated stock.
9 Lead time.
10 Returns to supplier.

The data can be extracted and used in whatever way the computer is instructed, which means that applications not envisaged at the time of the establishment of the database can be developed as and when the need arises. For example, it might be discovered that a listing of all items with an annual usage value of over £50,000 would be useful, or it might be necessary to identify items which are slow moving yet

**A radio data terminal fitted to an order picking station enables data to
be entered in 'real time'**
(Courtesy: Microlise Radio Terminals)

of high value, with the idea of reviewing the need to stock such items
in mind. A summary of all the components with the word 'bearing'
in their name, or a routine to remind the storekeeper to check on o⁻

maintain particular items could easily be devised once the database has been established.

Typically, data on purchasing aspects of the organisation's activities will also be maintained, such as supplier(s), price and so on, since computerisation enables a greater integration of purchasing and stores systems.

The use of the database in connection with a small selection of stores procedures is described below. The descriptions are of the general aspects of the procedures; most organisations will devise special additional routines which suit their particular activities.

Receiving

When a batch of material arrives an operator in the receiving section will key into a computer terminal the details of the order number and the vocabulary number and quantity of items received. The computer will then perform a number of checks, perhaps using a check digit to ensure that the number entered is a valid one (see Chapter 2), and to make sure that the quantity delivered is appropriate according to the order quantity. If special inspection is required, or certification is necessary, the computer will inform the receiver that this is the case.

Assuming that all is in order, the operator will key in the quantity of goods received, and the computer will make the necessary adjustments to the data on stock balances. Possibly at this stage the computer will, via a printer linked electronically to the machine, output a goods received note or similar document to be circulated to the various interested parties in much the same way as a manually prepared document might be used. Many systems these days dispense with the need for such a document, producing appropriate summaries for the accounts payable section, purchasing department and other interested parties of goods received, with appropriate order numbers and other relevant information. These reports may be printed lists, usually called 'hard copy', or made available for call up on to a computer screen in the appropriate department. The reports may be issued selectively, with, for example, user departments routinely getting information only on material for which they have been waiting, or information on prices being suppressed for the stores department.

Picking

When a user department or customer calls for a range of items, information on the material required will be fed into a terminal or workstation at the turning point. This may be manually keyed in from the requisition, or automatically read by an input device, which might be an optical character reader, a bar code scanner or a device which scans data recorded magnetically. Of course, for automatic reading to take place the information will have to be prepared and presented in the appropriate way by the user department or customer. Frequently, a combination of automatic reading and manual input is found to be effective. An example of this kind of data entry which will be familiar to many readers is when purchases are made by credit card Some retailers have devices which automatically read the information about the customer's account which is encoded on the magnetic strip on the card, but the salesperson still has to key in the individual transaction details.

The database will be scanned by the computer, and information as to the appropriate economic picking route and sequence will be output in the form of a picking list. At this stage any shortages may also be reported. When the goods are handed over to the client the transaction will be confirmed, and the records brought up to date, with stock balances adjusted, and a record made of the charge to be made against the user.

Stock checking

There will be a software routine which instructs the computer to print out, at the appropriate time, instructions as to the items to be checked, and their location. Like the picking list mentioned above, this instruction will probably suggest a sequence in which the operation should take place in order that wasteful movement is avoided. If the stock-taking is to be blind, then the printout will not give details of the quantities which the records show as available.

The printout will probably be designed and laid out in such a way that spaces are provided for the checker to enter on the paper the quantity found. When the checking round is completed, the information from the count will be input. If no discrepancy exists, the computer will accept the input and the database will be confirmed as accurate in respect of that particular item. If there is a discrepancy, then a recount will be required, and if, after an appropriate number of recounts there is still a significant difference, then a report to the appropriate manager for executive action will be made.

As has been mentioned, the examples given are general outlines only, and are only three of the many routines and systems associated with stock management.

The examples are given from a situation where the computer is ' line' and operating in 'real time', that is to say that when transactions are recorded the information is input to the computer straight away, and the data is processed immediately so that the records are always up to date and reflect the current situation. If the organisation is of any size, then some form of networking will probably be employed, with the facility to input data and to call for information to be available at various locations, such as the goods receiving area, issue points, the stock control office and so on.

With manual systems it is very difficult, and even when possible usually not economic, to maintain records concurrently with the transactions. Record keeping is normally done in batches following the physical transactions (post-posting), or prior to the transactions (pre-posting). A source of much frustration is the fact that records are seldom, if ever, a strict reflection of the true situation.

The process whereby records are brought up to date on a continuous day by day basis is frequently called the 'perpetual inventory' approach, and most manual systems follow this principle. However, only a computerised system relying on a database as outlined in Fig. 5.1 can maintain economically a true perpetual inventory.

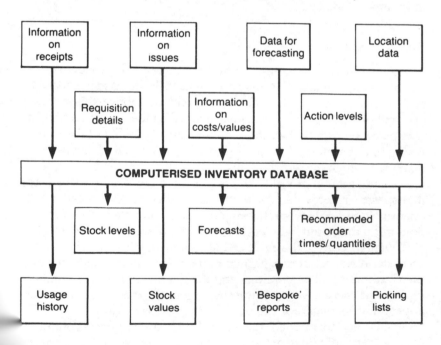

Fig. 5.1   The maintenance of data in a computerised system

ELECTRONIC DATA INTERCHANGE

Electronic data interchange, usually referred to simply as EDI, is the name given to the transmission and receipt of structured data by the computer systems of trading partners, often without human intervention. Many people apply the term 'paperless trading' to this process. The International Data Exchange Association defines EDI as 'the transfer of structured data, by agreed message standards, from one computer system to another, by electronic means'.

All kinds of data can be exchanged electronically, for example invoices, transfer of funds, enquiries, quotations, technical information and so on.

Many large organisations trade with each other through EDI links, and are enjoying the benefits which include reduced costs because of the automatic nature of the process, and the absence of a need for paper, telephone calls or fax transmissions.

Leaving aside the purchasing implications of EDI as being outside the scope of this text we can nevertheless see that there are still important implications for those concerned with the provision of materials. For example, the commonly used system where items are called off against an existing contract as and when the need arises is that the stores or stock control section informs the purchasing department who will in turn get in touch with the supplier, perhaps by telephone or post. Obviously this is a time consuming and therefore expensive procedure, and there is a distinct probability of mistakes arising as the message is handled by those along its route. With an EDI system linking the buying organisation with its supplier the replenishment can be triggered at the instant that the need arises, and the message is transferred from origin to destination without the possibility of corruption *en route*. A further benefit of an EDI link is that the computers of suppliers and customers can interrogate each other about stock levels, production plans and similar information so that activities are appropriately synchronised. As Fig. 5.2 shows EDI linkages can be internal or external.

EDI is not, in itself, a particularly complex idea, and there are few technical barriers to its implementation once the protocol by which the computers should communicate with each other has been established, and the equipment configured accordingly. The negotiation the commercial aspects of EDI arrangements between organisat' may be slightly more problematical. This notwithstanding, the ' EDI is growing rapidly, and the main beneficiaries are tho' cerned with the buying, selling and movement of materials

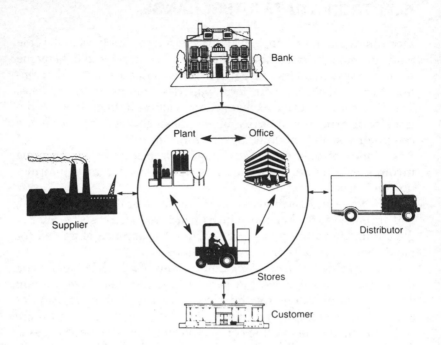

Fig. 5.2   EDI enabling internal and external communications

CURRENT DEVELOPMENTS

The world of computers and communications is a rapidly changing one, and a good deal of attention is currently being given to systems which enable direct communication between organisations without there necessarily being any human intervention. For example, electronic data interchange enables the computer at a car factory to relate production activity to stock levels, determine that a certain number of, say, dashboard circuits will be needed soon, and directly inform the supplier's computer of this state of affairs. Another interesting area is that of 'teletext', where data can be sent to a screen either as a broadcast signal, or through the telephone system or some other cable. A user can, for example, view a supplier's stock position and call material in real time, thus obviating the necessity for high stock of his own to allow for the delay inherent in conventional communications. A third example of computer technology finding application in the stores function is the remote terminal, a small, often hand-held device, which can be carried by the operator and used to input and access information on the main computer either through a telephone or by a radio link. Thus a salesman in the field can allocate stock the instant he makes a sale, or a stock checker can interrogate the system in an attempt to reconcile a discrepancy while located at the storage location of the items concerned. Many organisations are employing systems whereby the operators of mechanical handling equipment in the storehouse or stockyard receive information electronically as to what their next task or movement should be. The decisions as to how the movements should be planned and sequenced may be taken or aided by computer.

CHAPTER 6

Materials accounting

Adequate materials accounts are necessary for a variety of reasons, of which the following are the most important:

1 To indicate the value of stores in stock
2 To provide a basis for material costing
3 To provide the means of operating stock control by value

THE VALUE OF STORES IN STOCK

This is an important item in most concerns, and it is desirable to know at all times how much working capital is represented by stores in stock. When preparing a profit and loss account, it is essential to have the value of stock at the beginning and end of the accounting period. In the balance sheet, stock appears as an asset (a 'current' asset or, as it is sometimes called, a 'liquid' asset).

Although stock is a current asset it should always be remembered that it is not as liquid as cash, and that money spent on stock represents working capital which is tied up. It has been said that from the point of view of the organisation's top management, stock might be better thought of as a liability rather than an asset, because of the costs of funding stock. The expression 'working capital' may also be thought of as misleading, as materials sitting in a storehouse are certainly not 'working'. Nevertheless, from an accounting viewpoint, stocks are 'working capital' and an 'asset'. A simple example of the treatment of stock in company accounts is shown above.

For balance-sheet purposes, the normal rule is that stock should be valued at cost price or current market price, whichever is the lower. The reason for this is to ensure that the value of stock is not overstated because overstatement would have the effect of increasing the amount of profit shown, and such an increase would not be justified. If cost of materials in stock is in excess of the market value, then if the materials were sold, they would not realise the amount of money paid for them. In other words, they are not now worth their

Profit and Loss Account for the Year Ended 31/12/93

	£	£	£
Sales			500,000
Less Cost of sales			
Stock at start	117,000		
Purchases	220,000		
Available for sale	337,000		
Stock at period end	100,000		
Cost of sales			237,000
		Gross profit	263,000
		Less Operating expenses	183,000
		Operating profit	80,000

Balance Sheet as at 31/12/93

	£	£	£
Fixed assets			
Buildings (cost)		150,000	
Plant (less depreciation)		80,000	
		Net fixed assets	230,000
Current assets			
Stock	100,000		
Debtors	150,000		
Cash	20,000		
Less Current liabilities			
(Creditors)		120,000	
	Working capital		150,000
		Net assets	380,000
Financed by			
Share capital			300,000
Retained profit			80,000
			380,000

original cost price, and must therefore be shown at what they are worth, i.e. the market price.

On the other hand, if the market price at the time of the balance sheet is higher than the original cost price of the stock, it is considered prudent not to increase the stock value accordingly, because it is not advisable to take credit for an apparent profit when it has not, in fact, been realised.

BASIS OF MATERIAL COSTING

Stores accounts facilitate material costing in two ways. First of a
provide prices by means of which the cost of any particular i

be calculated. Secondly, a comparison of the total value of issue recorded in the stores accounts with the total value of material charges to various jobs or activities provides a check that all material has been properly costed.

Suppliers' prices. Prices are quoted by suppliers in various ways: net prices, or list prices subject to discounts, inclusive or exclusive of freight, customs, insurance or packages. For costing purposes we must arrive at a figure which will represent the cost actually incurred up to the point of delivery of the goods. To do this a 'purchase' price is calculated by taking the supplier's price as the base, deducting any trade or quantity discounts, and adding any other expenses not already included.

Trade discount. This is the discount granted by manufacturers to distributors. It is usually expressed as a percentage of the list price and may or may not vary with the quantity bought.

Quantity discount. Customers making bulk purchases are frequently allowed special rebates where large orders enable the suppliers to make savings in production or distribution costs.

Transport charges. As a general rule, suppliers' prices include the cost of transport but, where this is not so, such charges, whether paid to the supplier or to a carrier, are added to the basic price when calculating the purchase price. This is frequently necessary with bulky deliveries, or consignments from abroad where sea or air transport is involved.

Insurance. If any separate expense is incurred on insurance in transit, it is treated in a similar way to transport charges.

Customs duty. Any duties separately payable are added to the basic price. Value added tax is deducted provided the company is registered for this purpose.

Non-returnable packages. The supplier's price normally includes the cost of packages but, when a separate charge is made, it should be added to the basic price.

Returnable packages. If returnable packages are not charged separately, or if they are charged and credited at the same values they can be ignored. Where the amount credited on return is less than the original charge made, the difference is added to the supplier's price in arriving the purchase price.

lation of purchase price. The purchase price of any item is calculated follows:

| Supplier's list price { | *Minus*
Trade discount
Quantity discount
Value added tax | *Plus*
Transport charges
Insurance in transit
Customs or other duties
Package charges |

Example:

Supplier's quotation {
List price – £500 per tonne ex works.
Quantity discounts available –
50–100 tonnes – £10 per tonne.
100–250 tonnes – £20 per tonne.
250–350 tonnes – £30 per tonne.
Delivered in 50 kg non-returnable
boxes chargeable at £5 each.

In this case the buyer takes a consignment of 300 tonnes, and incurs a carriage charge of £3000 and insurance-in-transit expenses of £300.
The purchase price is calculated as follows:

		£
300 tonnes at supplier's price £500 per tonne		150,000
less: quantity discount £30 per tonne		9,000
		141,000
plus: transport charges	3,000	
insurance expenses	300	
packages (6,000 at £5)	30,000	33,300
		£174,300

£174,300 ÷ 300 = £581

The purchase price is, therefore, £581 per tonne.

Cash discount. It is a common practice for suppliers to allow a discount for cash payment within a limited time, e.g. 2½ per cent monthly account or 15 per cent for settlement within seven days. Cash discount is a financial transaction and is ignored when calculating the purchase price.

METHODS OF PRICING MATERIAL ISSUES

When the purchase price of an item has been determined as outlined above, it forms the basis of the prices to be used for the costing of issues from store. There are four main methods:

1 Cost price
2 Average price

3 Market price
4 Standard price

Cost price

Cost pricing is the system of using the actual purchase price of goods issued, and it may be applied in two ways: first in, first out (FIFO) or last in, first out (LIFO).

The most widely practised of these two is first in, first out, whereby each consignment received has its own purchase price and issues are made at the price of the first consignment until that quantity is exhausted. Issues are then made at the price of the second consignment, and so on.

Example:

Receipts			Issues			Balance	
Quantity	Cost Price per unit £	Value £	Quantity	Cost Price £	Value £	Quantity	Value £
100	25	2,500				100	2,500
100	30	3,000				200	5,500
			40	25	1,000	160	4,500
			60	25	1,500	100	3,000
			20	30	600	80	2,400
400	35	14,000				480	16,400
			80	30	2,400	400	14,000
			40	35	1,400	360	12,600
			240	35	8,400	120	4,200

It will be seen that, at any time, the value of the balance in hand is the amount of money which has actually been paid for that amount of stock, at the price of the latest consignments. This facilitates calculation of the value of stocks for balance-sheet purposes, because all items are already recorded at cost price. Another advantage of the FIFO method is that, since issues are charged at actual prices, no apparent profits or losses arise as a result of the pricing arrangements.

There are two common objections to the method. It is cumbersome and costly in operation, particularly if there is a lot of movement in purchase prices and, also, it does not provide a good basis for comparing job costs, as it is possible for material to be issued at the same ᵗⁱᵐe for two jobs, but at different prices.

ᵗʰe FIFO approach enables the balance sheet to give a fair commercial ᵛᵃˡᵘᵃᵗion of the stock balance, and is acceptable to the Inland Revenue.

The last in, first out (LIFO) method of pricing also uses actual purchase prices as its foundation, but issues are made at the cost of the latest available consignment. LIFO is not acceptable to the Inland Revenue as a basis for stock valuation.

Average price

There are several kinds of average prices, such as simple average, weighted average, periodic average, moving average, but for present purposes it is sufficient to consider the weighted average, which is by far the most common. The price is arrived at by dividing the total value of the stock of a given item by the total quantity, and it is necessary to calculate a new price for each commodity every time a delivery is received.

Example:

Receipts			Issues			Balance		
Quantity	Cost Price per unit £	Value £	Quantity	Average Price £	Value £	Quantity	Average Price £	Value £
100	20	2,000				100	20	2,000
100	30	3,000				200	25	5,000
			40	25	1,000	160	25	4,000
			80	25	2,000	80	25	2,000
200	60	12,000				280	50	14,000
			60	50	3,000	220	50	11,000
			120	50	6,000	100	50	5,000

The principal disadvantage is the amount of calculating work involved. This may be overcome by the use of mechanised systems which handle the arithmetic without difficulty.

There are, however, the advantages of minimising the effects of rapid or substantial price changes, and showing the stock remaining at cost price.

Market price

Market pricing is the system of pricing all material issues at the market price at the time of issue, and is sometimes referred to as 'replacement price'.

The method has the major advantage of keeping costs in line with current prices. Unfortunately, during a time of rising prices, the stock balance may be very much understated (in exceptional cases it appears as a negative figure); or on the other hand, if prices are falling rapidly, the stock remaining is seriously overvalued, and large sums have to be written off to reduce it to market value. There is also a good deal of work in obtaining information and keeping the market prices up to date.

Example:

	Receipts			Issues			Balance	
Quantity	Cost Price per unit £	Value £	Quantity	Market Price £	Value £		Quantity	Value £
100	25	2,500					100	2,500
100	30	3,000					200	5,500
			40	30	1,200		160	4,300
			80	30	2,400		80	1,900
400	40	16,000					480	17,900
			120	40	4,800		360	13,100
			260	45	11,700		100	1,400

It will be seen here that, as a result of rising prices, the stock balance of 100 is valued at only £1,400 or £14 each as against the latest market price of £45 each.

Standard price

A standard price is a predetermined price fixed on the basis of up-to-date knowledge of market prices and conditions. It is set for a given period of time, e.g. six or twelve months, and is kept fixed during that time, irrespective of the actual prices paid for receipts of material. At the end of the fixed period, the standard is reviewed, altered if necessary, and put into operation for a further period.

As both receipts and issues are valued as standard, there is no real need to show the total values of each transaction on stock records, because the value of stock on hand at any time is easily calculated by multiplying the quantity balance by the price.

Standard prices are generally used with the accounting technique known as 'Standard Costing' widely practised by larger organisations, and gaining acceptance in many smaller concerns.

The use of standard pricing is steadily increasing as a result of its obvious advantages:

1 Clerically, it is easier than any other method.
2 By eliminating variations in cost due to price changes, it gives a better indication of efficiency in the use of materials.

3 It avoids any delay in obtaining a price and therefore speeds up record posting and costing operations.

The only disadvantage worth mentioning is that, in times of rising prices, stocks are undervalued and in times of falling prices, overstated.

The use of pricing methods

The methods of pricing employed depend partly on the nature of the business concerned and partly on the nature of the materials. For example, standard prices are very common in mass-production factories and in the Armed Services, and cost prices are usually employed in jobbing shops. Market prices are suitable for many raw materials, standard prices are useful for most production items, average prices are convenient for tools, fixtures and spares, and it is normal to use cost prices for equipment or machines.

Several different pricing methods are frequently to be found in the same organisation.

Recovery of stores costs in issue prices

In some organisations it is the practice to recover the costs incurred in running the storehouses and stores office by inflating issue prices to an extent calculated to meet those costs in the course of a year. This is done simply by making a percentage addition to the value of materials charged to job or process costs. This is not a widespread practice in Britain.

ARRANGEMENT OF STORES ACCOUNTS

Like so many other aspects of stores work, the arrangement of stores accounts varies greatly in practice with the size and activity of the business, but all systems are designed to provide information about the value of stock held, the value of receipts and the value of issues.

The low cost of computers and the wide availability of good quality stores accounting software has had a large impact on the practice, though most systems share the features of the manual approach now described, the main difference being that information is stored and processed electronically rather than through the use of paperwork.

Three main records are involved:

1 Stock records for individual items

2 Stock control accounts for groups of items
3 Main stock account for the total stock

The stock records and stock control accounts together are referred to as the stores ledger; they do not form an integral part of the main double-entry books of account of the business and, for this reason, are described as 'memorandum' accounts.

The main stock account is an integral part of the books of account and is kept by the finance department.

Stock records for individual items

If stock records are kept in a form showing quantity, unit price, the value of each transaction and the total value of the balance on hand, they are themselves accounts for each individual item held. Receipts are treated as debit entries and issues as credits, and the value of stock on hand is, therefore, a debit balance. Adjustments or stocktaking results, price changes, errors or other reasons are posted from the basic documents as follows:

Increases	*Decreases*
Goods received notes	Issue notes
Transfer forms (inwards)	Transfer forms (outwards)
Return-to-store notes	Stores-advice notes
Stocktaking surplus vouchers	Stocktaking deficiency vouchers
Price-adjustment forms (increases)	Price-adjustment forms (reductions)
Write-on vouchers for correction of errors or other adjustments	Write-off vouchers for stock losses, correction of errors or other adjustments.

Stock control accounts

Stock record cards are normally kept in classification order in accordance with the coding system, and for each classification there may be a control account.

Accounts of this type are not entered in detail for each transaction in the same way as the stock records. Receipt documents posted individually to the records are summarised at intervals (say monthly), and one total posting only is made to the control account to represent receipts for the month. Similarly, issues are aggregated each month, and stocktaking discrepancies and price adjustments are commonly dealt with in the same way. Other adjustments, such as losses or correction of errors, are usually posted in detail.

Main stock account

This shows for the whole of the organisation the total value of receipts, the total value of issues, and the total value of the balance of stock on hand. In the same way as the stock control accounts 'control' the stock record cards, the main stock account 'controls' the stock control accounts. Its balance should, therefore, equal the sum of the balances on these accounts, and periodical checks should be made to verify that this is so.

With regard to the relationship of the main stock account to the stock control accounts and stock record cards it should be noted that:

1 The main stock account controls all the storehouse accounts.
2 The storehouse accounts each control their own classification accounts.
3 The classification accounts each control their own stock record cards.

Variation account

When standard prices are in use, some arrangements must be made to account for the difference between the actual purchase price of each consignment received and the standard price at which it has been taken into the stock accounts. This difference is known as a variation, and the method of dealing with it is as follows. First of all, a variation account must be opened. Thereafter:

1 If the cost of a consignment exceeds its value at standard price, the difference is debited to the variation account.
2 If the cost of a consignment is less than its value at standard price, the difference is credited to the variation account.

The following example shows the postings involved when suppliers' invoices are received. In practice this would not be done for each individual invoice, but for a totalled batch or group of invoices.

Invoice Summary	
	£
Total invoice value	575
Value of receipts at standard price	550
Variance	25
Creditors ledger – Credit	575
Stock account – Debit	550
Variation account – Debit	25

It therefore follows that, at any time, the balance on the variation account represents the total difference between cost and standard values for the period during which the account has been kept open. This balance is charged or credited to the profit and loss account.

One variation account only may be maintained, covering the whole of the stores in stock or, alternatively, a separate variation account can be kept for each classification. To some extent the movement on variation accounts gives an indication of the efficiency of purchasing.

When standard prices are reviewed and changes made, the whole of the stock concerned must be valued at the old standard price, and also at the new standard price at the time of the changeover. The difference between these two values must then be dealt with. If the value at the old prices is the greater, the stock account will be credited, and the variation account debited. Where the old value is less than the new value, the stock account will be debited and the variation account credited.

PROVISIONS

At the end of a trading period, when the profit and loss account and balance sheet are being prepared, the total value of stock in hand is obtained by extracting the balance on the main stock account. This figure by itself may not be inserted in the balance sheet without further consideration. It is frequently affected by one or more of the following factors:

1 Price
2 Obsolescence
3 Deterioration

Price

As has been said earlier in this chapter, the balance sheet is expected to show stock at cost or market value, whichever is the lower. If issues are made on a cost or average-price basis, the main stock account balance will represent the value of stock at cost. If there has been a significant decline in market prices, it will be necessary to calculate the difference and make a provision for the amount involved. The value of this provision is deducted from the main stock account figure to give the balance sheet figure. If current market values exceed cost, no action is required.

If issues are made at market prices, the value balance remaining on the main stock account represents neither cost nor market value. In times of rising prices, the balance is below cost and below market price and, in times when prices are falling, it may be in excess. It is necessary to consider making a provision either to reduce the value of stock (as outlined in the preceding paragraph) or, in exceptional circumstances, to increase the stock value. Arrangements to increase the stock value in this way by a provision are unusual, and action is justified only when the balance on the main stock account is obviously very much under cost or market price and there is no prospect of a fall in the market.

In the case of standard pricing, the balance on the main stock account similarly represents neither cost nor market value. The balances on the corresponding variance accounts, however, should give a reasonable indication as to whether the stock balance is above or below cost or market price and this can be used as a guide in deciding whether a provision is necessary and, if so, how much should be provided.

Obsolescence

In the course of time, items held in stock may become out of date and of no further use to the organisation. This is more likely to happen in some categories of stock than in others. For example, it is a normal feature of holdings of machinery spares, when the machines to which they relate are scrapped or superseded by more efficient models. When this is expected to happen, the stock controller should see that his spares holdings are run down in anticipation but, in practice, it is not possible to do this exactly, and some obsolescence, particularly in slow-moving stand-by spares, is more or less inevitable. At the point where it is known that operational machines are to be discarded, the spares are described as obsolescent. When the machines are finally scrapped and removed, the spares are then regarded as obsolete. Obsolescence is also commonly encountered in piece parts, bought-out parts, tools, gauges and fixtures when there is a permanent change in the production programme, involving discontinuing the product for which these items are held. Obsolescence is not confined to the categories of stock mentioned above; it can occur in any classification.

The method of identifying obsolescent or obsolete items and adjusting their values is dealt with in a later chapter but, in valuing the year-end stock for the balance sheet, regard must be had to the effect on the stock value of obsolescence which has not yet been exactly disclosed. In other words, provision must be made for the estimated value of items of stock in hand which, although they have not yet been identified, are in fact obsolescent or obsolete. This might be described as latent obsolescence. The provision is usually expressed as a percentage of the total stock, estimated in accordance with past experience. The amount of money involved is deducted when calculating the stock figure for the balance sheet.

Deterioration

Many items deteriorate in store and, in the course of time, must be written down in value or written off. In a similar way to obsolescence, a provision may be necessary at the year end for deterioration which has not yet been disclosed in detail. Sometimes obsolescence and deterioration are dealt with together as one provision only.

Stock in the final accounts

In accordance with the above, the net figure which is to be used for the purposes of the profit and loss account and balance sheet may be arrived at as follows:

	£	£
Value of stock as per balance on main stock account		1,500,000
less Provision for price adjustment	50,000	
Provision for obsolescence (2%)	30,000	
Provision for deterioration (½%)	7,500	87,500
Balance sheet figure for net value of stock in hand		£1,412,500

Appreciation of stock values. Some types of stock actually increase in value as time goes on; for instance, whisky in the process of maturing over several years, and timber in the course of seasoning. In these circumstances, it may be desirable to make a provision to enhance the value of the stock, but it should be done on a very conservative basis.

Goods received and not yet invoiced. Some invoices relating to purchases that have been taken into stock are not received before the books are closed at the end of an accounting period, and a schedule of these amounts is required. The value is included in the outstanding liabilities on the balance sheet.

CONTROL OF STOCK BY VALUE

It has been mentioned previously that stock control is necessary to conserve working capital. Control by quantity is, of course, designed with this in mind, but in order to make sure that it is operating effectively, it is desirable to have control in value. Stock control in quantity is only bound to give the correct overall result if every item is kept at the proper level. This is never achieved in practice, and a few expensive items out of balance can upset the whole situation. Value control is therefore necessary to show the overall position.

Stores charge

The first step is to establish which items are to be held on stores charge; that is to say, those items which will be represented by a monetary value in the stores accounts. As a general rule, complete equipments are not held on stores charge, but there are exceptions – it is not unusual to find that machines are so treated up to the point at which they are issued from store and put into use. In some instances where the usage of machine spares is intermittent or not of substantial value, they may be charged directly to cost as soon as they arrive without passing through the stores accounts. Instructions should be issued covering the time at which items are accepted on to stores charge (e.g. before or after inspection), and the time at which they are removed from charge (e.g. at the time when the issue is made from the storehouse, or after delivery and acknowledgement of receipt).

Stock targets

If stock is to be controlled in value it is necessary to define what stock values are intended to be held. One common method is to decide the total sum of money which it is proposed to provide in the form of working capital represented by stock. This total can then be split between the separate classifications, e.g. steel, timber, bought-out parts, general stores, etc. Some account must be taken of fluctuations in the value of consumption and, to do this, stock targets are best calculated, not in exact sums of money, but related to the rate of turnover and expressed as a number of weeks or months of average consumption. For example, if the value of consumption of steel was an average of £20,000 per month over the last year, and the target stock for steel was expressed as £60,000, if the consumption in the next year dropped to an average of £15,000, the target at the end of that time would obviously be inappropriate. It is therefore more satisfactory to specify the target stock for steel as being three months' supply calculated at any given time on the average consumption of the preceding year.

Stock control accounts

Stock control accounts have already been described. The form and method of operation of these accounts is subject to many variations to suit different enterprises but, for the purpose of illustrating their use in the control of stock by value, it will be assumed that there is one main stock account, storehouse control accounts for each stockholding point, and classification control accounts to show the value of stock in each vocabulary classification at each stockholding point.

These accounts are used in the following way:

1 It will be obvious from the main stock account balance whether the total value is satisfactory or not.
2 If the total stock is too high, it is fairly easy to see from the storehouse control accounts which of the stockholding points has shown an increase recently.
3 Totals in the classification accounts for the unsatisfactory storehouses can be inspected to find out which classifications have been responsible for the increase.
4 The source of the problem having been thus far established, reference can be made to the stock records to examine the quantity-control levels and take appropriate remedial action.

Where stock targets are in use, the control accounts provide the information to compare the actual values in any given classifications or stockholding points with the corresponding target figures.

Commitment records

It is evident that the value of goods on order has a bearing on whether stocks are likely to increase or decrease in the future. If the value of purchases is running at a rate in excess of current consumption, stocks will increase; on the other hand, if the amount being bought is less than the value of usage, stocks will fall. For this reason it is advisable to have a record in some detail of the value of orders placed.

One of the complications encountered is that it is first of all necessary to ensure that all orders placed are evaluated or, where this is not practicable, that at least an estimate of value is available.

A commitment record of some sort is essential in organisations where money is allocated annually, e.g. the voting of annual sums by

Parliament to Government departments; otherwise the amount allocated may be seriously overspent or underspent.

Commitment records can take either of two forms:

1   A periodic evaluation of outstanding orders.
2   A running record of orders placed, less the value of deliveries made.

Whichever type of record is adopted, it is usual to split up the value of orders and receipts into classifications in accordance with the stores coding system, and to compare the value of orders placed over a period in each classification with the corresponding value of consumption obtained from the stock control accounts.

Reporting information

Whoever is responsible for the control of stock by value must have regular reports of the balances on all stock control accounts at suitable intervals and accurate information about the value of consumption and outstanding commitments. At the same time information should flow in both directions. The stock controller should therefore see that storekeepers are informed at regular intervals of the value of stock, the value of consumption and, where possible, the value of outstanding commitments which relate to their particular storehouses. This enables all concerned to be aware of the current position and promotes cooperation in securing the desired results.

Action

When it appears from the value records that stock in any classification and/or in any storehouse is out of balance it may be necessary to hasten or delay deliveries, to place more orders, to cancel orders, to transfer stock, or even to dispose of material by sale. The stock controller should be given specific authority to issue the appropriate instructions, and should be held responsible for the stock value at all times.

BUDGETARY CONTROL

Where complete budgetary control is in operation the stock control will be integrated therewith and will form a part of it. The stores manager should be consulted before budgets are fixed so that he may offer advice concerning the rate of consumption, the rate of replenishment, and the economic value of stock to be held. The final budget should be agreed by him and either he himself or members of his staff should be nominated as controlling officers for the budget sections concerned.

ANNUAL AUDIT

The law in Great Britain requires that, for most larger organisations, there should be an annual audit. This requires a physical check on the stock situation, and appropriate procedures are described in Chapter 9.

CHAPTER 7

Approaches to the provision of materials

In the ideal world, stockholding would not be necessary. Demand and supply would be synchronised, and materials would flow to the point of use at a rate exactly matching the speed of consumption. A good deal of attention is paid to the need to minimise inventories, and some modern methods approach closely the ideal of 'stockless provisioning'. Stocks are not totally dispensed with though, and it is unlikely that they will be.

REASONS FOR HOLDING STOCK

Every organisation stores some materials of one kind or another for the following reasons:

1 Delivery cannot be exactly matched with usage day by day.
2 Economies associated with buying or manufacturing in large quantities more than offset the cost of storage.
3 Operational risks require the holding of stock to guard against breakdown or programme changes.
4 For work in progress where a completely balanced production flow is impracticable.
5 For finished products where the holding of a buffer stock between production and the customer is desirable.
6 Owing to fluctuations in the price of a commodity it is desirable to acquire stocks when prices are low.
7 In order that material may appreciate in value through storage, e.g. timber, wines and spirits.
8 In order that customers may be attracted by a range of products from which to select.

The weight to be given to each of these factors will depend upon the type of organisation; the determination of requirements and the approach to stock control will naturally be influenced by the nature of the firm's activity.

DEPENDENT AND INDEPENDENT DEMAND

In general, inventory items can be grouped into two categories:

1 Independent demand is present when requirements arise or a demand occurs in a way unconnected with any other organisational activity.
2 Dependent demand occurs when demand is related to some predicted activity, such as production or planned maintenance.

Some examples will make the distinction clear.

Example 1.

A wholesaler holds stocks of products for distribution to retailers. The motive for holding these stocks is to be able to satisfy customers' (i.e. retailers') demand for products – a demand which arises from outside the organisation and over which the wholesaler has no control. This of course does not mean that the wholesaler stocks items oblivious of the demand for them, indeed the successful wholesaler will be able to predict demand to some extent. It simply means that products are being stocked to meet demands arising in a way not connected to any other activity.

Example 2.

A manufacturing company assembles components into a finished product or products. Stocks of components are held because of decisions taken to produce specified quantities of these assembled products. Here the inventories are held to meet an internally set demand for the final products, and so they would be classified as demand dependent.

Of course, any stocks of final assembled products held by the company and offered for general sale will be demand independent inventory, as will such things as 'ad hoc' maintenance materials.

Example 3.

Sometimes items of inventory can be held for both purposes. For example, a company assembles finished products and provides an after sales service. Stocks of components are then held: to meet preset production demands, these are demand independent; to meet demands for service as and when they arise, also demand independent.

It is probably obvious that the inventory control systems that would be appropriate for situations where demand is independent would not be appropriate for dependent demand.

In the case of independent demand each stock item can be viewed singly Given some forecast of customer requirements per period, attention can then be directed towards the cost-minimising policy for stocking that item. We have well established models (of varying degrees of complexity) for dealing with this problem, in particular the Economic Order Quantity (EOQ) approach to be discussed later.

When demand is dependent, stock items can no longer be considered singly. If, for example, components are stocked in order to assemble finished products then there is an obvious need to consider the whole situation. Each component will need to be available in those quantities and at those times which will meet the requirements set by the demand for final products. In the next section we look at an approach to dependent demand inventory control known as Material Requirements Planning (MRP).

It is not the *nature* of materials which determine whether they are demanded dependently or independently, it is their *application*.

For example, stationery items held by a retailer for sale to the casual caller, or in an organisation's stationery store to be used as and when called for are items demanded independently. If, however, the stationery happened to be envelopes provided in predetermined quantities to meet the known needs of the payroll department then demand would be said to be dependent.

Lubricating oil may be provided so that vehicles can be serviced as and when the opportunity or need arises, though not in any predictable way; this would be an independent demand situation. Similar lubricants may be acquired and provided to enable a planned maintenance schedule to be met by undertaking work on a predetermined date. This is an example of dependent demand.

APPROACHES TAKEN IN PRODUCTION ORGANISATIONS

A typical approach to the provision of material in a manufacturing concern is:

1 A sales forecast is made and the manufacturing programme decided, and Bills of Materials are prepared based on each job.
2 The total requirements are then ascertained by extending these Bills of Materials.
3 Materials can then be purchased for delivery in time to meet the production line or batch requirements in accordance with the Works Order issued to meet the manufacturing programme.

4 As far as practicable, in a mass production concern particularly, materials should not be held in store, but delivered daily, or at most weekly, direct from the supplier to the machine line.
5 Bought-out parts will also appear on the Bills of Materials and should be dealt with in the same way as raw materials, if possible.
6 It is, of course, necessary for the materials department to keep close contact at all times with using departments and the planning office for knowledge of future programmes, with design departments for future developments and with the supply market regarding current and future supply positions and price trends.

Materials Requirements Planning (MRP)

This procedure, usually referred to simply as 'MRP', is an approach to stocks and scheduling that is widely employed in situations where demand is dependent, that is to say, where demand can be planned or predicted on the basis of a known programme of future activity.

The approach was pioneered by Joseph Orlicky, who described the approach as follows:

A Material Requirements Planning System, narrowly defined, consists of a set of logically related procedures, decision rules and records designed to translate a master production schedule into time-phase 'net requirements,' and the planned 'coverage' of such requirements for each component inventory item needed to implement this schedule. . . . An MRP system replans net requirements and coverage as a result of changes in either the master production schedule, inventory status or product composition.

MRP begins with a knowledge of how much end product is desired, and when it is needed. This information is broken down into the timing and quantity details for each component part or sub-assembly.

Basically MRP is most suited to a large manufacturing organisation which produces some components in-house, buys other components from suppliers and ultimately assembles them all into a fairly complicated finished product. Examples are the manufacture of cars, tractors, electricity generators, rifles, radio and television sets, washing machines and domestic cookers, to mention only a few.

The concept of the system is that production control and inventory management are integrated. This is done in such a way as to ensure that raw materials and components are only made available when they are actually required, and not before. At the same time a similar principle is applied to work in progress in the production areas. Each operation on a component is managed so that when completed, the next part of the production line will be ready to receive it and put it through the next operation without delay, and also without accumulating large quantities of work in progress between operations. Naturally, if this is well done, the amount of capital required to finance stocks of materials and work in progress will be minimised.

It is possible to operate a system with most of the features of the MRP approach manually, but this is only practicable if the product is a simple one, without too many individual components or production operations involved. True MRP systems generally depend on the use of computers, in view of the large amounts of data which must be stored, retrieved and manipulated.

The main features of an MRP system are as follows:

The Master Production Schedule (MPS). This is based on the build or assemble programme, and is a statement of what final products need to be made, and when. It drives the entire MRP system. The MPS is based on sales forecasts or customer orders, production capacity and the prioritisation of work. It is a matter of some complexity and difficulty to get the MPS right, yet right it must be, as the whole planning process is based on this document.

The Bill of Materials (BOM). This is a list showing all the raw materials or components required to make the final product. Usually it is a very complicated and formidable document. If we think about a tractor, we can see that it must be so because there are thousands of components. We can analyse parts of an imaginary Bill of Materials for a tractor, just to show how the document is constructed. It is arranged as follows:

1 The complete tractor is divided into major assemblies – say chassis, engine, transmission, steering, suspension, gearbox, electrical harness, etc.
2 The major assemblies are split up into sub-assemblies. In the case of the engine, for example, that major assembly will divide into sub-assemblies for crankshaft, engine block, cylinder head, engine gear and so on.
3 The sub-assemblies are again split into minor assemblies. Taking the crankshaft assembly as our example, one of the minor assemblies would be the piston.
4 Having arrived at the piston minor assembly, that is then detailed into individual components, such as the piston head, compression ring, scraper ring, small-end bush, small-end pin, connecting rod, big-end bearing, big-end nut and bolt, and tab washer. Thus we

arrive at the final details of the individual components which either have to be made in the firm's own production areas or bought from suppliers. In the instance of the piston minor assembly, perhaps only the piston head and connecting rod would be manufactured internally and all the other components bought from an external source.

These aspects of a Bill of Materials are shown in Fig. 7.1. The student will readily understand that a complete Bill of Materials for a tractor would comprise hundreds of pages of detail. The process of breaking down a product into a list of the various component parts, giving their quantities is called 'explosion'.

Now the essential principle of MRP is that raw materials or components are to be made available only when required, not before, and certainly not later! In pursuit of this principle, the manufacture or purchase of all these components must be coordinated to see that they

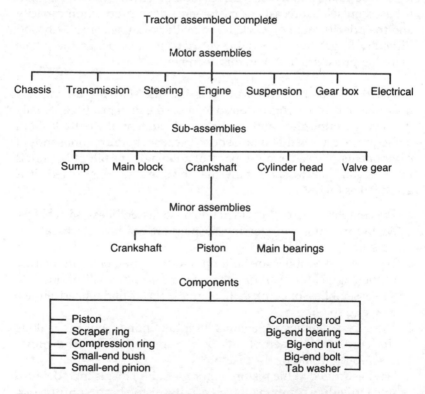

Fig. 7.1   Bill of materials. This diagram is for the purpose of illustration only and does not purport to be accurate in detail. Diagrams of this kind are called product structure trees

are on hand when the minor assemblies are to be produced. In turn, the minor assemblies are only required to be ready when the sub-assemblies are to be done. They in turn follow the requirements of the major assemblies and they follow the pattern of production of the final assembly – the complete tractor. So in theory, the provision of the smallest component is ultimately linked through the chain of assemblies to the number of complete tractors rolling off the end of the production line. This calls for a tight production control of what is made in the firm's own facilities. As regards raw materials and bought components, there must be a programme of scheduled deliveries from suppliers to match the needs of the production units.

The important issue here is the time of delivery. This must be emphasised because if delivery is too soon, stocks will accumulate and expenses will rise, but if goods arrive too late, production lines may be slowed down or even stopped – again with increased costs. It is a finely balanced process to get it right.

Referring back to the example given, if the lead time for supply of connecting rod forgings is four weeks from outside suppliers, and the machining time in the shops is one week, then ideally the order to the supplier should go out five weeks before the finished machined component is wanted. The time it is wanted can be found from the production control schedule, which will show in which production week the piston minor assembly is to be prepared. If for example that is week 35, then the purchase order for the forging must be received by the supplier in week 30.

The Inventory Status File keeps records of what is in stock, and allows the gross requirements to be adjusted to net requirements by taking into account the current stock position. The idea is to avoid stocks if possible, but if inventories do come into existence, the system will ensure that they are used in the right sequence.

The MRP program takes into account the total requirements for end products specified in the MPS, and 'explodes' this information into individual requirements for the component parts. The net requirements are then computed from the information in the inventory status file. Orders for the net requirements will then be generated for issue to suppliers or 'in company' manufacturing facilities at the appropriate time.

Reports will be generated by the MRP system which will present information in a format useful to those operating the system. The most important report is obviously the one which indicates how much

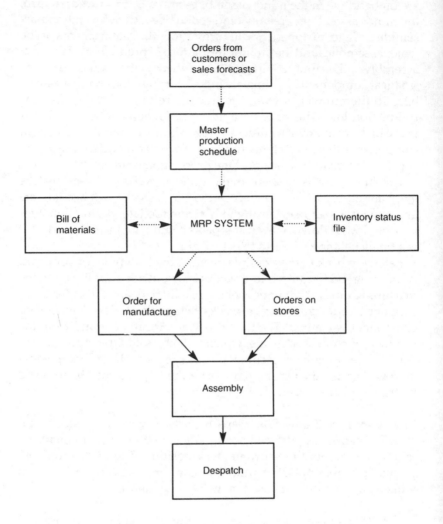

Fig. 7.2 Flows of information (⋯→) and materials (→) in a material requirements planning system

should be ordered and when, but a variety of others can be generated (see Figure 7.2).

An illustrative example of an MRP system

To show the basic principles of an MRP system in practice imagine a

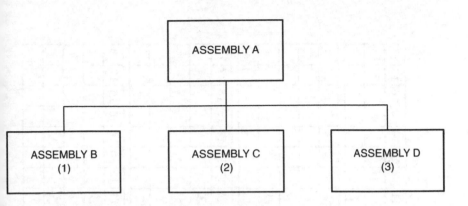

Fig. 7.3   Bill of materials for assembly A

company producing a finished item which we shall call assembly A. Each unit of assembly A is made from 1 unit of Assembly B, 2 units of Assembly C, and 3 units of Assembly D. We can show the Bill of Materials for an assembly A, in the form of an 'assembly tree' as shown in Fig. 7.3.

Suppose a decision is made to make available to a customer 1 unit of assembly A in week 12 in the manufacturer's production calendar. We might find our inventory status file showing that we have some, but not all, of our needs in stock. For example:

Assembly A: Inventory status file

Product	Gross requirements	Stock in hand	Net requirements	Lead time (weeks)
Assembly A	1	0	1	1
Assembly B	1	1	0	2
Assembly C	2	1	1	4
Assembly D	3	0	3	6

The gross requirements column is an indication of the total numbers of each assembly required, and the net requirements figure is the difference between this and the stock in hand for each part. This information can be used as the basis on which to prepare the Master Production Schedule (see Fig. 7.4). Obviously, in a situation as simple as the one described, there would be no real need for complicated computer aided planning though simplicity is of benefit when illustrating the basic principles of the system.

MRP MASTER SCHEDULE FOR __ ASSEMBLY A

	1	2	3	4	5	6	7	8	9	10	11	12	13	14	15	16	17	18
Quantity needed												1						
Production schedule											1							

ASSEMBLY B

	1	2	3	4	5	6	7	8	9	10	11	12	13	14	15	16	17	18
Gross requirements											1							
Stock on hand											1							
Scheduled receipts											0							
Planned order release																		

ASSEMBLY C

	1	2	3	4	5	6	7	8	9	10	11	12	13	14	15	16	17	18
Gross requirements											2							
Stock on hand											1							
Scheduled receipts											1							
Planned order release							1											

ASSEMBLY D

	1	2	3	4	5	6	7	8	9	10	11	12	13	14	15	16	17	18
Gross requirements											3							
Stock on hand											0							
Scheduled receipts											3							
Planned order release				3														

Fig. 7.4   MRP master production schedule

Manufacturing Resource Planning (MRPII)

As the name suggests, Manufacturing Resource Planning is capable of taking into account more than just the material resources of MRP. The other resources; human, financial and capital equipment can be planned using this technique.

MRPII has been defined as:

A system built around materials requirements planning and also including the additional planning functions of production planning, master production scheduling and capacity requirements planning. Further, once the planning phase is complete and the plans have been accepted as attainable, the execution functions come into play. These include the shopfloor control functions of input-output measurements, detailed scheduling and despatching, plus anticipated delay reports from both the shop and the vendors, purchasing, follow-up and control etc. The term 'closed loop' implies that not only is each of these elements included in the overall system but also that there is feedback from the execution functions so that the planning can be kept valid at all times.

Even more so than MRP, MRPII is a computer system, and there are many packages on the market, each different from the others, but

Class	Characteristics
D	MRP working in data processing department only. Poor inventory records. Master schedule mismanaged. Reliance on shortage lists for progressing.
C	Used for inventory ordering, not scheduling. Scheduling by shortage lists. Overloaded master schedule.
B	System uses capacity planning, shop floor control. Used to plan production, not manage the business. Help still needed from shortage lists. Inventory higher than necessary.
A	Uses closed-loop MRP. Integrates capacity planning, shop floor control, vendor scheduling. Used to plan sales, engineering, purchasing. No shortage lists to override schedules.

Fig. 7.5 Wright's classification of MRP/MRPII user

enabling the essential functions of an MRPII system to be performed. The benefits arising from the successful implementation of an MRPII system include shorter lead times, fewer stocks, and the ability to make realistic and accurate delivery promises to customers.

Few organisations are able to completely implement MRPII all at once, and a phased or evolutionary approach is usually adopted. The four point scale developed by Oliver Wright has come into general use as an indication of the level of implementation, class D being at an infant stage of development, and class A mature (see Figure 7.5).

Distribution Requirements Planning (DRP)

Although distribution is outside the scope of this book, it may be helpful to mention the development of Distribution Requirements Planning. In a sense this is the opposite of an MRP system, in that it is based on customer requirements at the point of use or demand. The idea is that the requirement 'pulls' the product through the organisation. DRP is employed by distribution planners (rather than production or manufacturing planners).

Logistics Requirements Planning (LRP)

Successful implementations of LRP are, as yet, few. The powerful and attractive idea is to combine the MRP and DRP systems to enable a comprehensive planning system which coordinates material requirements entering the organisation, other resource requirements connected with conversion and distribution requirements connecting with the customer.

The Just-in-Time approach

The Just-in-Time (JIT) approach to the provision of materials for production is based on the philosophy that waste ought to be eliminated where possible. The term waste applies not only to materials, but to time, effort, equipment and storage space; in other words it is all about efficiency.

JIT is not really a technique, or even a set of techniques. It is a way of thinking about the approach to production which draws upon a variety of ideas, methods and techniques in its implementation. JIT should be thought of as a philosophy which allows the adoption of appropriate techniques where necessary.

JIT is different from more traditional approaches to increasing productivity in that it concentrates on the non-value-added elements of production. Approaches such as method study and automation focus on the time that a product is actually being worked on, that is to say the time when value is being added. In practice though, for the majority of the time that they are in a production organisation, products are picking up cost rather than having value added. JIT concentrates on the areas where products are gathering costs, and is therefore concerned with techniques such as total quality control, reduction of batch sizes, reduction of set up and lead times, reduced inventories, group technology layouts and total involvement. These ideas will be explained later.

JIT is a 'pull' system in the sense that replenishment is triggered only when the amount available reaches a certain level, and stock is pulled through the system only when needed. The traditional method of ensuring that uncertainties associated with quality and/or delivery time failures do not give rise to disaster is to carry stocks by way of protection. This is not the only reason for carrying stocks, but it is an important one.

The well known 'ship and rocks' analogy (see Fig. 7.6) illustrates

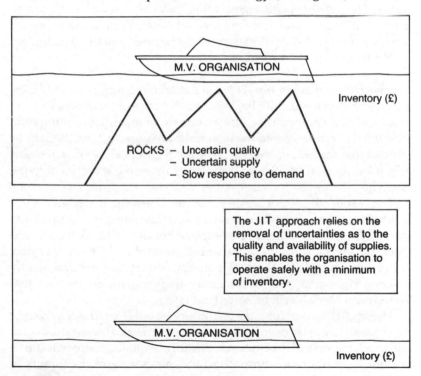

Fig. 7.6   The 'ships and rocks' analogy

the concept of JIT very well. In the first diagram the ship, representing the business, is kept off the rocks by the depth of water (representing stocks). Of course, these stocks have to be bought and held by the business, but it is an effective way of keeping the ship afloat. Although the provision of inventories is effective, it is not necessarily the most efficient. The removal of the rocks, representing the uncertainties about obtaining the correct material in the proper quantities is probably more efficient. Thus, in the second diagram the ship is still comfortably afloat but the depth of water (stocks) is substantially reduced.

The origins of JIT.   Elements of what we now call the JIT approach have been widely employed for many years in high volume mass assembly organisations. It has probably always been recognised that stockholding is expensive, and that efforts to match the rate of supply of components and assemblies to the rate of their consumption are likely to be worthwhile. Nevertheless, it was the Toyota company in Japan who developed the formal concepts associated with JIT in the 1960s. During the 1970s many other Japanese concerns started to employ JIT ideas, and towards the end of the decade the approach was beginning to be appraised, and in some cases tentatively adopted, in North America and Europe.

Necessary conditions for JIT.   Total quality control is essential: incoming material must not be defective. Because of the absence of any 'cushion' of inventory, incoming materials, or materials moving from one stage in operations to the next must not be defective. It might be argued that the idea of 'zero defects' is a theoretical and unattainable ideal, but in practice the probability of defective material arriving must be very low indeed.

The responsibility for quality will lie where the material, part or assembly is made, not where it is received. The emphasis is on quality assurance; the prevention of defects, rather than their detection and cure, through inspection of incoming goods. In addition, operators will be responsible for their own quality, attempting to build quality in on a right first time basis, rather than relying on the fact that defective materials will be sorted out later.

The small batch or lot sizes characteristic of JIT production reduce the probability of large volumes of defective material being produced, although because of the extreme criticality of quality there will still be a need for a rigorous approach to the monitoring of the quality of production or assembly as it takes place. Statistical Process Control (SPC) will be employed where practicable and appropriate. This is a technique whereby limits or ranges are set, and the quality of the output from the process is measured on a continuous or sampling basis. If the measured quality of the output of the process moves gradually towards or through the upper or lower specification limit then 'drift' is said to be taking place, and the process is stopped for readjustment. If the quality of output becomes inconsistent, with no pattern as such emerging, but with measurements sometimes falling outside the specification or range limits, then the indication is that quality is spreading, and remedial action will again need to be taken.

Fig. 7.7 illustrates the basic principles of charts in process control.

In order that the level of quality is appropriately high, in the sense that materials are to specification, for the JIT approach attention should be paid to the following factors: the quality of raw materials and components prior to further manufacture, the design of the product and production processes which must be right first time, the control of processes as outlined above, and of course the people, as

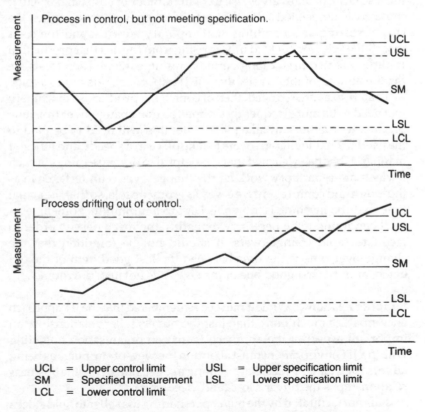

UCL	= Upper control limit
SM	= Specified measurement
LCL	= Lower control limit
USL	= Upper specification limit
LSL	= Lower specification limit

Fig. 7.7 Control charts as employed in Statistical Process Control (SPC)

overall responsibility for quality rests with each individual involved in production operations and their management and control.

Batch size reduction. JIT depends upon materials being available when they are needed, not before, and not later. This of course implies that if consumption of the materials, as is almost inevitably the case, is at a fairly steady rate, then production will ideally be at a similar rate. The reality is that this exact synchronisation will probably be impracticable, in that production machines and facilities are employed for a variety of different items, and that the rate of production will exceed the rate at which materials are used.

A traditional view of manufacturing is that the more you make of an item, the cheaper you can make it. The economies of scale associated with long production runs and high volumes are a powerful inducement to produce in large quantities, and to stock the excess production until it is needed. However, the production of materials in these large batches gives rise to a fair number of costs, in particular those costs associated with the costs of financing excess stocks, the cost of storing and handling the temporary surplus, and the costs associated with longer lead times arising from the fact that production facilities are tied up for long periods on single items. These costs are manifestations of the 'waste' that the JIT approach sets out to avoid.

If batch sizes are reduced, then of course the production machinery will need to be more frequently stopped so that change-over from one product to another can take place. Attention will need to be paid to the need to enable change-overs to take place in a speedy and efficient manner. It has been learned that it is helpful to organise things in such a way that preparatory work for the change-over is undertaken in as thorough and comprehensive a way as is practicable, so that the actual time that the machine is 'down' is kept to a minimum. Sometimes it has been found to be necessary to modify the machinery in order to facilitate rapid change-overs. It should not be forgotten that the change-over time is the time between the last good item of the old batch, and the first good one of the new. It is not just 'downtime'.

Supplier relations. While it must be remembered that the JIT approach encompasses much more than just the buyer/seller relationship, an important aspect of the approach is that an organisation operating within a JIT environment must abandon the view of suppliers as being adversaries, and the idea that anything a seller gains from the business relationship is the buyer's loss (and vice versa).

JIT is not facilitated by the buyer persuading the seller to hold stocks at his own expense on behalf of the buyer, only to be released when the need arises. However, the erroneous belief that this kind of arrangement leads to substantial reductions in stockholding costs seems to be widely held. In the short term the costs are borne by the supplier, but must be recovered from the customer if the supplier is to remain in business. JIT is not about shifting costs, but eliminating them.

A relationship of absolute trust must exist between the buying and supplying organisations, with the buyer expecting the production and delivery of materials exactly when called for, and without any defects. In exchange for attaining these difficult goals, the supplier ought to be rewarded with a fruitful long-term relationship with his customer. The whole idea is one of partnership, and the term co-makership has been coined to describe the type of mutually beneficial relationship that is sought.

The words 'symbiosis' and 'synergy' are often applied to the type of relationship described, with the relationship generating benefits for both sides; benefits which would not have arisen if the two sides had not worked together. It is sometimes suggested that an appropriate way of describing this kind of buyer/seller relationship is that it gives rise to a '2 + 2 = 5' outcome.

Given then that the ideal form of relationship is one of partnership, it follows that there is likely to be benefit in being as helpful as possible to one's suppliers, not only in connection with the development of products which can be profitably produced and used for the benefit of both, but also in connection with the exchange of information. The more quickly, accurately, and completely relevant information can be exchanged between buyer and seller the better it is for both. Electronic Data Interchange (EDI), whereby the computers used by trading partners 'talk' to each other, is proving to be very beneficial in this respect, and it is widely believed that such systems will become essential for all organisations operating together in a true JIT manner.

The kind of relationship described takes time to create and develop, of course, and requires a different approach from the traditional 'competitive bidding' situation, where each time a contract comes up for renewal qualified bidders are contacted and encouraged to make a better offer than that made by their competitors. While this approach is widely used, and is quite appropriate in certain circumstances, it can not be employed where long-term dependencies are to be created. It is common in organisations operating JIT to discover that buyers are single, or at most dual sourced, though of course these sources will have been chosen with great care.

Involvement. Since JIT is not a technique, but an 'approach' it is not something that can simply be learned about and then applied. It is a way of thinking about things, and as such it requires the involvement and commitment of all concerned. The phrase 'total employee involvement' is sometimes used to indicate this need, but the phrase might be misleading because of the distinction that is sometimes made between employee and management. The fact is that for JIT to work properly, everybody in the organisation needs to be involved. This involvement will extend outside the organisation, to include suppliers and contractors.

It is necessary for staff to be committed to the JIT approach, to understand the philosophy fully, to be flexible in terms of the activities and tasks they undertake, and to play a a full part as members of the corporate team. An organisation embracing JIT for the first time is unlikely to possess the appropriate culture, and a good deal of effort on the part of all concerned will be necessary. JIT requires fairly radical changes in working practices, and will in all probability require attitude changes too.

JIT requires flexibility in production. It also requires that people divert their energies to 'support' activities if there is no immediate requirement for work employing their mainstream skills. In other words, the workforce must consist of persons who can flexibly apply a range of skills, and who are ready to transfer from direct production operations to indirect support activities as and when the need arises. Therefore the implementation of a JIT programme will require a major investment in training, and the learning of new skills is likely to be a continuous process for all concerned. Of course commitment cannot be created simply through training. Involvement, participation and a sense of 'ownership' of the organisation and its activities will only come about if the conditions are right. There must be plenty of consultation between all involved, the involvement in decision making must be genuine, and be seen to be real, and communications between management and workers must be comprehensive (in both directions).

Payment and incentive schemes will be required which are generally competitive, and which reward excellence and thereby provide some incentive. Traditional piecework schemes are unlikely to work in a JIT environment, and any working practices based on demarcation are a barrier to successful implementation.

Kanban. Kanban is the control system that helps the JIT approach to work. The word kanban translates literally from the Japanese as something like 'signal', 'sign' or 'card'. The term kanban is not a synonym for JIT although early references to the JIT approach in the West used the expression kanban systems and this has caused some confusion. The word kanban should not be taken to literally indicate the use of a card; any system which automatically signals in some way that a product has been used and requires replenishing may be referred to as a kanban system.

The kanban may take many forms. It might be a small storage area on a bench, or workshop floor located between two stages of a production process. When an operator requires to use an item, it is taken from the kanban area, and this is taken as a signal to the operator upstream to replenish the item, so production is 'pulled' by actual use of the item having taken place.

Containers may be used, with or without cards, as the kanban. An empty container is taken as the signal for a replacement to be made available. This approach to kanban is similar to the 'two bin' approach to stock control covered elsewhere in this text. Of course, the kanban may be just a card attached to a production item or batch. When the material is brought into use the card is passed up the line to trigger further supply. There also exists a kanban system known as the double card system. In this application there are two kinds of kanban cards, conveyance (c-kanban) and production (p-kanban). As their names suggest, the c-kanban controls the movement of containers and materials, and the p-kanban controls the actual production or manufacture of materials.

These are just some of the ways in which the kanban idea is put into practice, but note that in these, and in all other applications of the kanban system, new items are not produced until existing ones are used. The system automatically prevents the build up of unnecessary inventories. Kanban systems rely on strict adherance by all concerned to the rules of the system, the principal features of which are likely to be that nothing is to be produced until the necessary kanban indicates that it is needed. In the event of there being no immediate requirement, staff should attend to cleaning, or maintenance, or other duties. On no account are materials to be produced in anticipation of a requirement. When production is signalled, only the prescribed quantity is to be produced.

Requirements for JIT.   The CIPS briefing publication 'Just in Time, the Purchasing Viewpoint' identifies the following needs as vital for JIT users:

- Multi-bay unloading facilities, physically and geographically coordinated with internal manufacturing or distributive stores needs.

- Rapid identification coding systems; (obviously bar coding best suits distributive sector needs but the application is widening).
- Changes in external factory access may be required to facilitate multiple unloading.
- Consolidators may be sought to collect, aggregate, kit marshall and deliver goods to the end user company, i.e. manufacturer or distributor warehouse. This gives the consolidation operation a unique insight into certain businesses and may qualify them to also provide final end-customer delivery.

JIT and MRP contrasted

As has been said, JIT is really a philosophy, and MRP a system, so they can not be directly compared. JIT is a 'pull' approach in that it concentrates on what has been used, and replenishes it. The focus is on actual past events rather than anticipated future ones. MRP, on the other hand, is concerned with plans, being based on the master production schedule. Materials are 'pushed' into the system to enable production to take place. The MRP approach is difficult to implement without the assistance of electronic data processing because of the large amounts of information which are involved. The JIT approach is rather simpler in concept (if not in operation), and may well be undertaken manually.

It is probably a mistake to view the two approaches as competing alternatives: they can be viewed as complementary to each other. MRP is employed to translate forecasts into plans, and the plans into detailed schedules. JIT is concerned with the application of plans and the management of schedules. It has been said that MRP is to do with the process of planning, and JIT with the approach to the execution of plans.

The full implications of the JIT approach go far beyond those concerned with inventories and their reduction or elimination. The purchasing considerations associated with good supplier relations and communications, zero defects, and delivery on time are generally well recognised and understood. As applied in Japan though, the focus is much broader than simply 'purchasing and stock control'. It is more like an approach to running the business, which gives rise to reduced inventories as a secondary result rather than a primary aim. The complete implementation of JIT probably involves reviews of design, engineering, inventories, production planning and control, supplier quality, process/production quality and manufacturing flexibility.

DIFFERING STOCK CONTROL NEEDS OF CONSTRUCTION, SERVICE AND RETAIL ORGANISATIONS

Construction organisations

1 A Bill of Quantities is typically prepared for each contract, giving full particulars of materials required, and there will also be a phased Construction Programme showing when the various parts of the job start and finish, e.g. foundations, steelwork, brickwork, cladding, glazing, electrics, heating installations, painting, etc., for a building project.

2 Delivery of material can be arranged in the proper quantities at the appropriate time on to the actual site in accordance with the information given on the Bill of Quantities and the Construction Programme.

3 An organisation of this kind does not usually hold stock at any permanent storehouse but buys as required for delivery to site, though of course a site or project stockyard will sometimes be necessary.

Service organisations

There are many kinds of service organisation, and hence many provisioning systems. Taking as an example a public service road transport organisation, a typical approach is:

1 Fuel and lubricant requirements are estimated from past experience and the forecast of number of trips and mileages. Storage tanks are kept at garages and replenished weekly on a long-term contract basis.

2 For spare parts for vehicles there is usually a planned maintenance programme whereby buses are withdrawn from service at regular intervals, engines and major mechanical parts reconditioned after fixed mileages and bodywork and upholstery renewed after a period of time.

3 From experience, spares scalings can be produced showing the number of overhauls over a year, and this spares scaling is used as the basis for determining the requirements in advance and arranging deliveries to repair shops at regular intervals.

By a combination of experience and technical assessment the average number of spares of different types used for each vehicle can be fairly accurately established and the number of spares required to maintain any given number of vehicles over a specified period can be estimated. This is what is known as spares scaling.

The following example has been simplified and abbreviated for the purposes of illustration:

Motor Vehicle Type ABC

		Number to be Carried in Stock		
Spare Part No.	Description	To service 1 vehicle	To service 6 vehicles	To service 12 vehicles	To service 100 vehicles
127861	Cylinder head	-	-	1	5
128642	Cylinder-head gasket	1	3	5	30
278930	Carburettor	-	-	1	6
306158	Exhaust silencer	-	1	1	6
321753	Tyres	4	20	36	280
407938	Headlamp bulbs	1	5	9	70
513882	Rear spring	1	2	3	18
684955	Engine complete	-	-	-	2

It should be noted that not only does the number of each type of spare vary with the number of vehicles being maintained, but the range of spares to be carried also depends on the same factor. Where very large numbers of vehicles are running it is normally desirable to hold the complete range but, where only a few vehicles are involved, it is not necessary to keep some of the major expensive or slow-moving items. Spares scalings are used not only for provisioning to serve existing equipment, but also as a guide to determine in advance what range and quantity of spares should be purchased when new vehicles are introduced.

Retail organisations

A typical approach is that:

1 Forward sales levels for broad categories of items are estimated (e.g. forecast sales for summer clothes, soap powders) by month.
2 The sales estimates are converted into unit terms, and inventory levels planned on a monthly basis.
3 Merchandise is selected for the various product categories – an activity that accounts for much of the work is retail buying involving choices of assortment and depth, particular lines, colours, size mixes, as appropriate.
4 As merchandise is selected, an 'open-to-buy' figure is determined on the basis of anticipated sales levels, less cost of acquisitions.
5 Selected merchandise is scheduled for delivery in appropriate quantities over the selling season.

6 Sales are compared to planned figures, and open-to-buy amounts and budgets adjusted where appropriate.

7 Price reductions are used to clear slow-moving stock and special buys for promotions are sometimes made.

THE EXTENT OF STOCKHOLDINGS

This is influenced by four main considerations:

1 Operational needs
2 Time required to obtain delivery of goods
3 Availability of capital
4 Cost of storage

Operational needs

The user's desire is for immediate availability of all materials, stores and spares which may be required under any circumstances, with no risk whatever of failure of supply. From an operational point of view the efficiency of the stores department is judged by whether material is forthcoming or not when it is required. In the event of a 'stockout' (i.e. no stock available in store), the consequences may be very serious. Failure to supply some stores may result merely in an irritating delay, but if there is a run-out of a vital production material, the whole of a production line may be stopped and great expense incurred.

Delivery time

As regards time of delivery, some goods can be obtained ex stock from suppliers but, in many cases, weeks or months must elapse between the date of order and receipt. Delivery time can be regarded as the period which a supplier requires to make delivery, whereas lead time, a term often taken to have the same meaning, is the period between recognising the need for replenishment and the new supplies actually arriving at the storage fixture. Lead time has been succinctly summarised as 'Min to Bin', and includes the time spent in preparing and placing the order, and in checking and placing incoming goods in store. The effect of this delay can be overcome by phasing deliveries commensurate with operational requirements in advance, but it will still be necessary to hold sufficient stock to avoid shortages in case suppliers fail to deliver on time, and also to cater for unexpected variations in operations.

Availability of capital

Goods in stock represent working capital, and the business will have to provide this capital either out of its own resources, or by borrowing from a bank or elsewhere. Capital is never unlimited and, from a financial point of view, it is most desirable to restrict the amount tied up in stock as far as circumstances will permit. Efficiency in this respect is normally judged by 'stockturn'. The stockturn is the value of issues for any given period divided by the average value of stock in hand during the period. It is expressed as a ratio; for example, if the issues of steel are £100,000 in a year, and the average value of stock on hand during that year has been £25,000, then the stockturn is 100,000/25,000, i.e. four, and the investment of a working capital of £25,000 in stock has supported consumption of a value of £100,000. It will be clear that the higher the stockturn, the more active and economical is the use of capital.

The importance of this must be fully realised. The value of stock on hand is frequently the largest single asset in the balance sheet.

Cost of storage

The factors comprising the cost of storage are as follows:

1 Interest on the value of stores in stock (i.e. loss of interest on capital tied up in this way), or the benefit which could be gained from employing the money more productively within the organisation.
2 Operating expenses of storehouses, including wages, depreciation, rent, rates, repairs, heating, lighting, etc.
3 Loss and deterioration of stock
4 Obsolescence
5 Insurance
6 Stock checking
7 Recording and accounting

These costs are substantial, and investigations made in various industries have shown that the annual cost of storage may be of the order of £20–30 per £100 of stock held.

ORDERING QUANTITIES

Up to this point, we have been considering the problem of provisioning largely from the point of view of avoiding stockouts or excessive holdings, and little has been said of the actual quantity which should be ordered at any one time.

The factors to be taken into account in this respect are:

1 Reliability of estimated requirements
2 Available storage accommodation
3 Cost of storage
4 Cost of ordering

Reliability of estimated requirements

For important commodities regularly consumed in large quantities, the estimation of forward demand is critical. Quite naturally, the longer the period for which an estimate is made, the less dependable the figure is likely to be; it is not too difficult to forecast what will be required for the next month, but to look ahead for a next year is seldom easy. Nevertheless, to obtain the best commercial terms, it is often essential to make fairly long-term contracts, and orders for quantities representing a year's supply are commonly placed once a year. Where this is done, the rate of 'call-off' is significant; it is desirable to see that the quantities which are delivered each week or month correspond as closely as possible with the rate of consumption.

Available storage accommodation

Whatever the quantities ordered, arrangements must be made to see that deliveries are not too great in amount to be accepted into the available storage accommodation. If this point is not considered carefully, goods which require covered storage may have to be kept in the open air, or rent may have to be paid for warehousing facilities outside the organisation.

Cost of storage

The cost of holding any particular item of stock is a somewhat elusive problem. It is first necessary to decide what factors are to be included in the cost – these have been outlined earlier in this chapter. Thereafter, it must be realised that the costs of storage are not the same for all items. For instance, the true expense incurred in storing, for example, bags of cement and ingots of tin is not proportional to their value. Another point is that temporary fluctuations of the levels of stocks within reasonable limits do not substantially affect some of the factors such as depreciation of buildings, rates, repairs and wages.

The storehouses will not be extended or curtailed in size and the staff will not be increased or reduced in number because of minor changes in the amount of stock on hand.

However, in spite of these difficulties, it is possible to arrive at the total cost of holding stock for a given period of time (say one year) and, by relating that total sum of money to the average value of stock held during the period, to calculate the average cost of holding stock as a percentage of the value of the goods themselves. The figure can then be regarded as the nominal cost of storage for any given item, and is usually in the range of 20 to 30 per cent.

Cost of ordering

It is not an easy matter to say what really is the cost of placing an order. In the first place we have to decide what processes are involved. Obviously the cost of running the buying office is one factor, but it is reasonable to suppose that entering the appropriate stock records and certifying and paying invoices are also a part of the cost of ordering. In the second place, orders themselves vary in character; some are easy to handle and some are very difficult, they may consist of only one item or several items, full tendering procedure may or may not be necessary, and so on.

The only reasonable way to arrive at the cost of placing an individual order is to ascertain the total cost of ordering over a given period and divide that sum by the number of orders placed. This does not give the precise cost of placing any particular order.

Acquisition cost

The acquisition cost of an item is the sum of the cost of ordering and the cost of storage. To keep stock as low as possible, frequent orders for small quantities must be placed; this means that, although storage costs will be low, ordering costs will be high. On the other hand, if large quantities are ordered at infrequent intervals, the ordering costs will be low but the storage costs high.

It is apparent that the most sensible course to pursue is to compromise and find some optimum order quantity which will produce the most economical combination of ordering and storage costs, that is to say, the minimum acquisition cost.

Where very high stock values are involved, the relative cost of ordering is probably negligible, but for items of modest value it may be significant.

RANGE

It has already been pointed out that stock control is concerned with the range of materials which should be carried in stock, as well as the depth in which materials should be held, though it is of course seldom the case that the question of what to stock can be answered solely by stock control staff. Decisions on range will normally involve consultations with others in the organisation, particularly in the case of a manufacturing concern, where design, engineering and production staff will typically be involved.

The basic aim concerning range should be to meet the whole variety of the stock requirements of the organisation with as narrow a selection of different items as is possible. Clearly this need to keep range as narrow as possible has much in common with standardisation, and is related to such topics as value engineering and of course classification and coding. Keeping the range of items stocked to a minimum gives rise to the following advantages.

1 Reduced risk, as there are fewer stock lines on which a shortage could occur.
2 Economies of scale; reducing breadth gives rise to increased consumption of adopted items, and hence better prices.
3 Reduced ordering costs.
4 Reduced stockholding costs, arising from fewer stock locations and lower *total* stock levels.

Many organisations have achieved great savings through undertaking variety reduction exercises, an activity which involves looking at the inventory, or a section of it, and asking questions such as:

1 What possible substitutes are there?
2 What range of sizes is essential?
3 Is the same part used elsewhere under a different identification?
4 Is it absolutely essential to stock the item?

While exercises of this kind are of very great value, it should be remembered that the 'savings' which ensue are, in a sense, evidence of earlier inefficiency, and that if the range of stock items had not been allowed to proliferate in the first place then the savings would not have been possible.

For this reason it is important to scrutinise very carefully all requests for new items to be introduced to stock, and some concerns employ a formal 'application for stock' system, requiring approval of the answers to a detailed questionnaire before stocks can be approved and acquired. A typical form might require such information as:

Full description of new item
Purpose for which required
Anticipated duration of demand
Reason why new item is required
Particulars of any general stock items to be replaced by the new
    item.

The form is carefully considered by the appropriate authorities, and
only when there is full acceptance that it is necessary to stock the item
concerned will action be authorised.

CONSIGNMENT STOCKING

Also known as consignment buying, supplier operated stores, and forward
supply, this arrangement is one where the supplier keeps a stock of
his materials on the customer's premises, and this stock is only drawn
upon as and when the customer needs material. In other words, while
the physical stocks are held within the buying organisation, the
ownership of the goods only passes to the buyer at the time of use.

Advantages for both buyer and seller are found in this approach,
the principal one being that the buyer has access to a range of stocks
without tying up his working capital, and the seller is sure of making
an immediate sale when the requirement for some of his goods arises.

Stocks of Maintenance, Repair and Operating (MRO) items, raw
materials and production items are sometimes held on a consignment
basis, and organisations in wholesaling and retailing commonly take
goods on a sale or return basis, which is, of course, a similar idea. If
an arrangement for stocking on a consignment basis is to be entered
into, it is advisable, for the protection of both parties, to formalise the
agreement by means of a contract, covering such questions as:

1 Exactly what is to be consigned?
2 Who is responsible for stock checking?
3 For how long will the arrangement last?
4 Who arranges insurance cover?
5 Who pays for items damaged while in stock?
6 Exactly when does title pass?
7 What happens to unused stocks at the end of the agreement period?
8 How and when does the supplier gain access to his stocks, for
    checking or inspection?
9 In the event of a dispute, who is to arbitrate?
10 Who pays for any necessary maintenance of stocks?

CHAPTER 8

Stock control techniques

The usual approach to the control of stock is the control of inputs to the stores; the stock controller in most circumstances will have little, if any, jurisdiction over outputs. Irrespective of the stock control system employed, the stock controller must consider the following points as well as those mentioned in connection with the extent of stockholdings when determining the rate at which material should be taken into stock.

Unit of issue

To control by quantity, the first step is to establish the units of quantity. These may be units of weight, such as kilogrammes, units of liquid measure, such as litres, units of length, such as metres, units of number, such as tens, or any other unit which is appropriate to any particular commodity. The unit of issue is the smallest quantity normally issued from a storehouse. A suitable unit of issue is fixed for each item of stock held and this unit should be employed consistently in all receipts, issue, recording and provisioning procedures.

Probable requirements

It is always necessary to form some estimate of future consumption. Past performance as indicated by the records is a very good guide, but it can be no more than a guide, and the stock controller must see that he has as much reliable information as he can get about future changes in production levels or alterations in technique. Therefore, he needs regular and effective contact with all user departments, and to be aware of planned activities.

Availability of supplies

To regulate the input of materials effectively, the stock controller must know what delivery period is likely to be required by suppliers of the commodities for which he is responsible. Here again, past performance will give him an indication of what to expect, but the situation can change rapidly, and a good liaison with the purchasing office is essential to obtain advice on the current state of the market and forecasts of future prospects regarding delivery times.

Frequency of delivery

The geographical location of the source of supply or the nature or bulk of the material affects the size and frequency of deliveries. It is unlikely that daily deliveries will be made from a distant source, and bulk materials normally dealt with in wagon loads will not be available in small quantities at short intervals.

Price discounts for quantities

Price is naturally very important and, if substantial supplies are regularly required, the buyer will seek to make bulk purchases, wherever possible, to get the cheapest unit price. The stock controller can play his part by organising his demands in such a way as to take advantage of this situation. Before placing orders, the amount of discount available should be compared with the extra costs of storage which may be incurred to make sure that it is, in fact, advantageous to make bulk purchases.

Cost of ordering

The clerical and administrative cost of placing orders is not negligible and, with items of low unit value, may be a significant factor. Such items should be ordered in sufficiently large quantities to avoid unreasonable expense in preparing large numbers of small orders.

Rate of issue

This is a question of meeting the practical needs of the operating function. For example, if the storehouse is supplying an overseas depot, it may be necessary to make up major consignments of substantial quantities or, again, in process or engineering factories, there may in many cases be a minimum quantity of materials suitable for economic batches in the production process.

Seasonal fluctuations

In some businesses, production is related to harvest times or weather, for example, fruit canning or clothing manufacture, and the input of materials has to be arranged accordingly.

Standard ordering quantities

Some articles are normally purchased in standard quantities, i.e. by the tonne, the hundred, the litre, and so on. For example, small wood screws are available wholesale by the hundred, and orders for less than that should not be placed, otherwise retail purchases will have to be made at high prices.

It is for the stock controller to see that his demands are expressed in the standard ordering quantities appropriate to the goods concerned and, if he does not do so, it is the buyer's duty to advise him.

Allocations

Where specific quantities of stock are set aside for special jobs or capital projects, this must be taken into account when controlling the amount in stock if the materials are also used for other purposes.

Obsolescence

Particularly in the case of specially prepared production materials or machine spares, regard should be had to the possibility of the item becoming obsolete and stocks should be maintained at a sufficiently low level to avoid undue risk in this respect.

High-value items

It is obvious that the greatest attention should be paid to the items of the highest value, but this common-sense approach is sometimes overlooked. Very frequently a large proportion of the value of stock is represented by a comparatively small number of expensive articles or materials with a very high rate of consumption, and the effect of fluctuations in these stockholdings is a major factor in the total stock investment.

PROVISIONING

Provisioning is the process of determining in advance requirements of materials, taking into consideration existing stocks, delivery times and rates of consumption so that the amount of stock in hand at any time will be in accordance with the stock control policy. The two major questions arising in any provisioning activity are:

1 When to order
2 How much to order

When these questions have been answered in respect of any particular commodity, the provisioner usually prepares some kind of provision-demand document, showing the quantity and delivery required, and passes this to the purchasing office to take the appropriate buying action. The departmental responsibility for provisioning in practice varies a good deal in different organisations. For example, in some Government departments there is a separate provisioning branch concentrating on this type of work alone, and in some engineering factories provisioning for production materials and components is undertaken by the production control, planning or progress departments. In most instances, however, provisioning is done by the stores department. The work is occasionally done by storekeepers themselves, but the larger type of organisation sets up a separate stock control section.

General stock items

The responsibility for provisioning general stock items lies entirely with the stock controller. He prepares demands to be sent to the purchasing office as and when required according to the information from the system and his own judgement.

Items which are not general stock

For items in this category, it is necessary for user departments to initiate the provisioning action by preparing a form generally known as a purchase requisition, giving full details of the material required. The document is passed first to the stock controller, and it is his duty to check that the items concerned are not, in fact, already in stock, that the description is adequate and that the demand is properly authorised and otherwise in order before he sends it on to the purchasing office for action.

APPROACHES TO CONTROL

Although there are many systems for the control of stock, both manual and automatic, there are really only two basic approaches on which these systems are based. Reordering will either take place when stocks fall to a predetermined level, or according to the situation discovered when levels are reviewed on a periodic regular basis. Sometimes these approaches will be used in combination, for example, it might be the case that the reorder level approach is employed with the backup of regular review of physical stock levels. The two approaches are commonly called the 'action level' method and the 'periodic review' approach.

The action level method

The basic method of controlling stock by quantity is by means of fixing, for each commodity, stock levels which are recorded in the stock control system and subsequently used as a means of indicating when some action is necessary. There are various kinds of stock levels, but the fundamental controls are minimum, ordering, hastening and maximum levels. It does not follow that all these are necessary or even desirable for every item, and they should be employed with discretion because the fixing of too many levels makes the work of provisioning unduly complicated.

The minimum stock level is the amount expressed in units of issue below which the stock of any given commodity should not be allowed to fall. When the level is reached, it triggers off urgent action to bring forward delivery of the next order, and it is sometimes called the 'danger level'. In fixing a minimum the main factor to be taken into account is the effect which a run-out of stock would have upon the flow of work or operations. For many items this effect is negligible, and it may be desirable to have a minimum stock level of 'Nil'. In other cases, such as raw materials or important spare parts for vital machines, the effect of a run-out might be to stop production entirely, and sufficient stock must be held as a minimum to avoid shortages at least in normal supply conditions.

The reorder level is the amount expressed in units of issue at which ordering action is indicated in time for the material to be delivered before stock falls below the minimum. Two main factors are involved in deciding the ordering level: first, the anticipated rate of consumption, and second, the estimated time which will elapse between the raising of a provision demand and the actual availability of goods in store after receipt and inspection, i.e. the 'lead time'. When the ordering level is reached for any item, before arrangements are finally made to buy a fresh supply, a check should be made to see if there are deliveries outstanding in respect of any existing order.

The hastening stock level is the amount expressed in units of issue at which it is estimated that hastening action is necessary to request suppliers to make early delivery. It is fixed between the minimum and the ordering levels.

The maximum stock level is the amount expressed in units of issue above which the stock should not be allowed to rise. The purpose of this level is to curb excess investment. In fixing a maximum the main consideration is usually financial, and the figure is arranged so that the value of the stock will not become excessive at any time. Other points affecting this level are the possibility of items becoming obsolete as a result of operational changes, shortage of storage space and the danger of deterioration in perishable commodities. When the level is reached, it is a signal to defer or cancel outstanding deliveries, if any. The use of maximum stock levels in 'action level' control is not widespread.

Review of stock levels.   In order to keep abreast of changing conditions after stock levels have been established in the first instance, they should be carefully reviewed at suitable intervals, e.g. quarterly, monthly or even weekly, and adjusted to meet any changes in the circumstances. Unless this is done, the levels originally fixed soon become out of date and the system of stock control is rendered ineffective.

When quantity control is operated in this way through the medium of stock levels, if a manual system is in use, the clerks entering the stock records are instructed as a matter of routine to examine each card every time a posting is made to see whether the levels are affected. Wherever this happens the cards concerned are either taken out and kept separately for subsequent attention, or marked or signalled in some way in accordance with the system of recording employed. It is then the duty of the stock control section to examine these items and to take the appropriate action, dependent upon which stock level has been reached. Where the minimum or hastening level is shown, a check is made to ensure that replenishment action has already been taken and that goods are on order. If this is so, the supplier is asked to hasten delivery. This may be done by the stock control section direct, or through the agency of the purchasing office. If, through some oversight, an order has not been placed, it is obviously necessary to do so immediately and to seek the earliest possible delivery. Where the maximum stock level has been reached, and there are any outstanding orders still undelivered, arrangements may be made for the supplier to delay the deliveries or to cancel the order. Where the ordering level has been reached, the action normally required is to initiate the placing of further orders on suppliers. A computerised system will, of course, automatically advise when stocks reach action levels.

The periodic review approach

It will be appreciated that, under the action level method of provisioning, commodities are ordered at unspecified intervals from day to day as and when ordering levels are reached. This means that orders can only be placed usually for one item at a time and this may not produce the best purchase prices. Very often it is possible to obtain discounts or more favourable prices for large-quantity purchases and the normal action-level method of control does not lend itself to this practice. Where a range of similar commodities can be ordered at one time the value of individual orders will be much greater and the possibility of

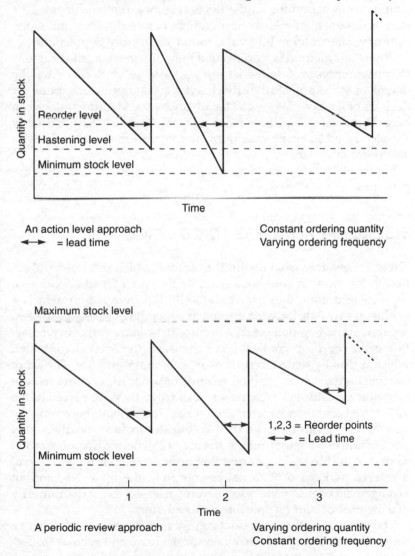

An action level approach   Constant ordering quantity
◄──► = lead time   Varying ordering frequency

A periodic review approach   Varying ordering quantity
    Constant ordering frequency

Fig. 8.1 Two typical approaches to control compared

lower prices more likely. For example, this would be the case if an order was placed for a large range of twist drills covering three months' requirements instead of placing single orders for individual drills from day to day. To take advantage of this situation, periodic review or cyclical provisioning may be introduced. In general terms this involves examining either the physical stocks or the stock records for a particular class of commodity at regular intervals and taking simultaneous action for all the items requiring replenishment. This may be done at intervals of one month, three months, six months, one year or whatever other interval is found satisfactory in practice.

Where this method is employed, if there are unexpected variations in consumption or if deliveries are seriously delayed, there may be danger of a stockout. On the other hand, if consumption unexpectedly declines or if deliveries are too far advanced, the amount of stock can become excessive. For these reasons, cyclical provisioning is usually supplemented by using maximum and minimum stock levels as an additional safeguard.

Figure 8.1 compares 'action level' and 'periodic review' approaches.

VISUAL APPROACHES TO CONTROL

There are several visual methods of control which still find application in the modern warehouse despite the widespread adoption of sophisticated computer-based methods. The 'two-bin' system is a useful and straightforward approach depending on the use of two separate storage containers, one in current use and another in reserve. When the 'current' container is exhausted, the second container, which is usually sealed in some way, is brought into use. The act of starting on the contents of the second container triggers the reordering process, and when the new stocks arrive they are placed in the vacant first container which is then sealed, the contents becoming the new 'reserve'. Variations on the two-bin idea include the division of one bin into two compartments, the use of reordering documentation as part of the bin sealing or dividing arrangement, or the location of a reserve package of material remote from the main bin, and an arrangement whereby the reserve is only released under the authority of a member of staff responsible for reordering.

The imprest method of visual control may be employed, where a set level of stock is predetermined for the item, and regular inspections are made so that the bin can be topped up to the correct level. This approach is often found to be useful where subsidiary stocks of material, perhaps on an open access basis, are kept apart from the main stock. Small fastenings in a manufacturing concern might, for example, be dealt with in this way.

The imprest level needs to be determined with some care. Too high a level might encourage wasteful use of the material; too low a level will lead to frequent replenishments (at some cost), and a higher probability of a stockout occurring.

The 'exchange' basis of control can be classified as a visual method, and is frequently employed in situations where a used item can be presented as evidence that a replacement is necessary, and an exchange can be made. Examples of appropriate applications of this method include the tool store, where a worn item can be exchanged for a serviceable one, or a clothing store, where soiled garments might be exchanged for clean.

PROGRAMMING DELIVERIES

In factories where there is a fixed production schedule several months ahead, the requirements of production materials are accurately determined well in advance. In such conditions it is often convenient and economical to place standing orders with suitable suppliers and to programme their deliveries of various materials or components at a given rate per day, week or month. This is common in the automobile and component industries. It gives the maximum certainty of delivery and simplifies the problem of provisioning to a great extent. Again, in order to avoid unexpected fluctuations in stock, it is usual to employ maximum and minimum levels to the individual stock items.

ORDERING QUANTITIES

Irrespective of the system of stock control in use it is clear that, if large quantities are ordered on an infrequent basis, then the risk of being out of stock will be diminished and the cost of acquisition will also be reduced. These savings will be offset by the higher average investment in stock leading to greater stockholding costs. If a policy of ordering 'little and often' is adopted, then stockholding costs will be reduced, while ordering or acquisition costs rise. The possibility of running out of stock may also be greater.

This situation can be illustrated by means of examples; consider the case of a chemical which is used on the following basis:

Purchase price	£1,000 per tonne
Rate of use	10 tonnes per week
Cost of storage	20% per annum
Cost of ordering	£20

If we order 2 tonnes each working day and we use it at once, the cost of storage will be zero, and the cost of ordering will be 5 (working days each week) × 52 (weeks) × £20 (cost of each order) = £5,200. Should we adopt an alternative policy in an attempt to reduce these costs, and order the 520 tonnes in 13 lots of 40 tonnes, with each lot being delivered just as the previous one is used up, we shall achieve some success. The annual costs will now mainly be made up of the cost of carrying an average stock of 20 tonnes of chemical, which will be 20% of £20,000, that is £4,000. In addition there will be sum of £260, being the cost of placing 13 orders. So, by ordering in this way at a total cost of £4,260 we save almost £1,000 each year.

In fact neither of the approaches outlined so far is an economic one; it will be possible to reduce the cost of even the cheaper alternative by more than 50% by ordering in lots of 10 tonnes, when the figures will be as follows: 52 orders @ £20 = £1,040, plus cost of carrying an average stock of 5 tonnes, which is 20% of £5,000 (£1,000). The total annual costs when ordering in 10 tonne lots is, therefore, £1,040 + £1,000 = £2,040.

Notice that the ordering costs and stockholding costs are approximately equal in this case.

Figure 8.2 shows a typical pattern of ordering and storage costs, and it can be seen from this diagram that the point at which the two lines intersect indicates the ordering quantity at which the sum of the cost of ordering and the cost of storage is at a minimum. In other words, the economic ordering quantity is the quantity at which ordering costs and storage costs are equal.

It is possible to apply a general formula in order to determine the optimum ordering quantity, which may be expressed as:

$$Q = \sqrt{\frac{200\ Ax}{y}}$$

Where Q = the value in £s of the most economical order quantity to place at a time

A = the value in £s of annual consumption

x = the cost in £s of placing one order

y = the cost of storage expressed as a percentage of the value of the average stock

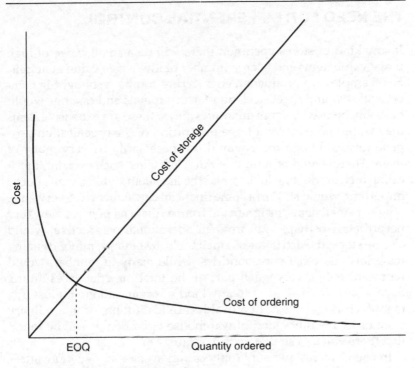

Fig. 8.2 **Optimum order quantity**

To manually apply a formula to each individual item of stock held in the average business would be laborious, and a common approach used to be to prepare a table based on the formula showing the optimum ordering quantity for various values of consumption. Various proprietary slide rules have been marketed to facilitate calculation of appropriate order quantities and programmable calculators can be useful. It is of course a simple matter to incorporate a suitable routine into the software for computerised stock control systems, and the majority of such systems will output a recommended order quantity based on current ordering and stockholding costs.

It must be recognised that the formula for the optimum ordering quantity should be used with discretion. This is because ordering costs and storage costs will, at best, be approximations, the recommended ordering quantity may not correspond with standard lot sizes, prices may not remain stable, and consumption might fluctuate.

THE NEED FOR DIFFERENTIAL CONTROL

In any kind of stores operation there will be a small range of high usage value items and a large number of low usage value materials. For example, in a production engineering company, bought-in components, bar and sheet steel, non-ferrous metals and castings would probably be used in large quantities. Since these are expensive items they would account for a large proportion of the organisation's expenditure, although there would not necessarily be very many of them. There would be a middle range of items, such as paint, lubricating oils, production tooling and the like, items which, while not so important, would still be of some financial consequence. A very wide range of small items, insignificant from a financial point of view (but nevertheless perhaps vital from an operational perspective) would also be stocked. Such items as small tools, fastenings, minor cleaning materials and other such sundries, while many in number, would represent only a very small part of the total material expenditure. Such a situation will exist in any kind of organisation, not just in a manufacturing context. In a health care institution, or in a military store or in any other kind of warehouse operation, it will be found that there will be a similar state of affairs.

In such circumstances it is only common sense to pay more attention to the high usage value items, controlling them very tightly, and thereby controlling the majority of the working capital which is invested in stocks. A widely used approach which enables this to be done is known as ABC analysis.

ABC ANALYSIS

ABC analysis is based on the 80:20 rule or as it is sometimes called, the Pareto principle, after the nineteenth-century Italian philosopher who illustrated graphically the fact that most of the wealth in Italy was owned by a small proportion of the population. Of course, there are many examples of such disproportion, for example, it may be found that a large proportion of sales are made by a small section of an organisation's sales force, or that a large percentage of a population inhabits a small share of the land area of a country.

As a rule of thumb it will be found in any store or stockyard about 80 per cent of the total value of issues in a year (or indeed any other period) will be accounted for by perhaps 20 per cent of the items. This 80:20 relationship is not necessarily an absolutely precise ratio for the relationship between usage value and the range of items stocked, so perhaps the frequently encountered term 80:20 *rule* is something of a misnomer, but nevertheless it is extremely rare for a greatly different relationship to be encountered.

The recognition of this disproportion enables a differential approach to be taken to categories of stock, with appropriate approaches to control being taken according to the usage value of each item.

ABC analysis, which is simply the refinement of the idea of there being two categories of stock into a series of three categories is widely employed.

Category A items, small in number, high in usage value – the 'vital few' from a financial point of view.
Category B items, medium number, medium usage value – 'normal' items.
Category C items, high number, low usage value – the 'trivial many'.

Figure 8.3 illustrates a typical ABC curve; it should be remembered that the 'break' points between classes A, B and C are arbitrarily set and can be placed at the points on the Pareto curve which suit the operator. The break points shown may, however, be regarded as typical.

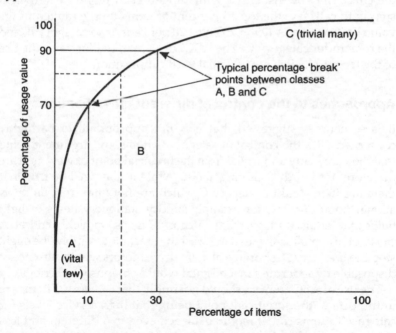

Fig. 8.3 Typical ABC curve showing 80:20 relationship

Conducting an ABC analysis

The derivation of an ABC analysis is a straightforward but laborious process, though many suites of stock control computer software contain routines which can conduct the necessary section and ranking of data. The process may be summarised as follows:

1 Calculate the annual usage value of each item in the inventory.
2 Rank the items in descending order of usage value.
3 Build up a series of sub-totals by entering the biggest usage value at the top of a list, then adding in each successively smaller usage value, generating a new sub-total time.
4 Using the total or combined usage value as the extent of the vertical axis, and the number of items in the inventory as the horizontal axis, plot the Pareto curve on graph paper.
5 Insert the A-B and B-C break points at suitable places.

The procedure outlined may, if wished, be simplified with only slight and perhaps insignificant loss of accuracy by sampling the usage values of the items stocked, and by plotting the curve by using usage values at fixed intervals from the cumulative usage value table rather than plotting every one. Indeed, the whole business of plotting the curve may be dispensed with altogether. It might be sufficient simply to call, say, the top 10 per cent of items on the ranked usage value list category A items, the next 20 per cent or so category B, and the remainder category C. The ABC curve merely illustrates the use of the technique; it is not essential for its application.

Approaches to the control of different classifications

It is sometimes suggested that it is not appropriate to be highly concerned with the control of category C items, the argument being that they are many and trivial from the financial point of view, and are therefore not worth bothering about. While it may well be true that there are items within category C which are not vital from an operational point of view, for example sundry stationery items or light bulbs of a certain wattage, many category C items are highly critical. A stockout of a small screw used in a washing machine assembly line might stop the line just as a shortage of main drive motors would; absence of disposable hypodermics in a hospital would obviously be serious.

The use of ABC analysis should not imply that category C items are unimportant, the significant point being that high service levels for category C items can, if required, be achieved in a different and less expensive way than for category A items. For A items, particularly in

A. High usage value	B. Medium usage value	C. Low usage value	
AV	BV	CV	V. Vital. Stockout would be disastrous
AI	BI	CI	I. Important, a stockout is highly undesirable
AN	BN	CN	N. Normal. Ideally stocks should be available, temporary shortage acceptable

Category	Approach to control	Frequency of stock check	Safety stock level
AV	Closely monitored control	High	Low
BV	Closely monitored control	High	Medium
CV	Automatic control	Medium	High
AI	Closely monitored control	High	Nil
BI	Supervised automatic control	Medium	Medium
CI	Automatic control	Low	Medium
AN	Closely monitored control	High	Nil
BN	Automatic control	Medium	Medium
CN	Automatic control	Low	Low

Fig. 8.4   Differential approaches to nine categories of stock

those A items where the unit value as well as the usage value is high, meticulous attention to every item will be the only economically feasible approach, whereas for category C lines it will be more cost effective to achieve high service levels by means of generous safety stocks.

The classification of stock according to criticality as vital, important or normal may be combined with ABC analysis with the aid of a three by three matrix as shown in Fig. 8.4.

CLASSIFICATION OF STOCK ACCORDING TO PURPOSE

It may be useful to consider stocks held by an organisation and to categorise them according to the purpose for which they are held (see

CLASSIFICATION OF STOCK ITEMS Item description . . . . Code no		Tick
A	High usage value	
B	Medium usage value	
C	Low usage value	
Vital	Extremely critical item	
Important	Stockout would cause serious problems	
Normal	Short-term stockout can be accommodated	
Bulk items	Special storage and handling needs	
Piece parts	Easily handled manually, though may be large quantities	
Unit loads	Delivered and handled in palletised lots	
Special	Particular handling and/or storage problems	
Perishable	Short shelf life; stocks must be kept low	
Intermediate	Shelf life a consideration, rotation necessary	
Durable	Deterioration in storage not a problem	
Steady	Demand continuous and smooth	
Lumpy	Demand intermittent and difficult to predict	
Dependent	Demand depends on production or other plan	
Independent	Demand does not depend on plan	
Seasonal	Demand varies according to regular pattern	
Trend	Demand rising or falling in predictable way	
Routine	Item stocked as normal, regular requirement	
Special	Item stocked for particular project or activity	
Insurance	Item stocked for emergency use	

Fig. 8.5 Stock may have to be classified in a variety of ways for storage, handling and control purposes

Fig. 8.5). The following list covers the main classes of stock, and suggests the approach to control which may be appropriate for each one.

Routine stocks. Stocks which are held, replenished and depleted in the normal course of business may be called routine items, or cycle stocks. The approach to the control of these items will depend on whether demand is dependent or independent; in other words, whether or not demand is known in advance because of the existence of a production plan, or some other kind of activity schedule. If demand is dependent, then stocks may be held at a very low level, and some kind of MRP approach will probably be employed in determining order times and quantities. JIT approaches are often found to be appropriate where demand is dependent. A typical example of a dependent demand situation is for embodiment parts where high volume flow or mass production is taking place. Where demand is independent, then stock levels will be determined by forecasting rather than planning, although 'leading indicators' such as the level of economic activity or population trends may well be employed. The retailing of consumer goods is an example of a situation where demand is independent.

Work in progress stocks. In many kinds of organisation inventories of materials in a part finished or partially assembled state are held. These are unavoidable stocks, arising mainly as a result of the fact that different production operations or processes operate at differing speeds, or that different batch sizes are accommodated by different operations. To a large extent, direct control of these stocks is impracticable; the volume and timing of such stockholdings will be driven by the planning and control of production. Nevertheless, the costs associated with stocks still arise from these inventories, and attention should be paid to the need to avoid unnecessarily high levels or too much delay.

Buffer or safety stocks. These stocks are held on a 'just in case' basis and are intended to be drawn upon if anything goes wrong with the proper control of the routine stock. Safety stocks are a particularly expensive form of inventory, in that they will seldom be drawn upon if the system of control does not fail in some way. The extent to which buffer stocks ought to be carried depends more on the cost of being out of stock than on the costs of ordering and carrying stock. There is no real point in protecting against the occasional stockout by means of buffer stocks if the cost of this protection is greater than the stockout cost. Unfortunately, of course, the cost of a stockout is usually difficult to assess accurately.

Care should be taken in connection with the physical safety stocks to ensure that they are rotated properly. If the stocks are segregated in some way from the main stocks they may lie undisturbed for a long time, and deteriorate until they are of little or no use.

Insurance stocks. These are items, usually of high value, or long lead time, or both, which are held in case some breakdown or other misfortune occurs which can only be remedied by calling these materials rapidly into use. Major spare parts for capital equipment, or submersible pumps for emergency operations in the mining industry would be examples of insurance stocks. Unlike most kinds of stock, the idea is that insurance stocks should not be used. They are only issued if some mishap has occurred; hence the name insurance.

As with buffer stocks, the main basis for deciding whether to carry insurance stocks is the cost of not having them when needed, rather than the intrinsic costs of buying and storing them.

Because of the rather special nature of insurance stocks, and the fact that they are often of high value, some organisations treat them as items of capital equipment, and they are reported in the organisation's accounts as fixed assets.

Seasonal stocks. These are held over and above normal stocks to cope with expected higher demand at certain times. A construction company might increase its stocks of foul weather clothing as winter approaches, or a supermarket chain would increase its stocks of luxury foods in time for Christmas. The usual approach to dealing with seasonality is to apply some manual override to a forecasting system which is producing figures derived from a de-seasonalised underlying trend. Seasonal stocks of natural products, for example apples in autumn, are a particular problem for producers and distributors, and have to be planned for and organised well in advance.

Redundant stocks. Most organisations, however well regulated, have small stocks of materials which are of no use to the organisation. That is not to say that they have no value, and it is an obvious matter of common sense to try to diagnose redundant stocks as promptly as possible, and to take steps towards their disposal, preferably by way of sale, but even dumping of material which is of no further use to the organisation is less costly than keeping it on the books, and in store, where all kinds of expensive routine effort is expended on housing, recording, checking and other activities. Redundant stocks arise for all kinds of reasons, for example, over-ordering, changes in production plans and activities, being superseded by newer items and by the user adopting different methods and materials and so on. Scrap and unserviceable materials might be thought of and dealt with in the same way as redundant stocks.

There is often some resistance to the disposal of redundant stocks, as an accounting transaction, known as 'writing off' needs to be undertaken, and the costs allocated to the stores or some other department. There is sometimes a tendency to leave redundant stocks alone, despite the fact that they are unlikely to be used, as it is less trouble that way. This is, of course, a short-sighted and expensive policy.

FORECASTING DEMAND

Forecasting is the process of estimating future quantities required, using past experience as a basis. It is fairly easy to predict the pattern of demand for some stock lines. For example, if an item is obsolescent, demand will almost certainly decline as time goes on; if a special sales campaign is to be started, demand should rise. Seasonal items such as bathing suits or fuel for heating purposes will have a fluctuating demand. Very often, however, the position is not so obvious, and can only be found by keeping records of past performance and projecting them into the future by forecasting.

The easiest method of forecasting is to take a simple average of past demand as follows:

Month	Actual Demand
May	40
June	30
July	80
August	70
September	120
October	140
Total for six months	480

(a) Simple average forecast demand for November:

$$\frac{Oct.}{6} + \frac{Sept.}{6} + \frac{Aug.}{6} + \frac{July}{6} + \frac{June}{6} + \frac{May}{6} =$$

$$\frac{140}{6} + \frac{120}{6} + \frac{70}{6} + \frac{80}{6} + \frac{30}{6} + \frac{40}{6} =$$

$$\frac{480}{6} = 80 \text{ per month.}$$

We could then use 80 as the forecast demand for November. For the month of December we would discard the figures for May, and add on the *actual* November demand and repeat the process. This is known as simple 'moving' average because the oldest period's figures are discarded and the latest added to the series each time the calculation is made. The method has the disadvantage that it gives equal weight to the oldest period (May) and the newest (October) and therefore does not reflect the trend with reasonable accuracy. If we substitute a 'weighted' average for a simple average, we can give more importance to the more recent figures as follows:

(b) Weighted average forecast for November:

$$\frac{1}{2} \times Oct. + \frac{1}{4} \times Sept. + \frac{1}{8} \times Aug. + \frac{1}{16} \times Jul. + \frac{1}{32} \times Jun. +$$

$$\frac{1}{64} \times May$$

$$= \frac{140}{2} + \frac{120}{4} + \frac{70}{8} + \frac{80}{16} + \frac{30}{32} + \frac{40}{64}$$

$$= 70 + 30 + 8\frac{3}{4} + 5 + \frac{15}{16} + \frac{5}{8} = 115\frac{5}{16} = 115 \text{ approx.}$$

This is the technique of 'exponential smoothing'. In the example the 'weighting factor' is ½ and is technically known as the 'smoothing constant', usually indicated by the first letter of the Greek alphabet, 'alpha' written α. This constant α is a value between 0 and 1. The higher it is the more emphasis is placed on the most recent demand figures, and therefore the more sensitive the resulting forecast will be to the latest trend of demand. In practice, the values most commonly used for α are 0.1, 0.2 and 0.3. If we substitute α for ½ in equation (*b*) above, it would read:

Weighted average forecast for November $\Big\}$ $= \alpha$ Oct. $+ \alpha (1 - \alpha)$ Sept.

$$+ \alpha (1 - \alpha)^2 \text{ Aug.} + \alpha (1 - \alpha)^3 \text{ July}$$
$$+ \alpha (1 - \alpha)^4 \text{ June} + \alpha (1 - \alpha)^5 \text{ May}$$

This can be simplified as:

New average demand $= \alpha D + (1 - \alpha)$ Old average demand

where D = the *actual* demand for the most recent period (i.e. in this case Oct.). This is the basic equation for exponential smoothing. It has the important advantage that apart from the constant α only two figures are needed to make the calculation – the actual demand for the latest period and the old average demand calculated last time.

Trend.   There are four basic patterns of demand:

1 Steady trend
2 Fluctuating trend
3 Rising trend
4 Falling trend

The equation:

New average demand $= \alpha D + (1 - \alpha)$ Old average demand

normally gives good results but a further refinement is to take more careful account of the trend specifically by adding a further similar equation:

New average trend $= \alpha$ Current trend $+ (1 - \alpha)$ Old average trend

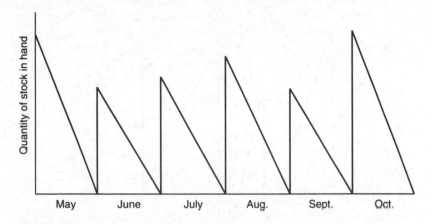

Fig. 8.6   Perfect forecasting

The principle is the same, and the current trend is the difference between the new average demand and the old average demand.

Errors. However sophisticated the system of forecasting may be, it will not be 100 per cent accurate and there will be a difference between forecast and actual. This is known as forecast error, and allowance must be made for it. In a perfect situation where the forecast was 100 per cent correct every time, and where the supplier always delivered promptly the pattern of stock would be as in Fig. 8.6.

This shows a nil stock just as each new consignment arrives at the beginning of each month. In practice, we know this is improbable and an actual stock performance looks more like Fig. 8.7. This shows two sources of error – unexpected major variations in demand – high in June and July and low in October, and late delivery by the supplier in July and September. These circumstances are the common experience and therefore we must have a 'buffer' or 'safety stock' so that we shall not run out of supplies.

Safety stock is obviously related to the accuracy of forecasting, and is in fact a function of the forecast error, which can be predicted by an equation very similar to those used for demand and trend:

New average forecast error =
   α Current Error + (1 − α) Old average forecast error

If the forecast error is large, the safety stock will also have to be large and if the error is small, a low safety stock is indicated. The level of service desired must also be taken into account. At a service factor of 98 per cent, there should be 98 chances in 100 that stock will not be

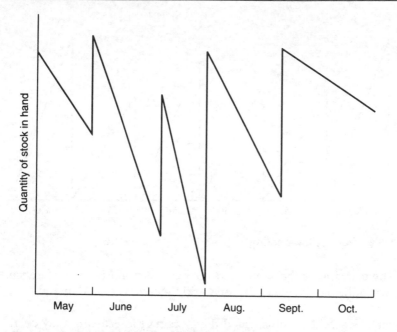

Fig. 8.7   Actual experience of stock fluctuation

unavailable when called for. One hundred per cent service might be impracticable, but the higher the service factor the more the value of the safety stock necessary. Safety stock is therefore calculated by multiplying the new average forecast error by a constant K, which represents the service factor. Stock control systems based on the exponential smoothing method of forecasting are most satisfactory when applied to finished goods held for distribution or resale – for example, a central warehouse serving a chain of grocery supermarkets or chemist shops, a wholesale paint warehouse, or a builders' merchant business. The technique is not usually suitable for the control of raw materials and bought-out parts for manufacturing organisations or construction companies, where demand is strictly related to a preplanned operational programme, but even in these concerns, it may be usefully applied to general consumable stores.

THE USE OF PROBABILITY IN INVENTORY CONTROL

In situations where demand is independent, decisions as to how much to stock will be based on our view of the probabilities of different levels of demand arising. These probabilities will be, to some extent, subjective. That is to say that some opinion or judgement will be employed in their determination. We may be using the pattern of the past to help us make our decisions (forecasts), or we may be relying on our experience, skill or feel for the job. Our view will be carefully determined, it will not be merely a guess, but on the other hand we will not be certain.

If the demand for something fluctuates randomly over a period of time then the concept of 'expected value' can be used to determine the appropriate level of stock to carry. The idea is illustrated by the following example:

A merchant buys fresh fish from the wholesale market at £2 per kg and sells it for £5 per kg. He is never sure how much to buy, but he knows that if he buys too much he will have to dump his surplus at the end of the day and lose the £2 per kg that it cost him. On the other hand, if the does not buy enough he will forgo the £3 per kg profit that he might have made if he had been able to satisfy all of his customers.

The merchant has kept records of demand for the past 100 days, and has analysed them as follows:

Daily sales (kg)	No of days
9 or less	0
10	10
11	20
12	40
13	30
14 or more	0

He can tell from these figures that there is a high probability of selling 12 kg, a much lower probability of selling 10 kg, and it is improbable that he will sell 9 kg or less, or 14 kg or more.

He can also see that there is a greater probability of selling 12 kg than any other quantity, but there is, nevertheless, a 60 per cent probability that he will sell a different quantity from 12 kg, and if he does then some costs arising from overstocking or understocking will arise. What should he do? He needs to work out the conditional profit and the expected profit of each possible policy. Conditional profit is the amount of profit he will make if a particular combination of stock level and demand occurs.

If, for example, he buys 11 kg, and demands on that particular day are for 13 kg, then his profit will be:

Income from sales, 11 kg at £5 per kg   £55

Less cost of fish, 11 kg at £2 per kg	£22
Conditional profit	£33

If he buys 13 kg, and demands are for 11 kg then his profit is:

Income from sales, 11 kg at £5 per kg	£55
Less cost of fish, 13 kg at £2 per kg	£26
Conditional profit	£29

The expected profit is simply the conditional profit which would arise from any particular combination of purchases and sales multiplied by the probability of that combination actually occurring. So, as we have seen, the conditional profit arising from buying 13 kg and selling 11 kg is £29. However, the probability of demand being 11 kg is 20 per cent, so the expected profit is £29× 20%=£5.80.

A table can be constructed showing the conditional and expected profit as follows:

		Buying Policy							
		10		11		12		13	
kg	%	CP (£)	EP (£)	CP (£)	EP (£)	CP (£)	EP (£)	CP (£)	EP (£)
10	10	30	3	28	2.8	26	2.6	24	2.4
11	20	30	6	33	6.6	31	6.2	29	5.8
12	40	30	12	33	13.2	36	14.4	34	13.6
13	30	30	9	33	9.9	36	10.8	39	11.7
TOTALS	100		30		32.5		34.0		33.5

CP = Conditional Profit   EP = Expected Profit.

The total expected profit arising from a policy of buying 12 kg is £34, which is higher than any other total. A policy of putting 12 kg into stock each morning is the appropriate one.

THE SETTING OF REORDER LEVELS

Suppose a stock item has a one week lead time. Past demand over 100 weeks has been checked and found to average 5 units per week. The lowest weekly demand was 3 units per week and the highest was 10 units per week. The pattern of weekly demand for the 100 weeks in summary was as follows:

Demand per week (units)	3	4	5	6	7	8	9	10
No of weeks with each demand	10	35	25	17	6	4	2	1

This table gives an indication of the probability of given levels of demand being exceeded. For example, 8 units per week would be exceeded in 3 weeks out of the 100 weeks, that is, there is a 3 per cent probability of demands greater than 8 arising.

Since these are the demands in the lead time they can be used as possible reorder levels. If a reorder level of 8 is set, the probability of stockout is 3 per cent, if the reorder level is 9, the probability of stockout is 1 per cent, whereas if the reorder level were reduced to 6 the probability of stockout would be 13 per cent. The protection offered increases as the probability of stockout falls. The greater the reorder level, the more costly is the stockholding cost, but the lower the stockout cost.

Suppose this item had a price of £500 and the stockholding cost was 20 per cent per annum. Thus every additional unit in the reorder level would add £100 per annum to the cost. How much would the added protection be worth? If the item in question was a critical one and any stockout arising cost £2,000, then on the information provided:

Reorder level	Probability of stockout (%)	Expected cost (£)
6	13	260
7	7	140
8	3	60
9	1	20
10	0	0

The expected stockout costs would be liable to arise every time an item was on order, so the annual cost would depend on the number of orders placed per annum. Suppose this was one order per annum, then the above costs would be the annual stockout costs. Increasing the reorder level from 6 to 7 would cost £100 per annum in increased stockholding but a reorder level of 7 gives increased protection so as to reduce stockout costs from £260 to £140, so 7 is preferable to 6 as a reorder level.

Increasing the reorder level from 7 to 8 costs more than the saving through the improved protection, so that in this instance a reorder level of 7 would be appropriate.

If there were 4 orders being placed in a year, expected stockout costs per annum would be quadrupled giving:

Reorder level	6	7	8	9	10
Annual stock-out costs (£)	1040	560	240	80	0

In this instance it is worth opting for the increased protection offered by a reorder level of 9, but not worth raising it further to 10. So, in this example 9 is the best reorder level.

This sums up the idea behind the setting of reorder levels, but in practice items will probably be grouped according to such factors as criticality and order frequency.

THE PROVISION OF SAFETY STOCKS

Safety stocks provision can be compared to the purchasing of insurance against risk of loss or damage to a possession. If the risk is perceived to be negligable, then insurance cover is unlikely to be bought, though if a significant possibility of loss is envisaged then some form of cover will probably be acquired.

If an appropriate stock control system is employed in a situation where future demand is always accurately predictable, and where suppliers always meet their promised delivery times, and where deliveries are always defect free, then safety stocks will not be necessary except, perhaps, to provide some cover for fragile or otherwise vulnerable materials which might suffer damage in production. Indeed, if the above circumstances are present then stocks of any kind might be eliminated, not just 'safety' stocks. A JIT system might be a viable alternative to stockholding.

Much, probably most, inventory management takes place in an environment where there is some degree of uncertainty. Protection against shortages or stockouts is a primary responsibility of the stock controller, and fundamental questions to be addressed are: How much does protection cost? and, having found the answer; How much protection do we wish to provide? It is a question of insurance, as previously mentioned.

If no safety stocks are provided, then it is probable that there will be zero stock preceding at least half of all deliveries of stock materials. The system will be designed to ensure that replenishment takes place exactly when existing stocks are exhausted, so a zero stock situation on receipt of a new delivery can be taken as evidence that the system is working well. There is, however, a very high probability that demands will be made during the out-of-stock period, and there will be a failure to supply. It has been suggested that, without safety stocks, there is a probability of 0.5 that there will be a stockout before each delivery.

Of course many inventory controllers provide safety stocks without necessarily calling them that, or even realising that that is what they are doing. If a pessimistic view is taken of a supplier's ability to deliver on time, or if stock and reorder levels are increased a little 'to be on the safe side' then safety stocks are being provided, albeit informally. It is surely preferable to be as scientific and analytical as possible in determining policies and procedures which enable supply and demand to be matched economically, and to consider 'insurance' cover as a separate question.

It is not really practicable to offer hard and fast decision rules for the provision of safety stocks. Whilst is feasible to attempt to calculate the cost of stockholding, and to use this figure in computing the costs associated with the provision of safety stocks, it is not so easy to attribute costs to failures to supply on demand. These costs can range from a figure close to zero (no 1 litre tins of paint in stock, but 2 × 500 ml can be issued), to many thousands of pounds (shortage of a small component for the main printed circuit board (pcb) stops production in a television factory). As can be seen, the cost of a shortage may bear little relationship to the price of the item.

An appropriate strategy for safety stocks ought to be employed, taking into account the following four main considerations.

1 The reliability of supply.
2 The predictability of demand.
3 The cost of carrying additional stock.
4 The cost of failure to provide.

SIMULATION

When it is not possible either to forecast future consumption from the pattern of past demand (perhaps because no pattern is discernible), or to relate requirements to production schedules or other indicators of planned activity, a technique which may be of value to the stock controller is simulation. Simulation is an attempt to duplicate the essence of a system without actually operating the system, and may take the form of physical analogue simulation, such as that accomplished with a flight simulator or digital modelling, usually with the assistance of a computer, and it is this latter approach that we are concerned within stock control.

It would clearly be uneconomic and impracticable to seek to determine an optimum policy in stock control by trial and error changes to actual policy, because to do so would be very expensive, and any savings achieved in arriving at the optimum might be more than outweighed by the costs involved in getting there.

It might, however, be practicable to take an experimental approach to 'simulate' the actual situation by using a technique which allows us to experiment with and manipulate a representation of it, and thus develop satisfactory solutions or procedures at a relatively low cost (see, for example, Fig. 8.8). There are many kinds of simulation; the 'business games' employed by academics to give students an opportunity to see what effect different decisions might have on business performance will be an example familiar to many readers.

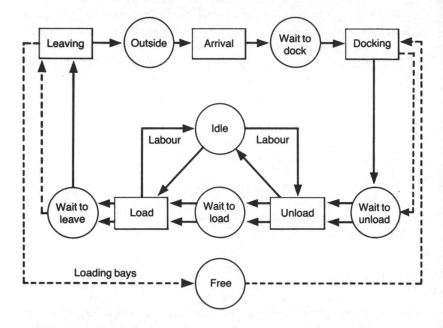

The warehouse is to have a loading platform with 5 loading bays. Trucks arrive at random intervals and have to queue if there is no free bay. After docking at the bay the trucks may again need to join a queue for the necessary labour for unloading and reloading. The major components of this system are:
(1) Loading bays   (2) Trucks   (3) Labour
Each of these has an activity cycle which includes activity (loading, working etc) and inactivity (queuing). Both active and inactive states take random time periods to complete, i.e. the truck will go through an indeterminate amount of time waiting and an indeterminate amount of time being serviced. The components of the system (loading bays), will be sometimes active, sometimes idle. The task of simulation will be to see how these components interact with each other. If we can make observations about the probabilities of different waiting/busy states and service times then we may be able to generate much useful information about how the loading bay might work if we varied the number of loading points, amount of labour and other factors.

Fig. 8.8   An example of a problem which might be solved by setting up a simulation

In the determination of stockholding policy the 'Monte Carlo' approach to simulation is often found to be useful. The name 'Monte Carlo' is given to any technique which uses a chance process to solve a problem. A basic illustration of Monte Carlo simulation in stock control is perhaps best given by means of an example.

The table below indicates the probabilities, learned from past experience, that a certain spare part will be required during the overhaul of a machine.

Probability.	Number Required
.4	0
.32	1
.12	2
.08	3
.05	4
.02	5
.01	6
.00	7 or more

The components cost £10 each to buy and store. Any component not used will be disposed of as scrap for £2 on completion of the overhaul. If, during the overhaul, more components are needed than are held in stock, a penalty of £100 is incurred through having to obtain material at short notice. How many components should be held in stock to minimise expected costs?

In order to simulate this situation we might use a range of random numbers from 0–99, each single number having an equal probability of 'coming up'. A die is a random number generator, the numbers 1 to 6 each having an equal probability of being uppermost when the die comes to rest after being shaken and cast. We cannot use a 100-sided die, such a device would be impracticable, but we can use a computer to generate random numbers, or we might use a published list of random numbers. Such lists can be purchased, and they appear in many statistics textbooks.

We can then allocate random numbers according to the probabilities which we know to exist as follows:

Number of parts required	0	1	2	3	4	5	6	7+
Probability	.40	.32	.12	.08	.05	.02	.01	00
Random number	0–39	40–71	72–83	84–91	92–96	97–98	99	

The next step is to use random numbers to reflect the probabilities of the different numbers of parts being required, and to calculate the cost for various stocking policies, remembering that there are three factors to take into account:

Purchase cost	£10
Scrap value	£2
Penalty cost	£100

Testing a stocking policy of carrying three parts in stock we might draw a random number of, say, 27, indicating that no parts are needed. The costs would therefore be £$(3 \times 10) - (3 \times 2) = $£24. Another trial might give a random number of 74, indicating a demand for 2 parts, and a cost of £(3 × 10) − (1 × 2) = £28. A random number of 97 would indicate a demand for 5, and a cost of £(3 × 10) + (2 × 100) = £230. A simulation using a random number stream of 1000 gave the following average costs for various stocking policies.

Number Stocked	Cost of policy (£)
0	136
1	82
2	52
3	40
4	39
5	44
6	51

A policy of stocking four parts yields a minimum expected cost of £39. The sensitivity of the stocking policy to changes in costs of ordering or stockout, or to changes in scrap values can be determined by changing the values and rerunning the simulation.

CHAPTER 9

Stock checking and stocktaking

The terms 'stocktaking' and 'stock checking' are often regarded as meaning the same thing but, for the purposes of this chapter, it is proposed to consider 'stocktaking' as the complete process of verifying the quantity balances of the entire range of items held in stock, and 'stock checking' as any other check on physical quantities which may be applied either regularly or intermittently. Stock audit is the name given to the process of reconciling stock records when an external agency is involved.

Stock represents cash and, invariably, cash is looked after very carefully. A cashier is appointed to control it; and it is locked up in safes when not in use. The cash office is fitted with a counter and a grille to make sure that no one other than the cashier's staff has access to the money. Every time cash is received or issued it is counted, and the balance in hand is checked at frequent intervals. Cash books are kept in detail to record all transactions and, if any of the checks made discloses a discrepancy, the most searching inquiries are pursued to find the explanation. Cash is regarded as so important that, in the event of any substantial deficiency arising, it is normal to call in the police.

Now since stock is the equivalent of cash, it might be suggested that it should be carefully protected, counted and checked in a similar way, but there are many organisations where the arrangements display a looseness and lack of system which would not be tolerated in the cash office, in spite of the fact that the value of stock is frequently very much greater than that of cash held.

PHYSICAL SECURITY

If stock is to be adequately safeguarded, it must be properly located in secure buildings or stockyards to which unauthorised persons are not allowed access, arrangements must be made for the custody of storehouse keys, and security precautions exercised during non-working hours.

All these matters are dealt with in another chapter, but they are mentioned here because they are an essential prerequisite of any satisfactory system of stock checking or stocktaking.

RESPONSIBILITY FOR STOCK

The person immediately responsible for the care and custody of stock should be clearly designated; it will normally be the storekeeper in charge of a storehouse or section. The storekeeper's responsibilities should be made known to all concerned, and he must be given proper authority and facilities to fulfill his duties. No stocktaking or stock checking should take place without the storekeeper's knowledge, and no discrepancies should be declared unless an opportunity has been given to investigate the position.

PURPOSES OF STOCKTAKING

Physical stocktaking is the process of counting, weighing or otherwise measuring all items in stock and recording the results.

The reasons for doing this are as follows:

1 To verify the accuracy of stock records.
2 To support the value of stock shown in the balance sheet by physical verification.
3 To disclose the possibility of fraud, theft or loss.
4 To reveal any weaknesses in the system for the custody and control of stock.

The size and number of surpluses and deficiencies revealed by stocktaking is a good criterion of the efficiency of storekeeping methods, control and procedure generally.

There are two methods of stocktaking: periodic and continuous.

PERIODIC STOCKTAKING

By the periodic method of stocktaking, the whole of the stock is covered at the same time at the end of a given period, usually the end of the financial year. Theoretically, stock should be taken at the close of business on the balance-sheet date, but in a large concern, it may be quite impossible to do all the work in one day, and the operation has to be extended over several days. The stocktaking need not be done only once a year; it may be carried out as often as seems desirable.

For a satisfactory stocktaking, a good deal of preparation is necessary. First of all, a programme should be drawn up and agreed with all concerned, including the finance department and the auditors; secondly, stocktaking sheets or cards have to be prepared in advance; thirdly, all personnel concerned must be instructed in their duties.

The arrangements made should deal with all aspects of the job and, in particular, the following points:

1 Appoint one person to control the whole operation.
2 While stocktaking is in progress, do not have the storehouses open for normal business.
3 After the end of the working day before the operation begins, no more issues should be made and no receipts recorded until the stocktaking is complete. The numbers of the last receipt and issue vouchers should be noted, and all documents up to and including these numbers posted to the records. At this point all the records can be ruled off and no further postings are made until the results of the stocktaking have been entered.
4 Take all normal stock including packages, scrap, residues, items on loan and goods under inspection.
5 Have stocktaking sheets under the control of one individual, consecutively numbered, and issued to the staff on duty as required. No duplicates should be allowed and, at the end of the job, all stocktaking sheets must be accounted for.
6 Record separately damaged, deteriorated or used items.
7 Make each person taking stock responsible for a particular section or clearly defined area of the storehouse or stockyard, and record everything that is to be found in that area. Stocktakers should proceed in an orderly manner, and mark each bin or rack as it is dealt with to avoid the chance of checking any item twice, and to ensure that nothing is missed.
8 Any items held which are not the property of the business ought to be marked or labelled in advance.
9 List separately any goods which have been received but not yet taken on charge (e.g. still under inspection).
10 Special arrangements must be made to include in the total list of stock all items belonging to the business which are not on the premises at the time of the check. This concerns free-issue stocks in the hands of suppliers, goods sent out for repair or processing,

or stocks at outlying operational sites. It is usual to write to the holders of such stock to obtain written confirmation that these items are in their possession.

11 Return to store all items issued 'on loan' either internally or externally before the stocktaking begins.

12 Show the method of check, i.e. count, weight, measurement or estimation on the stock sheet for each item.

13 Record quantities in terms of the normal unit of issue for the stock concerned. This can be ensured by inserting the appropriate unit of issue on the stock sheets before distribution.

14 The method of pricing should be known and, if possible, it is desirable to enter all prices in terms of units of issue on the stock sheets in advance.

15 Where several widely dispersed stockholding points exist, stores in transit at the date of stocktaking must be taken into account.

Stock sheets

The following is typical of the information which should appear on the sheets or computer printouts used for stocktakings:

1 Serial number of stock sheet
2 Date of stocktaking
3 Location
4 Vocabulary number
5 Description
6 Unit of issue
7 Quantity of stock found
8 Price per unit of issue
9 Value of stock found
10 Stocktaker's signature
11 Remarks column for comments about condition of stock or any other special notes.

When the physical side of the work has been completed, all stock sheets should be collected and arranged in classification order, the value of each entry extended and a total shown. By adding up these totals the value of stock in each classification can be obtained. The sum of these classification totals will give the grand-total value of stock on hand as verified by physical examination.

Suitable precautions must be taken to make sure that all stock sheets are returned and that the arithmetic is checked. Where stock records are kept, the next step is to compare the individual entries on the stock sheets with the appropriate record cards and enter the actual quantity found at the stocktaking date on the records. Where this quantity does not agree with the balance shown on the record cards, two points should be noted:

1 The physical stocktaking figure is the factual one and, therefore, takes priority and the balance on the card must be amended.
2 Major discrepancies require investigation to discover, if possible, why they have arisen. All established surpluses and deficiencies should be valued and written on or written off respectively, to ensure that the balances on the control accounts are adjusted to agree with the total value of stock verified by the physical stock-taking.

CONTINUOUS STOCKTAKING

Continuous stocktaking is the method whereby stock is taken continuously throughout the year in accordance with a predetermined programme so that each item is physically verified at least once in the course of the year, or more frequently if required. It can only be done if complete detailed stock records are kept showing receipts, issues and balances on hand (i.e. if there is a 'perpetual inventory'). The programme should be so designed that a certain number of stock items are taken on every working day. It may be thought necessary to have certain valuable or fast-moving stocks examined more frequently than other items. It is also wise to arrange that the operation is scheduled to finish a month or so before the end of the financial year so that, if work is delayed owing to unforeseen circumstances, there is time in hand to complete it before the year end.

The methods of physical check are the same as those employed for periodic stocktaking, but there are significant differences in other respects, as follows:

1 There is no need to close down the stores or the works while stocktaking is in progress.
2 The normal posting of receipts and issues on the stock records can continue without interruption.
3 The work can be done by a few specially appointed, experienced and trained stocktakers completely independent of the storekeeping staff.
4 Stocktaking results may be entered on the stock records from day to day as they arise, and any discrepancies disclosed can be thoroughly investigated in detail. This is an important advantage because one of the main weaknesses of the periodic stocktaking

method is that all the discrepancies are declared at once, and time to deal with them properly is necessarily limited.

5 Assuming that the continuous programme of stocktaking has been satisfactorily completed according to plan, the balances on the stock control accounts can be accepted for balance-sheet purposes without any special year-end physical check, and there need be no delay in the preparation of the final accounts, as far as stock is concerned.

STOCKTAKING PROCEDURE

'Blind' stocktaking

This is the name given to the system whereby the person taking stock is given no prior information about the vocabulary numbers, descriptions, stock-record balances or locations of the items to be checked, and is not allowed access to stock-record cards or bin cards. The theory is that the check will be more reliable as the stocktaker has no knowledge of what is supposed to be in stock. He or she has to locate and identify stores for themselves, is obliged to count every item, and is not open to any temptation to skimp work by accepting identifications of quantities as appearing on the stock-record cards. This system is laborious and slow, it requires more staff and, unless the personnel concerned are experienced and have a first-class knowledge of the physical characteristics of the stock held, errors are likely to arise because of faulty identifications.

A modification of blind-stocktaking procedure is to provide the stocktaker with locations and identifications, but to withhold from them the quantity balance on the stock records. This is a reasonable compromise and speeds up the work substantially.

It must be said, however, that if a major stocktaking operation is to be done in a short space of time, the quickest method is to give the stocktaker all available information including quantity balances on stock records. This assumes, of course, that he or she is a conscientious and trustworthy employee. It has three main advantages:

1 Where a stocktaker finds a major discrepancy on the first physical count, it can be rechecked straight away.
2 Where a trifling discrepancy is found, it can be ignored and unnecessary adjustments avoided.
3 It simplifies clerical work where the stock agrees with the card balance.

Teamwork

It is a common practice for stocktaking to be done by teams of two people, for the following reasons:

1 Where quantities are not large, the counting or weighing can be done by one person, and the clerical work by the other.
2 Where large items have to be measured or weighed, two people can usually operate more satisfactorily than one.
3 Where two people are concerned, they will to some extent check each other's work, thus minimising errors.

Stocktaking by storekeepers

It is advisable to enlist the help of storekeepers in the process of stocktaking. Because of their knowledge of stocks and where they are kept, they are able to find and identify items quickly. The ideal team (*see above*) is a storekeeper and another person who is not on the storehouse staff, thus combining speed of operation with independence of check.

Occasionally storekeepers are required to take stock of their own stores for balance-sheet purposes without outside assistance or supervision, but this practice is not recommended. To make storekeepers responsible for their own stocktaking not only exposes them to the temptation to conceal genuine discrepancies to avoid criticism of their work, but provides opportunities for deliberate fraud. It is much more satisfactory to have the stocktaking done by full-time stocktakers, internal audit or finance department staff, or some other independent persons.

Counting scales. To avoid the need for counting individually large numbers of small items, such as individual detail components, use may be made of counting scales. These are scales so designed that one article placed in one pan will balance several times its own weight in the other pan. For example, if the ratio of the scales is 1 to 100, then one item in the smaller pan will balance 100 similar items in the larger pan. It is easy to see that large quantities can be checked quickly in this way. Within reason, scales can be obtained to provide any required ratio.

Estimation. For some bulky items such as solid fuel, sand, cement, gravel, etc., weighing is out of the question because of the time and expense involved, and exact measurement may also be impracticable; resort must be had to estimation but, wherever possible, a surveyor or other suitably qualified technical person should be asked to assist.

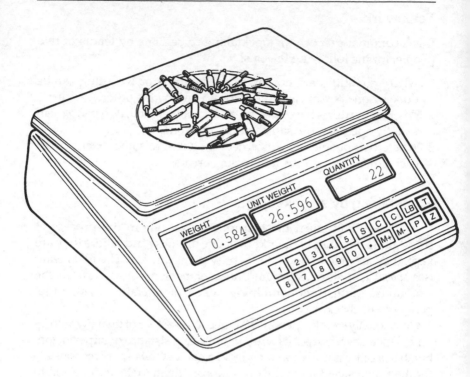

Fig. 9.1   Counting scales

Stock certificate

Irrespective of whether stocktaking is carried out by the periodic or by the continuous method, at the end of the financial year a stock certificate is signed by a senior member of the management. This document is a declaration of the value of the stock on hand, and usually there is a list attached showing the amount involved in each storehouse and/or in each classification. The certificate is further supported by all the individual stocktaking sheets.

Sampling

An alternative to a 100 per cent count of all items held in stock is to employ the sampling approach. Usually employed in computerised items, and where items are of low unit value and not classified as 'attractive', such a system can be very cost effective.

What usually happens is that items are classified into groups or sets, and the computer is instructed to produce an indication of which items should be checked according to specified statistical sampling levels; this information then being passed to the stockchecker. A physical count will be made, and the extent and level of discrepancies will be compared with the parameters laid down within the system. If these discrepancies fall within limits, then no further action will be taken and, if discrepancies exceed these limits, then a 100 per cent check of items within the group will be required. In some systems, a double sampling procedure is followed, so that in the event of a first sample not demonstrating clearly whether discrepancies are so great as to warrant a full check a second sample is taken for verification.

The sampling approach to stocktaking does of course depend upon the application of the statistical principles associated with probability, the devising and implementation of a suitable scheme will be a complicated and time-consuming business.

Paperless systems

Electronic data processing technology and the use of bar coding makes it possible to stocktake without the use of any document. The introduction of radio linked, integrated, hand held computer terminals with built in bar code scanners means that the operator can receive instructions from the main computer as to which items should be counted, and their location.

The operator will first scan a bar coded location label fixed to the front of the rack, bin or shelf to confirm that he or she is in the right location. The computer will signal confirmation that the location is correct. It may be appropriate to scan a second bar coded panel attached to the actual stock, particularly where a random location system is employed. This will confirm that the right item is in the location. The count can then take place and the operator will key in to the hand held terminal the quantity found. If this tallies with the computer record, the terminal will indicate that there is no discrepancy, and inform the operator of the next location to be checked. If there is a discrepancy then a second count will be required. If this second count fails to resolve the discrepancy, then the item is 'flagged' on the main computer for detailed investigation.

It will readily be seen that such a procedure brings a range of benefits. Stocktaking is 'blind', so that operators will not see the quantities they expect to see, and they can not take shortcuts by simply entering the right quantity without counting. An appropriate route for the checker can be computer planned, and where sampling is taking place, the computer can determine an appropriate sample range of items to be checked. The possibility of error is considerably

Fig. 9.2   A hand held radio terminal

reduced by the machine reading of bar codes rather than the human reading of labels.

TREATMENT OF DISCREPANCIES

Surpluses and deficiencies

When the amount of stock found by physical examination fails to agree with the balance on the stock records, a discrepancy exists. If the stock found exceeds the recorded figure there is a surplus and, conversely, if the physical stock is less than the book figure, there is a deficiency.

Minor discrepancies.   There are limitations to the accuracy of stock-taking, particularly where large numbers or quantities are concerned, whether the check is by count, weight or measurement. For example, in measuring 1,000 metal bars of random length no two people are likely to get the same result to the nearest foot. Similarly, in weighing half a tonne of loose bolts, some slight variation may be expected because of the degree of accuracy of the sales or the reading of them. If, therefore, discrepancies of small proportions appear to be found in such circumstances, it is often as well to leave the book stock unaltered unless the amount of money involved is significant. This point applies particularly where the methods of measurement are known not to be of great accuracy, e.g. the use of dipsticks in large tanks or, more obviously, the stocktaking of loose piles of sand, coal or bricks, where only an estimate can be made.

Storekeeper's agreement. Stocktakers should not declare a discrepancy on any item without first giving the storekeeper concerned the opportunity of investigation. This is a sensible precaution for several reasons:

1 There may be duplicate locations of which the checkers are not aware, but the storekeeper should know of them.
2 It can be expected that storekeepers have a better practical knowledge of their stock than anyone else, and they may be able to correct errors on the part of the stocktakers, particularly errors of identification.
3 It gives the storekeepers an opportunity to explain or correct the difference if they can, and ensures that they are aware of discrepancies which may reflect upon the performance of their duties.

When a storekeeper has been called in and fails to explain a difference, he or she should sign the stock sheet to indicate agreement that the discrepancy is genuine.

Investigation of discrepancies

After the stocktaker and storekeeper have agreed that a discrepancy exists, the procedure depends upon the nature and value of the discrepancy. Large amounts are more worthwhile investigating than small sums, more concern is felt about deficiencies than about surpluses and, where discrepancies may have arisen through 'breaking bulk' (i.e. making a large number of small issues over a period from a bulk stock, especially by weight), they are not perhaps thought worthy of any detailed inquiry. The degree of investigation is, therefore, a matter of judgment in the circumstances of each case. The following list of steps to be taken should be considered, bearing this point in mind:

1 Examine the transactions since the date of the last check to make sure that there are no errors or obvious omissions or duplications in recording.
2 See that there has been no confusion over units of issue.
3 Examine stores kept in neighbouring locations to see if a balancing discrepancy exists on another item.
4 Check the basic documents (i.e. receipt, issue, transfer, return-to-store notes, etc.) for any exceptionally large or apparently unusual transactions.
5 Have the physical stocktaking verified by an independent senior official.
6 Interrogate the storekeeper to find out if there is any explanation or suspicions as to how the discrepancy has arisen.
7 Examine the results of the last stocktaking to see whether there was a discrepancy on that occasion. In odd cases it may be found that a deficiency at one stocktaking is followed by a surplus on the next, and this may be because the first check was inaccurate.
8 Make inquiries of user departments in case there may have been issues from or returns to store without documentation outside normal working hours.
9 In serious cases, where theft or fraud is suspected, call in senior management.
10 Where necessary, review and tighten up physical security measures and documentary procedures.

Adjustment and reconciliation

After investigation, both stock records and accounts require adjustment in respect of declared discrepancies. This may be done direct from stock sheets or by a special Discrepancy Report form, listing all the items concerned showing:

1 Vocabulary number
2 Description
3 Unit of issue
4 Quantity as per stock record
5 Quantity found on physical check
6 Differences between 4 and 5 showing surpluses and deficiences separately
7 Unit price
8 Value

It is normal practice for discrepancy forms to be approved by the stock controller or some other appropriate authority before the

Col.1	Col. 2	Col. 3	Col. 4	Col. 5
	(Discrepancy summary)			
Classification No. and Description	Value of Surpluses £	Value of Deficiencies £	Value of Net Surpluses £	Value of Net Deficiencies £
01 Steel	257	127	130	-
02 Timber	12	131	-	119
03 Paint	-	6	-	6
04 Petrol and oil	18	25	-	7
05 Machinery spares	-	132	-	132
06 Bought-out components	175	25	150	-
07 General stores	3	56	-	53
Subtotals			280	317
Total Net Deficiency			-	37

adjustments are made to the accounts, and the discrepancies are summarised to show the net surplus or deficiency on each classification; see the discrepancy summary table.

In the example given, the values in columns 4 and 5 would be debited to the stock control accounts for the classifications concerned in the case of net surpluses, and credited in the case of net deficiencies as follows:

			£
Stock control account 01 (Steel)		Dr.	130
Stock control account 02 (Timber)		Cr.	119
Stock control account 03 (Paint)		Cr.	6
Stock control account 04 (Petrol and oil)		Cr.	7
Stock control account 05 (Machinery spares)		Cr.	132
Stock control account 06 (Bought-out components)		Dr.	150
Stock control account 07 (General stores)		Cr.	53

OBSOLESCENCE AND REDUNDANCY

Obsolescent

An item is said to be obsolescent when it is going out of use but is not yet completely unusable. For example, let us suppose that a logistics firm has been running trucks of model XYZ, and it is decided that in future all replacement vehicles are to be model ABC from a different manufacturer. From the date when this change is announced, most of the spare parts in stock for model XYZ become obsolescent. This does not mean they are immediately worthless, because they can be used for repairing the lorries to which they belong as long as these models are in service. On the other hand, the number of XYZ trucks maintained will decline as time goes on, and they will all eventually be disposed of. It is extremely unlikely that the spares in stock will be used to the very last item and there is an expectation that some of them will be on hand when all the XYZ lorries are withdrawn. Therefore there is a likelihood of loss by virtue of the fact that these remaining spares will have to be sold and probably fetch only scrap value. Those materials which are currently available from suppliers, but which are due to go out of production might also be termed obsolescent.

Obsolete

An item is regarded as obsolete when it is no longer usable by the business concerned, because of a change in operational practice or production methods. For instance, in the example quoted above, when all the XYZ trucks have disappeared, the XYZ spares will no longer be obsolescent, but obsolete.

Redundant

When the quantity of an item in stock is more than is reasonably necessary to provide an adequate service to the production or operational activity, the excess over the normal holding is said to be redundant. This has the same meaning as surplus. For example, if the use of reams of copy paper in an office is running at the rate of 50 per month and there are 6,000 reams in stock, there is obviously some redundancy, because the stock would last for 10 years. Redundant stock may arise as a result of changes in operational methods, or may be due to mistakes or inefficiency in stock control or purchasing. The disposal of redundant stock is dealt with in Chapter 11.

Review

In most organisations, some degree of obsolescence or redundancy is inevitable. It is particularly severe in manufacturing concerns where the design changes frequently (e.g. cars, domestic appliances, televisions), and also in organisations such as transport undertakings or the Armed Forces, where rapid technical development is going on and large quantities of spares are used for the equipment in service.

It is therefore desirable to review all stock held from time to time to identify items which are obsolete and redundant and this is usually undertaken once a year. The review may be combined with the normal stocktaking operation or done independently, on a periodic basis or on a continuous basis.

It is usual to conduct the review classification by classification. Apart from the fact that this is the most methodical approach, it also provides the maximum opportunity to suggest alternative uses for items which are no longer required for the purpose for which they were originally bought. For example, in looking at the steel classification it may be found that, owing to production changes, 12-mm diameter round bar is no longer required, but there is still a heavy demand for 10-mm diameter bar to the same specification. It might be more economical to use the 12 mm in place of 10 mm until the existing stock is exhausted, rather than to dispose of it outside the organisation.

Use of an inventory record system

It should be noted that the listing of obsolescent, obsolete and redundant items is done from the control system. There is no need to look at the physical stock in the storehouse until after the goods concerned have been listed, and then only for the purpose of deciding whether specific items can be used for alternative purposes, or to estimate disposal values.

Before the review begins, the manager responsible should find out what recent changes there have been in production or operation and what changes are imminent. From this information he will be able to determine which major items of materials or spares are likely to become obsolete and redundant, and these can be paid special attention during the review. In addition, all slow-moving stock should be particularly examined to ascertain whether it is still required or not.

Preliminary list of obsolescence and redundancy

The result of detailed examination of the stock records is to produce a preliminary list of items which appear to be obsolescent, obsolete or redundant. The next step is to investigate these items on the following lines:

1 *Obsolescent.* For machinery or equipment spares, make a fairly generous estimate of the probable usage of each item up to the time when it is expected to become obsolete. Submit the balance for disposal immediately, because the sooner they are sold, the more likely they are to fetch a price better than scrap value. In the case of raw materials consult the production department with a view to

using as many items for alternative purposes as it is economical so to do (e.g. the example of 12-mm and 10-mm bar quoted above).

2 *Obsolete.* List for disposal without further inquiry.

3 *Redundant.* With the cooperation of the operating department first scrutinise these items to see if they can be put to alternative uses and, if not, agree what proportion of the stock is to be retained.

4 *Slow-moving stock.* Give special attention to items where there has been no movement for six months or more.

With the assistance of the maintenance or user departments, 'stand-by' spares for machinery or equipment still currently in operation should be identified and the record cards endorsed accordingly, if this has not already been done in a previous year. For all other slow-moving items, the user departments can advise whether they wish the stocks still to be retained and, if so, why. In this category it is as well to be conservative and, after all the investigations have been made, it is a matter of judgment as to how much is disposed of immediately. It may be thought prudent even to wait until some slow-moving items have appeared on the list for two or more successive years before finally disposing of them.

Final list of obsolescence and redundancy

When the preliminary list has been investigated as described above, a final list should be made showing particulars of all items which it is proposed to write down or write off. In some organisations a committee consisting of representatives of purchasing and stores, finance and user departments is set up to agree the final list, which is usually approved by a senior member of the management before the accounts are adjusted and before anything is disposed of.

The following information is typical of that appearing on final lists of this kind:

1 Vocabulary number of each item
2 Description
3 Quantity in stock
4 Quantity to be retained
5 Quantity to be disposed of
6 Original book value of 3
7 Recommended book value of 4
8 Recommended book value of 5
9 Amount to be written off
10 Comments (e.g. remarks on condition, or slow movement of stock or suggestions for methods of disposal)

After approval, the amount to be written off is credited to the appropriate stock control accounts.

Deterioration of materials in store

It sometimes happens that materials in stock deteriorate for any of the following reasons:

1 The inherent nature of the material is such that it deteriorates in the course of time, e.g. fresh fruit, unstable chemicals.
2 Inadequate storage conditions, e.g. cement gets damp and solidifies, steel becomes rusty, stationery becomes dirty.
3 Damage in store through accident or bad handling, e.g. electric light bulbs may be dropped and broken, plasterboard is easily damaged.

Where this happens, the stock will not be worth the value at which it stands in the accounts, and adjustments must be made to rectify this state of affairs by reviewing the stock concerned and making an estimate of the value to be written off according to the amount of deterioration which has taken place for each individual item. This operation can be carried out as the occasion arises or, alternatively, at the same time as the stocktaking or in conjunction with the review of obsolescence and redundancy. In special circumstances, for example, if there has been a fire or a serious flood in the storehouse, the review of stock for deterioration may be a completely separate exercise.

STOCK CHECKING

Checking receipts

Receipts into store are sometimes checked for quantity by weighing, counting or otherwise measuring. Mutual 'partnership' type arrangements with suppliers have reduced the amount of incoming inspection, both of quality and quantity. We must have a good foundation for all subsequent operations by ensuring, as far as is practicable, that the quantities taken on to the system are correct in the first instance. In some organisations the process is carried further by checking not only the incoming consignment but also the remaining stock already on hand at the time that the new consignment is put away in its place in the storehouse. Whether this is worth doing or not is a matter of opinion in the circumstances involved. It depends upon factors such as the value of the item, the nature of the goods, the extent of the stock balance, the reliability of the records and the availability of labour and time.

Checking issues

It should be a matter of routine for the storehouse staff to check the quantities and descriptions of all issues made before they are handed over. It is also common practice to expect the recipient to counter-check the quantity received and to sign for it. This provides a reasonable assurance that quantities taken off stores charge are correct.

Spot checking

Spot checking is the practice of making random checks of some stores items at irregular and unspecified intervals. It is often done by senior stores officials in the course of their supervisory duties, but can also be operated in parallel with the stocktaking programme, irrespective of whether the periodic or continuous method is in use. Where the main stocktaking is carried out annually on a periodic basis, spot checking throughout the year is the best safeguard against malpractice during the period between stocktakings and also helps to minimise the year-end adjustment. Where stocktaking is continuous, spot checking during the year of items which have already been completed under the main programme is a similar precaution against irregularities arising in sections known to have been covered in the current cycle.

To get the maximum benefit from the labour involved, spot checks should be mainly, but not entirely, confined to items of high value, and it may be worthwhile to check the major items several times in the course of a year.

CHAPTER 10

Storehouses and stockyards

It is impossible to give any detailed advice or rule-of-thumb method for the siting and construction of stores buildings, because of the variations in circumstances in different organisations. The needs of individual businesses differ enormously; a large central store may be required, sometimes a series of small storehouses is necessary, sometimes only one small storehouse, and there are a number of instances where special facilities such as tanks and bunkers are essential. Very often there is no alternative but to accept existing buildings and try to make the best use of them.

Even when the building of new storehouses is envisaged, the situation is usually complicated by existing conditions to some extent. The site may be governed not by what is desirable but by what land is available, the buildings may have to be designed to harmonise with existing premises, and there is always the overriding consideration that, from the financial angle, the facilities to be provided must be in accordance with the funds which can be allocated for the purpose.

It therefore follows that a comprehensive examination of all kinds of storehouses is impracticable and this chapter must be confined to giving some general guidance on a number of points which are commonly encountered in connection with the buildings in which stocks are housed.

NEW STORES BUILDINGS

It is proposed to discuss the construction of new storehouses on the assumption that there are no unusual restrictions on the site or size of the buildings, and that the only financial consideration is to put up a structure which will be reasonably economical in relation to the service it is expected to provide. Although it is not practicable to deal with the details of every type and size of storehouse, many of the factors are common to all. Generally speaking, the bigger the building the more complicated it will be, and the greater the problems of construction and operation. Therefore, in order to give the broadest picture, it is intended to examine in some detail the siting and construction of a large-scale building used as a central storehouse, and serving a number of outlying units.

LARGE CENTRAL STOREHOUSES

Preliminary investigations

The first step is to collect information on the following points:

1 The number and location of the outlying units which are to be served.
2 The number of items of stock to be held.
3 The division of this stock into:
   (a) small items which can be accommodated in drawers or trays,
   (b) binnable items,
   (c) goods which can best be stored in pallet racks,
   (d) heavy articles which must be placed on the floor,
   (e) crated, boxed or cartoned stored which can be stacked without racking,
   (f) items which require special racks or fixtures,
   (g) goods which must have separate or unusual storage facilities,
   (h) materials which can be kept outside in the stockyard.
4 How much material will be received and issued each day.
5 What major handling equipment will be used, i.e. overhead or mobile cranes, fork-lift trucks, conveyers, etc.
6 How many road vehicles will have to be (a) unloaded, and (b) loaded, and at what times.
7 If rail transport is necessary, how many trucks will be required inwards and outwards, and at what times.
8 Whether it is intended to use canal or inland waterway transport.
9 Whether seaborne traffic is envisaged.
10 The number of staff to be employed.

From the above information it will be possible to estimate the size of the building or buildings and the approximate total site area, and also to give a general indication of where the site should be.

Site

The decision on the site is affected by many factors, of which the most important are listed below:

1 The storehouses should be as near as possible to the geographical centre of the area to be served, or to the biggest stores-consuming unit. The selection of the optimum location is an important decision, and a variety of techniques may be employed in this selection.
2 If road transport is to be a major feature, the site must have good road access. It should not be in an area congested with traffic but, if possible, on or near a trunk road with good cross-country communications.
3 Where rail traffic is to be handled, the storehouse should be near a main line and the site must be sufficiently extensive and level enough to allow for the construction of adequate sidings.
4 If canal or inland-waterway facilities are required, it is self-evident that the storehouse must be built on the banks of a canal, lake or river.
5 Where direct access to seagoing ships is necessary, the building will have to be on the docks at a port.
6 The site should, if possible, be reasonably level, well drained and not too far from essential services such as water and electricity.
7 The site ought to be of sufficient size for its intended purpose, with adequate space for manoeuvring vehicles, an area available for an outside stockyard if required, and some extra room for possible future expansion.
8 The land should not be too expensive.

Construction

When the site has been chosen, the next problem arising is the size, shape and construction of the storehouse. This deserves the closest possible attention because the building will probably be in use for many years, and mistakes made at the outset may be the source of continuing inefficiency for a long time.

Single-storey and multi-storey buildings. As a general rule, single-storey construction is best for large storehouses for the following reasons:

1 The cost per cubic foot of storage space is usually much cheaper because the shell can be of lighter construction than is possible with a building having upper floors.
2 The weight-carrying capacity of an upper floor is always limited by structural considerations.
3 Material-handling costs are likely to be less than in a multi-storey building where goods have to be transported up and down between floors.

4 More use can be made of natural daylight.
5 Adequate ventilation is easier to arrange.
6 Modern 'high rise' equipment enables the efficient use of vertical space from a single ground floor.

The use of multi-storey buildings may be more favourable in special circumstances such as:

1 Where the stores are required to serve production or process shops already operating in a multi-storey building.
2 Where land available is restricted in area or extremely costly.

Bearing in mind the arguments outlined above, it is now proposed to continue with the consideration of storehouse construction on the assumption that we are dealing with a single-storey building.

Floors. The floor is a very important feature of any storehouse because not only does it have to carry the weight of all the stock held, but it also has to provide a suitable surface for the operation of wheeled vehicles, whether manually or mechanically operated. The floor must therefore be of adequate strength and have a good, hard, smooth finish with a minimum of obstructions. Modern practice is to use concrete, and there is no really satisfactory alternative. The first step is to decide whether the floor is to be at ground level or not, and this depends very largely on the handling methods employed. Where overhead cranes or mobile jib cranes are in use, the floor is best at ground level, because these machines unload vehicles from above, and the height of the lorry or truck platform is of no consequence. On the other hand, if fork-lift trucks or conveyors are in operation, it may be found worthwhile to have the whole of the floor raised above ground level to the height of the platforms of road or rail vehicles so that they can be loaded and unloaded with the minimum of lifting. Where this is done, it is necessary to provide one or more ramps from ground to floor level, of a gradient and width adequate to allow access to the storehouse for any vehicles such as fork-lift trucks, tractors or hand-trolleys.

The next step is to calculate the anticipated floor loading and design the foundations and floor accordingly. The floor should have a non-slip surface and may be treated with special compounds for dust prevention to minimise the problem of keeping stock clean and free from dust and grit. Storehouse floors are sometimes painted in the interests of cleanliness and good appearance, but the value of this is doubtful. When first completed, a painted floor looks very attractive, but heavy traffic soon wears the paint off in patches and, unless there is continual repainting, the floor will look less satisfactory than if it had not been painted at all. There are a number of specialist contractors who are expert in laying or installing floors with the necessary characteristics of being flat and level, and with the fine and durable surface finish needed by modern equipment. The degree of precision required is great, and the provision of an appropriate floor can be a very substantial fraction of the total cost of a new storehouse.

Structure. The design of the framework depends upon whether it is to bear only the weight of the building itself or whether it is expected also to carry overhead cranes, conveyers or monorails. With overhead cranes, a minimum height to the eaves of about eight metres is necessary to allow sufficient room for stacking materials underneath the level of the crane hook, and there must be a supporting structure strong enough to carry both the crane and its maximum load. For storehouses not employing overhead lifting gear, the height of the building should be sufficient to permit the use of double-tier binning, i.e. at least 4.5 metres to the eaves. This question of height is worth considering carefully because the height of a building can be increased by a few metres without a proportional increase in overall cost. It is, of course, unwise to build too high and incur unnecessary expense for additional heating and lighting.

The most suitable building materials should be used. Brick walls are best at floor level to avoid accidental damage from vehicles and equipment, but most of the sides and roof can be clad with corrugated steel or other sheeting.

In order to cope with changing requirements, a storehouse layout should be flexible and, for this reason, permanent internal partitions should be avoided.

Doors. Provision should be made only for those doors which are essential. They should be wide enough and high enough to admit all vehicles or handling equipment, and capable of being securely fastened and locked. A common feature of large storehouses is that roller shutters or doors of considerable size are provided in the receipt and issue bays or at opposite ends of the building. This is good for ventilation in summer but, in winter, if these entrances are kept open for long periods, there will be draughts and substantial heat losses. They should be designed so that they can be quickly and easily opened and closed, preferably by a power-operated mechanism, and small doors should be incorporated so that employees can have easy access during times when it is not necessary to have the main door open. Another problem with large doors is that rain may drive in underneath in very bad weather. This can be prevented if the bottom is not flush with the floor when closed, but slightly below floor level, and suitable drainage is provided.

Receipt and dispatch docks. There should be a receipt dock and dispatch dock with facilities for loading and unloading vehicles, preferably under cover.

Offices. Suitable offices or enclosures should be provided, adjacent to the receipt and dispatch docks, for the storekeeping staff responsible for handling, checking and documenting consignments inwards and outwards. Portable steel partitioning is the best form of construction for internal storehouse offices of this type in case it may be necessary to change their location in the future to cope with unforeseen developments.

Lighting. The fullest possible advantage should be taken of natural lighting. In most storehouses, shelves or racks are placed along the walls and, therefore, side windows should be at such a height that the light from them is not obscured by these fixtures. Roof lights are almost a necessity in a large storehouse, and the best use can be made of the roof space in this way by installing continuous glazing with wired glass – a type of glazing which is also suitable for side windows. As far as is practicable, the layout of the storage area should be arranged so that gangways and passages get the full benefit of natural light. Sufficient opening panels must be installed to provide adequate ventilation, and all openings should be capable of being securely fastened.

As regards artificial lighting, certain minimum requirements are stipulated in the Factories Acts, but the best practice requires higher standards than these. The installation ought to be designed in accordance with the layout of binning and racking so that the maximum amount of light shines into the storage compartments, and lighting fittings are not in the way of any cranes or other handling equipment.

Heating. In the majority of storehouses outside the tropics some heating facilities are required. There are many types of heating systems available, but those using steam or high-pressure hot water are probably the most suitable. One of the main problems is to arrange the heaters and pipes so as to avoid interference with bins, racks, gangways and handling equipment. To this end, fan-driven unit heaters suspended from the roof can usually be installed with the minimum interference with the storage layout, and flat radiant panels which can be placed high up on side walls or suspended from roof members are also convenient.

In special circumstances, e.g. where sensitive explosives or chemicals are in stock, or where there are natural products or other materials especially liable to deterioration, a complete system of air conditioning with temperature and humidity control may be necessary.

Fire risk. It is reasonable in any circumstances to see that the construction of a building takes account of the possibility of fire but, where the materials in store present an exceptional risk, it is wise to avoid the use of timber in the construction as far as possible, and cladding which has been treated with a bituminous compound or other inflammable mixture is also undesirable: there are a number of proprietary heat resistant sheets. Water mains providing an adequate supply should be located in a suitable position, and provided with sufficient hydrants; an overhead sprinkler system may be installed.

Ancillary services. When a major storehouse is being designed, the ancillary services listed below should not be overlooked and their siting, construction and layout should be included in the overall plan.

1 Boiler house
2 Electricity substation
3 Offices
4 Garage and fuel supplies for stores transport
5 Clocking stations
6 Toilet and cloakroom facilities
7 First Aid centre
8 Canteen
9 Parking space for cars and cycles
10 Clubroom or other recreational facilities

Extensions. As far as local circumstances will allow, it is desirable to arrange the site and construction of new storehouses so as to make reasonable provision for the possibility that the buildings may have to be extended to cope with changing conditions.

STOREHOUSES SERVING ONE FACTORY OR OPERATING UNIT

Many of the features of construction and layout for storehouses of this type are similar to those involved in large central stores. Points deserving special mention are as follows:

Site

The site of the storehouse depends partly on the bulk and nature of the goods involved, the transport facilities and the factory layout. Where large quantities of heavy materials are to be handled (e.g. steel joists, cement, sand), it is usually advisable to place the storehouse at one end of the factory nearest to the main road or railway line. This also applies if the production processes are accommodated in a single large shop operated on the flow principle. On the other hand, if the manufacturing facilities are distributed over a number of separate buildings, it is probably best to locate the storehouse as near as possible to the shops served by it.

Construction

The type of construction of the stores building may have to conform to the general design of other adjacent buildings.

Separate accommodation. The question often arises as to whether the storehouse should be an entirely separate building or whether it should be attached to or even occupy a part of one of the production shops. In favour of a separate building it may be said that:

1 The storehouse will be more independent in its operation.
2 There need be no overlapping or confusion between transport for stores and for production.
3 The stores staff will have full control of their own handling equipment.
4 The security of stock should be improved.
5 There is little likelihood of encroachment on stores space by the production function. It very often happens, where the store is part of a main production shop, that all or part of the stores area is eventually required for the extension or improvement of production facilities.

Against the erection of a separate building are the following arguments:

1 It will probably be more expensive.
2 Where a storehouse is integral with another building, sharing transport or handling facilities is very often practicable, e.g. where

there is an overhead travelling crane in one of the production shops, if the storehouse is in one of the end bays, it may use the same crane. If the stores building were separate, an additional crane might be required.

3 A store inside the production shop is more readily accessible to users and should be able to provide a quicker off-the-shelf service and also to minimise transport delays.

Mezzanine floors. Where horizontal space is at a premium, but vertical space is available, the use of a mezzanine can be a cost effective approach to the provision of storage accommodation. A mezzanine effectively doubles the available floor space, and can improve access to materials. Its disadvantage is that natural lighting will be restricted in the lower area.

A mezzanine under construction in an aircraft maintenance hangar
(Courtesy: the Mezzanine Floor Co. Ltd)

HIRING OF STORAGE ACCOMMODATION

Decisions on storehouse organisation are sometimes influenced by the following factors:

1 Lack of capital to build or extend storehouses
2 Lack of space on site for building or site of difficult shape
3 High rents and rates in urban areas
4 Seasonal fluctuations of bulk stocks
5 Temporary inflation of stocks in other special circumstances

For any one or a combination of these reasons, it may be advisable to hire storage accommodation elsewhere. There should be a written agreement on the hiring covering at least the following aspects:

1 Whether complete buildings are to be hired or if not which part
2 The period of hiring and the length of notice on termination
3 If buildings are to be heated and lighted
4 Who will provide the labour, handling equipment and transport
5 Responsibility for dilapidations and damage to buildings and stock
6 Responsibility for accident, fire and theft precautions
7 Insurance of buildings and stock
8 Access for stocktaking

Similar considerations apply to hiring open storage space.

STOCKYARDS

The importance of adequate stockyard facilities as a part of the storekeeping function will now be discussed, with emphasis on their construction and layout.

Buildings for housing stock are expensive, and certain heavier and less perishable materials may be kept in the open for a reasonable length of time without serious deterioration. The following are typical examples:

Structural steel sections and plate; heavy steel bars; rails; metal pipes; large iron castings; stoneware pipes and fittings; timber; bricks; sand; gravel; coal and coke; precast concrete products; heavy cable; large electrical insulators; outdoor plant and machinery; scrap of various kinds awaiting sale.

Unfortunately there is a tendency in many places for open-air storage to receive less attention than the storehouses themselves, and the arrangements are quite often casual and inadequate. The following is a list of some of the common shortcomings of outside storage facilities:

1 Stock is scattered over a wide area, making proper control very difficult.
2 The absence of fencing or other means of enclosure increases the risk of theft, fraud or unauthorised issues.
3 Road and/or rail access is inadequate. In particular, road surfaces are often unmade, thus slowing down transport and hindering the use of mechanical-handling equipment.
4 Badly drained surfaces frequently become waterlogged, causing undue deterioration of stock and making access very difficult in bad weather.
5 Lack of artificial lighting impedes efficient working during the winter months, and makes night work impracticable.
6 There is an excessive employment of manual labour.
7 Material is stacked on the bare earth and, in course of time, becomes overgrown by vegetation, or corroded.

Where significant quantities of stocks are held in the open, a proper stockyard should be designed, constructed and operated in an efficient manner. If this is well done, the following advantages will be apparent:

1 Good planning saves space.
2 Enclosure of the area improves security.
3 If a gatehouse and weighbridge are provided, there is a much more satisfactory control over vehicles delivering or collecting. The proper booking in and out of all carriers and the recording of gross and tare weights minimises the possibility of fraud, which is always a serious danger.
4 Adequate drainage facilitates movement in the yard and avoids deterioration of materials.
5 Satisfactory road and rail access speeds up the turn-round of vehicles.
6 When goods are properly stacked and labelled, stocktaking is easier and more accurate.
7 An efficient layout permits the use of modern handling methods and this in turn usually produces significant economies in the employment of labour.

CONSTRUCTION OF STOCKYARDS

Site

The location of the yard is determined by the disposition of road and rail facilities and the position of existing buildings. Subject to this consideration, the stockyard should be immediately adjacent to the main storehouse, and adequate and unhindered road access (and rail access, where necessary) should be regarded as very important. If the best site available is not already levelled and well drained, arrangements must be made to do this.

Surface

The nature of the surfacing depends to some extent on the kind of materials to be stocked and the type of transport and handling equipment employed. The three types of surface normally in use are as follows, the depths of foundation and finish being varied to suit local circumstances:

1 *Ashes*.   A bed of consolidated clinkers or ashes, finished off with fine ashes and rolled. This is one of the cheapest methods, but unfortunately also the least efficient, because the surface is easily cut up by heavy transport. It may be regarded as reasonable for stacking areas, but is not satisfactory for roadways. In particular, it is unsuitable for fork-lift trucks.

2 *Tarmac*.   A bed of hardcore, rolled and consolidated, covered with a layer of tarmac and finished off with a cost of fine tarmac, rolled. This costs about three times as much as ashes, but is much more satisfactory. Drainage of surface water is more effective, the area is easier to keep clean, and it stands up to traffic. One drawback is that very heavy stacks of material may tend to damage the surface, particularly in hot weather.

3 *Concrete*.   A bed of hardcore rolled and consolidated, topped by a layer of concrete reinforced by steel fabric. The cost of this is about four or five times that of ashes, but it is probably the best finish for normal purposes. It drains well, provides an excellent foundation for stacking material, will bear any traffic within reason, and requires less maintenance in the course of time than either ashes or tarmac.

In most stockyards, access roads and gangways occupy rather more than half the total area and it is sometimes thought worth while to economise on the initial cost by a compromise whereby the roads are concrete or tarmac and the stacking areas are of ashes.

Lighting

The installation of lighting is only worthwhile if it is necessary to operate in the early mornings or late afternoons or if a night shift is worked. Subject to the size of the yard, conventional lighting is best placed round the perimeter, arranged to shine inwards, but an interesting modern development is to have tower-mounted floodlights of the type found in football stadiums.

Fencing

Unless the yard is within a factory or other premises which are already adequately enclosed, the provision of a fence or other surround is important for good physical control and security. Many kinds of fencing are available. One popular arrangement is to have galvanised or plastic-coated chain-link fencing about 2 m high with steel or concrete posts. Sometimes the posts are cranked to carry two or three strands of barbed wire above the chain-link fencing, thus increasing the total height and giving more protection against trespassers.

Gates

The number of gates should be kept to a minimum and all gates should be lockable. Railway gates must be provided if required.

STOCKYARD FACILITIES

Railways

It is always advisable to have railway lines sunk to road level in the yard, so as to avoid interference with internal movement of other vehicles. The siding facilities to be provided depend upon the weight of traffic but, where possible, a dead-end single-line siding into the stockyard should be avoided, because this will restrict the rate at which wagons can be handled.

Roads and gangways

These should be of concrete or tarmac, as far as funds permit. The width must be appropriate to the vehicles and loads carried, and the detailed arrangement of the roads and gangways depends very largely upon the type of mechanical-handling equipment in the yard. For example, with an overhead gantry crane or tower-mounted mobile crane, probably no more than one road is needed and gangways, if they are necessary at all, will only have to be wide enough to permit

Cantilever racking in an oilfield stockyard

the slingers to get about among the stock; but with a fork-lift truck installation, there must be sufficient gangways to ensure that no material is beyond the limited reach of the forks, and all these gangways have to be wide enough to allow access for the fork-lift truck, carrying a load.

As far as the main access roads or gangways are concerned, a system of one-way traffic is desirable, at least for vehicles delivering or collecting consignments. This avoids congestion and allows traffic to flow smoothly.

If one-way traffic is not practicable, care must be taken to see that there is enough room for large vehicles to turn round at dead ends, and lay-bys may be needed to allow lorries to pass each other if the road is narrow.

Tub and trolley tracks

Tubs or trolleys on narrow-gauge tracks are sometimes employed in industrial concerns such as mines and quarries. If they are used for transporting materials from the stockyard to the workings, a narrow-gauge circuit may be required in the yard. The rails should be sunk to ground level in the same way as for main-line tracks.

Stacking areas

The mechanical-handling equipment in use governs the layout of stacking areas in the same way as it affects the arrangements of roads and gangways. Stacking areas should be clearly defined and roads and gangways kept clear.

Gatehouse and weighbridge

In order to supervise the comings and goings of vehicles and to prevent unauthorised entry into the yard, it is desirable to have a gatehouse. This can also serve as a place to keep receipts and issue documents and records, and it is frequently combined with a weighbridge for recording the gross and tare weights of all vehicles. The gatehouse may be regarded as the control point of the stockyard.

Storehouse

Wherever circumstances will permit, the stockyard should be located immediately adjacent to the main storehouse. This allows the staff of storehouse and yard to use common facilities, such as offices, cloak-rooms, toilets, canteens, etc.; it improves supervision in the yard and also makes it easy to switch labour between the storehouse and stockyard as the workload fluctuates.

BUILDINGS AND ENCLOSURES WITHIN THE STOCKYARD

In large yards it may be necessary to have certain buildings inside the perimeter; for example:

Cabins or offices
Toilets
Garages for vehicles or equipment
Sheds or covered areas.
Cement stores

To keep the yard tidy and to prevent losses, steel swarf, scrap, sand, gravel, etc., are best housed in open-fronted brick-built bins. Separate locked enclosures are occasionally provided for especially expensive items such as electric cables, or goods particularly liable to be stolen, such as non-ferrous scrap.

Buildings or enclosures ought not to be scattered around the yard, but should be sited as close together as possible, preferably near the gatehouse, to facilitate supervision and control.

CHAPTER 11

Stores operations

SECURITY

Security of buildings and stockyards

Storehouses ought to be of reasonably substantial construction. Doors provided should be restricted to the minimum number necessary for efficient operation and fitted with adequate locks. All windows and skylights must be capable of being securely fastened and, if there is any obvious danger of unauthorised entry (e.g. where the windows overlook a public highway), additional protection in the form of bars or wire mesh may be advisable. The internal layout is usually arranged to provide an issue counter or issue bay segregated from the main storage area and, wherever possible, enclosed. Stockyards should be surrounded by an adequate fence with locking gates, and the number of gates should be restricted to what is necessary for effective working.

Custody of keys

The following are typical precautions taken regarding the custody of keys. All keys belonging to the storehouses and stockyards are numbered and registered, and written instructions are issued nominating the persons responsible for them. During off-duty hours, keys are kept in a locked key safe in some convenient place such as the lodge at the entrance gates of the establishment, and everyone collecting or depositing a key is required to sign the register on each occasion. The number of duplicate keys is carefully restricted and they are deposited in the keeping of some senior officer who has a safe. In the event of keys being lost, mislaid or stolen, the fullest possible inquiries are made and, if there is any uncertainty, a new lock is fitted.

Access to premises

The storekeeper in charge is responsible for the care and custody of all materials from the time of delivery until the time of issue. He therefore has the authority not only to exercise supervision over his own staff, but also over all other persons who have occasion to visit the premises for any purpose whatsoever. In the interests of security, access to storehouses and stockyards must be strictly limited. Apart from storehouse employees themselves, people collecting goods should not normally be admitted into the storage area, but kept on the 'public' side of the issue counter, and drivers and others making deliveries confined to the receipt dock. Similarly, in a stockyard, personnel not employed in the yard should not be admitted unless they are in charge of transport, and then only under the supervision of a member of the staff.

During closed hours, arrangements should be made to have a watchman on duty inside the stores premises or, alternatively, to have visits made at short intervals either by a patrolling watchman or by the works police, or by a specialist security firm.

Marking the stores

In order to minimise the risk of pilfering, it is sometimes advisable to mark stock items with the name or initials of the firm or another convenient symbol of identification so that, if anything is stolen, it may subsequently be traced and the mark will serve to prove that the article is the firm's property. Wherever possible, the buyer is asked to ensure that requirements on marking are included on purchase orders and the work is done by suppliers but, if this cannot be arranged, it may be necessary for the marking to be undertaken in the storehouse. Discretion should be exercised in this matter; many items, e.g. forgings, castings, heavy steel, special components, etc., are not worth the trouble of marking, but articles suitable for domestic use, such as hand tools, soap, towels, clothing, toilet rolls, electric lamps, etc., will usually repay some attention. For valuable portable equipment such as micrometers, surveying instruments, ammeters, etc., and for such items as vehicle tyres and batteries, the principle of marking may well be carried so far as to give each individual item a registered serial number and to check that all articles of this kind are eventually returned to store when their useful life has expired (in many cases a manufacturer's serial number is available for this purpose). Invisible inks which are revealed by ultraviolet light are useful for security purposes.

Segregation of pilferable items

It is prudent to take extra security precautions in respect of 'attractive' goods which are generally recognised as being especially subject to pilfering (the type of article referred to in the paragraph above on marking). Separate locked enclosures are often provided inside the main storehouse for commodities of this kind, and they are placed under the care of one particular storekeeper who is entrusted with the keys and accepts the responsibility for the safe keeping of the stock.

Electronic surveillance

Closed-circuit television, video recorders, hard-wired alarm systems, ultrasonics and 'beam interruption' systems all have a place in ensuring the security of stocks.

Statutory and other regulations

Storekeepers should be aware of statutory requirements, by-laws or other official regulations affecting the safety of storehouse premises or their contents, e.g. explosives regulations, petroleum regulations.

Inspection by supervisors

At regular intervals a senior supervisor, such as the stores manager or chief storekeeper, should inspect storehouse and stockyard premises and equipment to satisfy himself that they are in good order and that physical conditions are up to the required standard.

KNOWLEDGE OF MATERIALS

It is most desirable for stores staff to have a good general knowledge of the principal materials used in the organisation to which they belong; what the natural sources are, the processes involved in manufacture, relevant technical terms, methods of measurement, common defects and the purposes for which the materials are eventually used. This is particularly important if the storekeeper has any responsibility for the inspection of consignments on receipt. The knowledge possessed by the average good storekeeper in this respect is often taken for granted, but it should be appreciated that it is acquired as the result of an intelligent study of his materials accompanied by practical experience of handling and storing them.

PREVENTION OF DETERIORATION

It is well known that most materials will deteriorate in store in the course of time, and the fact that a building is provided for storage is in itself an acknowledgement that some degree of protection is required.

Suppliers' packages

The standard of packaging by manufacturers nowadays is steadily improving. Most suppliers are anxious to make sure that their products arrive in good condition and will be fit for use when required. To this end many small items are carefully packed; for example, roller bearings are greased, wrapped in impregnated paper and put in separate, sealed cardboard boxes. On arrival in the storehouse, packages of this kind are very often broken open to check the goods in detail. In the interests of stock preservation this must be avoided and, as far as possible, suppliers' special packages should remain intact in the storehouse until they are to be issued for use.

Order of issue

The rate of deterioration naturally varies with the material concerned, but one fact is quite certain – the longer an item is held in stock the more risk there will be of trouble in this respect. For this reason, it is an elementary rule of good storekeeping that stock is to be issued in the order in which it was received, i.e. the oldest stock is disposed of first. Where the 'shelf life' of a material is very short (e.g. photographic films and papers) the date of receipt is sometimes shown on individual packages so that the storekeeper can report items approaching the end of the safe storage period.

Heating

Damp is the storekeeper's worst enemy; it accelerates the corrosion of metals, solidifies powders and discolours paper. It follows that, for nearly all storehouses, an effective space-heating installation is a necessity to avoid damp and the damage it causes. In circumstances where the storage of valuable and sensitive materials is involved, it may be necessary to go so far as to have the storeroom fully air-conditioned, with temperature and humidity control; this is sometimes done for high-precision metal components and for some textiles and plastics.

Preservation and packaging

The storage of materials involves not only custody or safe keeping, but also the preservation of materials against premature deterioration. Preservation involves the use of protective coatings of various kinds, proper packaging for storage, and appropriate storage methods.

Protective coatings may be permanent, such as paint, galvanising or anodising; permanent coatings are normally applied during manufacture. Many temporary coatings are also employed in storage, most of these being oils or greases of various kinds, applied by brushing, aerosol or other spray, or dipping as appropriate.

Packaging, apart from its basic and obvious function of protecting material whilst in transit to a store, also has to fulfil the function of assisting in the preservation of material in stock, and should always be specified with this in mind. Some examples of the packaging needs of different types of goods follow:

1 Rigid packaging is needed to allow efficient stacking and handling. Examples: canned food, plastics parts of irregular shape.
2 Packing in small boxes is required to keep material tidy, and to allow items to be issued and accounted for in economic lots. Examples: pencils, small arms ammunition.
3 A dustproof, but not necessarily waterproof barrier is required. Examples: stationery, clothing.
4 A waterproof barrier is required. Examples: pallets of bagged rock salt or cased machinery standing in the stockyard.
5 A water-vapour proof barrier is required; goods must be in a sealed package, perhaps enclosed with a dessicant (moisture absorbing agent). Examples: electronic equipment, delicate instruments.

Detailed protective measures

If a heated and well ventilated storehouse is provided, the majority of items require no special treatment, particularly if they are fast moving, but some materials are exceptionally liable to deterioration and each presents its own problems. The following comments illustrate a few of these cases.

Cement. As intended, cement solidifies if it gets damp. It must, therefore, be stored in a dry, heated building and should be kept off the floor because even in a warm storehouse there will be a certain amount of condensation at times on concrete floors. Cement is normally supplied in stout paper bags but if, by any chance, it is stored loose, it requires even more care.

Electronic components. These may be exceptionally fragile and are also susceptible to damage from moisture. The presence of a magnetic field may also cause damage, and certain components are adversely affected by exposure to neon lighting.

Timber. Timber is particularly susceptible to rot if it becomes wet, and is attacked by fungi of various kinds. Sawn timber is best stored inside or in open-sided sheds, and boards should not be stacked solid but interleaved with scantlings so that air can circulate throughout the stack.

Metal. All metals are more or less liable to corrosion, especially iron and steel. If they are to be kept for long periods it is necessary to protect them with a coating of oil, grease or some slushing compound produced for that purpose. This applies particularly to bright-finished steel bars and to material stacked in the open. An exception to the rule is iron castings, which may actually be deliberately put outside for the purpose of 'ageing', i.e. allowing time for the internal structure of the metal to become fully stable, but in this case surface corrosion is not of any importance.

Photographic materials. These need to be kept away from light, and must not be exposed to extremes of heat or cold.

Tyres. If tyres are stored in piles one on top of another, the weight may damage the internal fabric, and this method of stacking is to be avoided. Tyres should be kept upright on their treads in suitably designed racks. Too much heat is harmful to all articles made of rubber, and tyres must, therefore, be kept away from heat sources, e.g. boilers and radiators.

Agricultural produce. Crops of various kinds are often in store for long periods between harvest and, if they are not properly looked after, are liable to germinate or to be attacked by mould or insect pests. Bagged grain must be kept dry and may require dusting with insecticide or rot-prevention compounds at intervals. In some cases this involves unstacking, treating and restacking.

Machinery and equipment. If there is a need to hold machines or expensive equipment for a period of years, to keep them in good condition they may be 'cocooned', that is, they are completely enveloped in an airtight covering of a suitable plastics material.

Textiles. It is well known that textiles may be subject to damage by moths and, if they become damp, they may be affected by rot. This can be overcome by treating them with mothproofing chemicals and wrapping bales in airtight packages. If rolls of cloth are stored for a long time, it may be necessary to unroll and inspect them at intervals.

STOREHOUSE LOCATION SYSTEMS

Numbering of locations

In a large storehouse, the personnel cannot be expected to remember where everything is kept and some form of location system has to be devised. Basically this is a question of saying where in the building each item of stock is kept, but it must be done in a systematic manner.

1 The storehouse area is divided into sections, each of which can be given a letter or a number.
2 Each stack of storage fixtures in a section is also lettered or numbered commencing from one end.
3 Each bay of shelving or racking forming a stack is similarly identified.
4 Finally, each individual bin opening has a number.

A system of this kind will provide a location symbol of the following type: A.24.3.17, conveying that the item in question is to be found in section 'A', stack number 24, bay number 3, bin number 17.

The location of an item may be thought of as its 'address' in the form of house, street, district and town. The location system is usually supported by a location index, which is a complete list in vocabulary-number order of all items held and their locations. In view of the fact that in a busy storehouse locations may often have to be changed and new items put into stock, the index is best kept either on cards or on some form of strip file so that it can be rearranged without difficulty. The location index may be held in the storehouse itself or the stock-record cards in the office may be marked up with locations to serve the same purpose. The information can, of course, be kept in both places although this should be avoided unless there is good reason for it. Generally speaking, it will be found necessary to have the index in the storehouse if issues are to be made before the issue documents are posted to the stock records (post-posting). On the other hand, if the documents are entered on the records before the issue is physically made (pre-posting) there will not be the same need for an index in the storehouse, since the location of each item can be entered upon the issue document by the record clerk for the information of the storekeeper.

Fixed location systems

The expression 'fixed location system' denotes the traditional idea of 'a place for everything, and everything in its place'. The storage location of each item is more or less static. The code or vocabulary number of the material stocked is usually the basis for the determination of the location of each item. This approach, which might be well exemplified by the way in which books are stored in a public library, has several advantages. Chief among these is the fact that stores personnel will quickly and easily learn their way about the stores because there is a recognisable pattern to the various locations and they are not continually changing. Also, because items of a similar nature will be adjacent to each other in the stores vocabulary, they are also likely to be stored near to each other, thus further assisting the stores staff in finding material. They only need to know where broad categories of goods are placed, rather than individual items.

There are, however, a number of problems which arise when using a fixed location system.

1 In just the same way that redundancy needs to be built into a coding system to allow the introduction of new items, spare storage capacity needs to be provided on a 'just in case' basis if regular major relocations of stock are to be avoided.
2 The system does not recognise the different 'handleability' or 'storeability' characteristics of different items; it is therefore inevitable that difficult items will be located out of sequence.
3 Exceptions will also need to be made if popularity storage is to be employed. In other words, if those items which are very frequently used are to be located near to the issuing point in order to make life easier for storehouse staff to achieve a rapid response, these items will be out of sequence.

Where large stocks are carried it is sometimes considered desirable to split the total into two parts – bulk and detail. Most of the stock, especially large and heavy items, is then kept in the bulk store, and small quantities of every item in use are in the detail store. This arrangement reduces walking and selection time and enables a quicker service to be provided.

Random location systems

Where stores are fast moving, or storage space is scarce and expensive, it may be advantageous to employ a random location system. The term 'random' is rather misleading in this context; it should not be taken to mean 'disorganised' or 'without pattern', as random location systems depend on a systematic and very highly organised approach to the placement of stock.

There are several random location systems in use, most of them dependent on computers in view of the substantial amount of record keeping that the approach entails. Most systems involve the use of racks with standard size openings to accommodate pallets, trays or other containers. The sections, aisles, bays and individual bins are given location numbers in the usual way. When a delivery is received it is placed in the first available space and the location is recorded on the computer. When an issue is required the location can be called up by the stores staff on a VDU at the counter. As soon as a location is emptied it is immediately available for new receipts of any item; it will simply be necessary for the computer files to be amended to enable the cross-referencing of an item with its location.

Where circumstances are suitable this system does allow maximum use to be made of the available storage space, though it has its limitations if there are major differences in the sizes, shapes or weights of the materials being stocked. The random location system is particularly suitable for fast moving items which are not unduly bulky, and finds application in distribution warehouses, assembly shops and work-in-progress stores. It has the drawback that reference to the computer to determine the location of an item is necessary before an issue can be made, but most systems require the record to be amended on issue anyway. Because of the great efficiency in the use of space and the ease with which electronic data processing systems can be employed to maintain the necessary records, the practice of random location is steadily growing.

FLOW

Due attention must be given to the way in which materials will flow through a storehouse or stockyard in view of the fact that considerable savings of time and space can be made if the need for materials to move in opposite directions in the same area of the store is removed. The principle is the same as that employed by those responsible for traffic management in most cities; a 'one way' system of movement reduces congestion considerably.

The ideal arrangement for an industrial store will give a straight line flow, with material arriving at one end of the building and being dealt with in a separate receiving area before being located in the bins or fixtures. Issuing takes place at the other end of the building, material flowing in one direction and having to negotiate as few corners as possible. Many stores buildings are not, however, purpose-made and are therefore difficult or impossible to organise so that a straight line flow takes place. When this is the case, a 'U' or 'horseshoe' flow is often found to be a satisfactory alternative. Figures 11.1 and 11.2 illustrate the principles of the two systems.

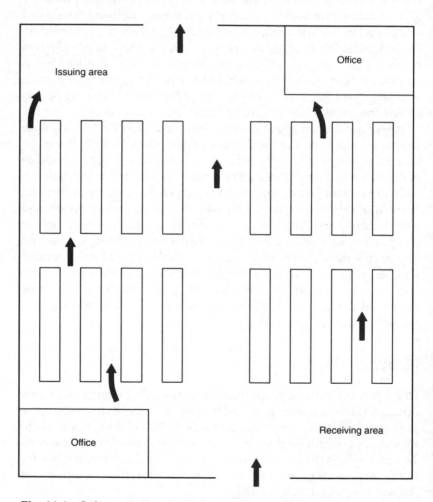

Fig. 11.1 Schematic layout of store with 'straight line' flow

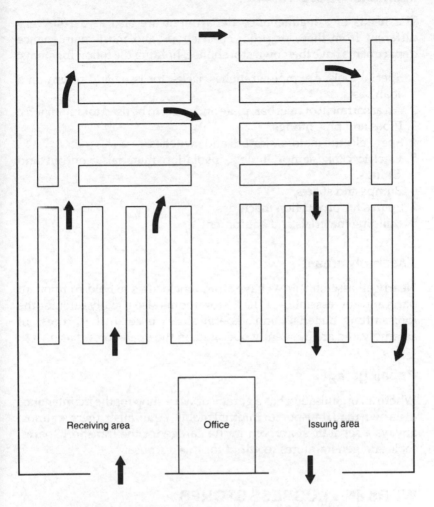

Fig. 11.2   Schematic layout of store with 'U' or 'horseshoe' flow

DEPARTMENTAL STORES

Irrespective of whether there is a central storehouse in an organisation or not, separate storehouses are frequently required to serve the needs of individual departments; these are known as departmental stores and are normally located inside the main departmental building or adjacent to it. Examples of this type of stores facility encountered in engineering production factories are given below.

Maintenance department

The needs of a maintenance department are also as a rule very different from those of production shops and most maintenance departments have their own storehouse, holding the following items:

1 Special tools, e.g. pipe-wrenches, jacks, for issue and return on a loan basis.
2 An assortment of steel bar, plate and sheet to be used for repair jobs.
3 Pipes and pipe fittings.
4 Spare electric motors, starters and switches.
5 Electric cable, lamps, bulbs, insulation materials, conduit and fittings.
6 Pumps and spares.
7 Spares for production machines.
8 Building materials and equipment.

Assembly areas

Nearly all assembly areas have stores enclosures to hold component parts and sub-assemblies. These storerooms also usually cater for the tools, fitting materials and general stores used in the process of assembly and are frequently operated on the open-access basis.

Repair garages

Where an organisation has a garage or workshop for the maintenance of its own road transport or internal mobile equipment, there is almost always a separate storeroom in the garage for the transport spares, tools and general stores required for this purpose.

WORK-IN-PROGRESS STORES

In a machine shop or fitting shop where a completely balanced flow of production is not possible, there may be a need for one or more enclosures to hold work in progress away from the shop floor, and storerooms are located at appropriate places in the production line. Subject to the nature of the components being produced, they are usually best operated by using the normal trays or tote boxes employed in the production shops, working on a random storage basis.

SUB-STORES

A sub-store is the generic term used to describe any stockholding point where the materials held are supplied entirely from some other major storehouse or a central storehouse.

SPECIAL STORAGE FACILITIES

Most materials which are unsuitable for outside storage can be accommodated in a normal storehouse building and are not subject to any particular regulations. Some items, however, require separate treatment and even the construction of specially designed storage facilities. Examples are: cement in bulk, grain, flour, fuel oil, petroleum, explosives. Certain products, such as the last two mentioned, are also subject to statutory regulations about methods of transport, design of buildings and safety precautions. The stores department will be responsible for ensuring that all appropriate rules relating to storage are observed, and the staff should be familiar with official regulations concerning any commodity normally stocked. It is not possible within the limits of this book to give a detailed survey of all the different materials and circumstances that are to be found in practice, but the following notes on explosives and petroleum will serve to give a reasonable indication of the nature of the problem. These comments are by way of illustration only, and do not purport to give an exhaustive account of the requirements of the various Acts concerned.

Storage of explosives

The sale, storage and conveyance of explosives are governed by statutory legislation. Three types of store are covered, namely:

1 Magazines, for more than 4,000 lb of explosives
2 Licensed stores, for amounts up to 4,000 lb
3 Registered premises, for amounts up to 60 lb

The regulations quote special requirements which vary in detail for each of these types of explosive store, but the following provisions are typical:

1 A police certificate must be obtained for the purchase of explosives and the storehouse must be licensed annually by the local authority.
2 Stores are to be sited at certain minimum distances from other buildings and 'works'. The distances depend on the amount of

explosive carried and the nature of the other buildings or 'works', and vary from 75 feet to 704 feet.

3 Conditions regarding the construction of the storehouse cover substantial building, security against unauthorised entry, provision of a lightning conductor and requirements about the avoidance of damp or the presence of iron, steel or grit.

4 The safety precautions to be followed in operating the store include rules about protective clothing, no smoking, the forbidding of iron or steel implements or fittings, provision of approved lighting, warning notices to be posted, and persons under 16 years of age not to be employed.

Storage of petroleum spirit (gasoline)

The storage, transport and handling of petroleum spirit is also controlled by statutory legislation, and is subject to official inspection.

Petroleum spirit is defined as any petroleum which gives off inflammable vapour at less than 73° F, i.e. which has a flash point of below 73° F. This excludes paraffin but does not limit the definition of petroleum spirit to motor spirit only.

A licence is required to store more than 3 gallons in containers of more than 1 pint capacity. Licences are granted by the local authority, who may impose conditions as they think fit, and licensed premises are subject to inspection. Any accidents involving petrol which result in loss of life or personal injury must be reported to the Secretary of State.

The usual regulations regarding filling and emptying of tank vehicles are as follows:

1 The vehicle must be attended, the engine must not be run while filling or emptying, the delivery hose must be sound and the vehicle earthed.

2 Storage tanks in any installation must be clearly numbered, and each tank's delivery pipe and dipstick must bear the same number.

3 The storage tank shall be attended during delivery by a competent person (not attending the vehicle); before delivery commences this person is to ensure, by dipping, that there is sufficient room in the tank for the quantity to be received, and must complete a certificate to this effect. He will ensure that no escape or overflow of petrol occurs during delivery.

4 Two copies of the certificate referred to are to be made out. One copy is given to the vehicle driver and the other copy kept by the licence holder.

Conditions imposed by local authorities vary from place to place, but the following are typical:

1 No explosives to be stored in the petrol store building.
2 Persons under 15 not to be allowed access to the store.
3 No smoking or naked lights allowed dangerously near the store.
4 All electric apparatus in the vicinity to be flame-proof.
5 Fire extinguishers and sand to be provided as specified.
6 Notices 'Danger, Petroleum Spirit, No Smoking, Switch Off Engine' to be displayed in the vicinity of pumps.
7 Tanks (which must be steel or iron) to be enclosed in concrete of 15 cm or more in thickness.
8 Drum stores must have wells capable of receiving at least 75 per cent of the total quantity authorised to be stored.
9 Tanks to be pressure-tested and preservative-coated.
10 Vent pipes to be provided as required by the inspector.
11 All vessels used for storage to be marked 'Petroleum Spirit – Highly Inflammable – No Smoking'; the store containing cans and drums to be similarly marked in a conspicuous manner.
12 Cans and drums not to be stacked so as to obstruct the retaining wall.

Storage of other hazardous materials

Many kinds of materials need to receive special consideration in connection with storage, in view of their dangerous nature. The stores staff should be familiar with the risks associated with materials under their control, and appropriate standard warning signs should be applied to the packages and their locations (see Figure 11.3).

Fig. 11.3 A selection of warning signs for the packaging of dangerous substances

CENTRALISATION OF STORAGE FACILITIES

Small firms have no difficulty about deciding their form of storage organisation – one or two storehouses suffice to meet their needs – but as we move up the scale to consider the requirements of major industrial concerns or national and international organisations, the problem of whether to centralise or not becomes increasingly acute.

The existence of a storehouse of any kind is, in itself, evidence of centralisation in so far as all storehouses are set up for the purpose of serving a number of 'customers' dispersed over the surrounding area. It follows that the question is not whether to centralise; that is inevitable. The real point is: what degree of centralisation will be most economical and satisfactory in practice? The answers found to this query are many and various, and sometimes seem contradictory. Some concerns have a highly centralised storage layout, and others of similar size in the same line of business operate on a decentralised basis. The fact is that most cases are governed by past history and performance. Although the opportunity does occasionally occur, it is seldom possible to plan, build and operate storehouses from scratch.

The problems of centralisation usually arise by degrees as the business develops and expands through a period of years – perhaps many years. In the course of time, storehouses will have been built, handling facilities provided and procedures established; all these things must be taken into account in the reckoning as to whether more or less centralisation is desirable. Basically the issue is the fundamental question which confronts all stores departments: how to provide an effective service to users with the minimum of cost. Therefore it is necessary to examine all the arguments for and against centralisation and, where possible, to evaluate the advantages and disadvantages in money. This last is not too easy because many of the considerations, although very real in practice, are found to be somewhat elusive when one comes to put a price upon them. It is simple enough to calculate the cost of transport involved in a proposed centralised system and compare it with what is currently being spent, but how is the recognised advantage of centralised inspection and testing to be evaluated if little or no inspection is going on at the moment, and what assurance can there be that calculations on stock reductions are reliable? In the long run some factors can be evaluated in money with reasonable accuracy, some can be estimated intelligently and some must be taken for granted.

CENTRAL STORES

A central store is generally recognised as one which acts as a 'whole-sale' supplier to other unit, departmental, or sub-stores operating on a 'retail' basis issuing goods directly to users. This is not to say that central stores never make issues to users because, in appropriate circumstances, they may be required to perform this function in addition to replenishing their subsidiary storehouses. There are three main types of central store:

1 Where there is a large factory or process plant more or less within one perimeter fence, a central store serves departmental and/or sub-stores in various places within the factory, using internal transport only, e.g. a car factory, an oil refinery, a steelworks. Central stores of this type normally stock tools, fixtures, and general stores, but the extent to which they hold raw materials or piece parts depends on how many of these items have a common use in several sections of the factory. As a general rule, work in progress is not held centrally.

2 Where the organisation consists of a number of establishments engaged on similar work and within daily travelling distance of a central point, a central stores may be set up at that point, e.g. coal mines, transport depots, electricity stations, gasworks. Such a store normally holds the bulk of most materials, spares, tools and general stores in use in the organisation. The only items not held centrally are those which incur very high transport costs, such as pit props or heavy steel, or spares for installations peculiar to one operating unit. It is necessary to have a first-class transport system to provide a satisfactory service.

3 Where the organisation is widespread throughout the country or is international, a central store may be used to hold the bulk stocks or common spares for vehicles, plant or equipment, or stocks of items manufactured by the industry for assembly or service in different locations, e.g. airlines, shipping companies, tractor manu-facturers. Central stores of this type do not usually hold raw materials, general stores or work in progress. Here again the transport arrangements must be well organised, and air freight is often involved.

Advantages of a single central storehouse

1 A wider range of goods is provided for all users than can be held in any smaller storehouse.

2 Stocks of tools, fixtures, equipment and spares can be kept to a minimum.
3 Better and more scientific methods of stock control can be practised.
4 Economies in storage space are likely to be obtained; goods in bulk always take up less room.
5 The use of modern handling methods is facilitated.
6 Better purchase prices are possible because of bulk buying and delivery to a single point.
7 Inspection and testing of goods can be more efficiently organised.
8 Opportunities for standardisation are improved.
9 Stocks can be turned over with greater regularity and thus deterioration in store is minimised.
10 It may be possible to provide the same level of service to customers with a lower total value of stock compared with dispersed storehouses.

Disadvantages of central stores

1 Extra transport costs may be involved.
2 More staff may be required.
3 If the organisation is not good, there may be recurrent shortages at the point of usage.
4 There is a tendency for stock investment to rise if the creation of 'private' sub-stores is not rigidly controlled.
5 More documentation is sometimes necessary.
6 There is a risk of greater loss by fire.

These advantages and disadvantages will now be examined in some detail in the following paragraphs.

Range of items available. The number of lines stocked at a central point will be greater than the range of any given type of stores held at a unit, so that centralisation offers to users a much wider choice of items 'off the shelf', and there is less likelihood of run-outs.

Stock control. Provisioning is more likely to be efficient when centralised, because variations in the frequency and rate of consumption of common-user items tend to level out over a number of consuming points and more time can be spent on the calculation of optimum ordering quantities, stock levels, etc., for each individual item. This should lead to a reduction in the total value of inventory. A case in point is machinery spares. Under a dispersed arrangement each unit manager thinks it prudent to hold his own spares to meet any emergencies, and he may have some very slow-moving items which have been bought as an 'insurance' against the possibility of breakdown. Assuming that similar machines are in operation at more than one unit, the centralisation of spares will produce an almost automatic stock reduction in the course of time, because slow-moving spares will be purchased only in such quantities as are indicated by actual total consumption figures.

As against the prospect of stock reduction by centralisation, there is a danger of the opposite effect arising if the organisation is not efficient. Failure to control unit stocks at reduced levels to correspond with a centralised system will soon cause an increase in the total holding, and failure to make prompt and regular deliveries from the centre can easily lead to embarrassing shortages at units when the required material is, in fact, available in the main storehouse.

Storage space. Material held in bulk at a central point will occupy less room than the same material stored in several dispersed locations, but the economies obtained depend on how much space is already available. If centralisation releases some storage space at outlying units it is very often quickly taken up by bringing into the unit storehouse materials which have previously been left outside.

Handling methods. The question of handling is allied to the economical use of space. Purchase of expensive machines for each unit may not be worthwhile for the amount of work they are expected to do, but machines are more easily justified at a central store where large quantities are being handled. A point to be watched in this connection is that, whatever methods are used in the central store, the facilities at unit storehouses must be capable of unloading deliveries, e.g. there is not much to be gained by sending a 2 tonne unit load to an outlying storehouse if no equipment is available to lift it off the truck, and it has to be manhandled piece by piece. One of the main drawbacks of central storage is that materials have to be handled twice, once at the central point and once at the place of usage. This often makes the centralisation of heavy or bulky materials uneconomical.

Purchase prices. Central purchasing does not necessarily imply central storage also, and bulk buying can be successfully organised without concentration of stock. It must not be assumed that large quantities automatically mean cheaper prices; much depends on the methods of marketing in the trade and the nature of the goods.

Nevertheless the placing of large contracts is normally expected to bring the benefit of a lower price, and it is true to say in many cases that the discount obtainable is greater if deliveries by the supplier are required to be made to one central storehouse only, and not to a large number of dispersed stockholding points. This advantage is offset to some extent by the need subsequently to provide transport to the place of usage.

Inspection and testing. Numerically, the majority of items purchased are only superficially examined and this may possibly be all that is necessary when dealing with reputable suppliers. Where important production materials are concerned, however, or where safety considerations are involved, inspection and testing requirements can be of great consequence. When purchases are made to published specifications, then, if the buyer is to be sure of getting value for money, some effort must be made to inspect deliveries to see that they do comply with the specification. It is more economical to build and equip one central testing house which will be fully employed than to set up a separate outfit at each of several out-stations. This is a very strong argument in favour of centralisation in organisations where a great deal of importance is attached to inspection and testing.

Standardisation. When materials are centralised, the complete range is held in one place and the number of varieties of similar items is easily seen. Thus the possibility of economy by standardisation is more readily evident and the necessary information to undertake the job is immediately available.

Avoidance of deterioration. This is related to the idea that lower overall stocks will be required with a concentrated storage organisation. If the stocks are lower, it follows that the turnover will be quicker and goods are less likely to lie in store for a long time. In this connection it should be noted that overstocking due to unexpected reductions in the rate of consumption is more easily detected when stocks are centralised than when they are not.

Transport. The cost of transport to outlying units is a major point against centralisation, and the expense involved if the out-stations are widely dispersed may possibly more than offset all the advantages to be gained from favourable factors. Deliveries from central stores to units must be organised on a routine basis to make the best use of transport, and unit-stock levels should be arranged to avoid emergency calls for material required urgently, because demands of this kind usually result in uneconomic use of vehicles.

THE ASSESSMENT OF STORES EFFICIENCY

Before the question of stores efficiency can be addressed we need to consider the question of 'efficiency from whose point of view?' A look at the following examples of goals for stores efficiency will help to illustrate the point.

Financial

1 Minimise capital 'locked up' in stock, keep 'range' and 'depth' down.
2 Keep operating cost low.
3 Avoid obsolescence, deterioration and loss.
4 Maintain high stockturn.
5 Ensure appropriate investment in accommodation for stocks.
6 Employ efficient mechanical handling equipment.
7 Minimise expenditure on manpower and overheads.

Warehousing

1 Ensure space is efficiently used.
2 Keep handling to a minimum.
3 Ensure stock rotation.
4 Avoid accidents.
5 Ensure adequate staffing.
6 Ensure that personnel are trained.
7 Employ effective handling aids and methods.
8 Centralise where possible and appropriate.

Service considerations

1 Avoid stockouts.
2 Respond promptly to requests.
3 Ensure material issued is as fresh as possible.
4 Issue without undue formality.
5 Respond immediately to changing requirements.
6 Locate materials near to point of use.

Control considerations

1 Maintain accurate and comprehensive records.
2 Replenish on an economically correct basis.
3 Regular audit to take place.
4 Careful attention to returns, rejections and other exceptions.
5 Update records as promptly as possible following issues or receipts.

The set of lists could be extended, for example, to include goals which would be important from the personnel point of view, and the individual entries on each list might be supplemented, but what appears above will suffice to illustrate the point that the performance of the stores function will, in all likelihood, be viewed differently from different parts of the organisation.

The important point here is that some of the functional goals are contradictory; the finance function will want to keep stocks low; this will obviously militate against the desire of the customer or user department who is concerned that service levels should be kept high. Another example of this conflict is that the user department will require material to be issued in as fresh or new a condition as possible, whereas those concerned with storage will, in order to rotate stock, issue the oldest first. Again, the service consideration of keeping materials close to the point of use might conflict with the financial aim of keeping stores operating costs low.

This problem of conflicting objectives must be carefully considered when any attempt is made to measure of assess stores performance. It should be remembered that problems of this kind are not confined to the stores area; the phenomenon of 'suboptimisation' is widely recognised in management generally, and attempts are made to ensure that a particular functional area, in pursuing its own relatively narrow goals, does not come into conflict with the broader corporate aims of the organisation.

Reverting to the stores situation, an overall statement of the aim of stores and stock control activity would be difficult to phrase in a form appropriate for all organisations, but our concern will be with *efficiency*, getting things done in an economic manner, and *effectiveness*, ensuring that what we do achieves the desired result.

Broadly speaking, we might say that the stores, in conjunction with purchasing and stock control, exist to provide the organisation with an appropriately regulated flow of correct materials at a minimised total cost.

THE MEASUREMENT OF STORES EFFICIENCY

There are many approaches to, and systems for, the measurement of efficiency in stores. Most of these involve the analysis of records of activities over a period of time, and the application of some kind of formula or ratio analysis, designed to highlight any changes in efficiency. The following list gives some of the figures commonly used in efficiency measurement schemes:

1   Average stock levels (£)
2   Number of issues per year
3   Average number of stores employees (yearly)
4   Annual operating cost of stores function
5   Proportion of stock which is slow moving
6   Damage, loss or deterioration of goods in stock
7   Incidence of discrepancy between records and stock levels when stocktaking
8   Number of items requiring identification
9   Rate of turnover of stock (stockturn)
10 Service level
11 Surplus stocks. The quantity and value of stocks which are not needed.

Having decided what variables to measure and, bearing in mind that the activity of measurement itself costs time and money and should not be overdone, we can apply the measurements as indicators of performance. This can be done in several ways, the simplest being a comparison over time, comparing the situation as currently measured with the situation a while ago. Clearly, a deteriorating service level or a surprising fall in the stockturn figures would be cause for concern, and would give rise to an investigation of some kind.

It might be useful to consider changes in the relationship between variables. A rising stock level might seem to be rather disturbing in itself, but when viewed alongside a volume of production and sales rising at an even greater rate the situation might not seem to be so bad. Sometimes it is the relationships between, rather than the absolute values of, the variables which are important.

Examples of ratios frequently encountered are:

1   Stocks: sales ratio
2   Issues per employee per week
3   Issues value per employee per year
4   Average value per issue

5 Stores employees per £1,000,000 stocks
6 Cost per issue

A further way in which the measurements might be employed is as a basis for comparison with other similar companies (interfirm comparison) or comparison with industry or sector standards. An organisation selling shoes in the High Street would be very interested in learning, say, the stockturn figures of a competitor as a basis on which to compare. Performance against budgets or targeted figures is another fairly widely used way of applying the measurement of variables.

Probably the most frequently used indicators are stockturn and service level. A specific note on each of these indicators might be useful.

Rate of turnover of stock

This, often referred to simply as 'stockturn', is a measure of the velocity with which the capital represented by the stock flows through the store. If a particular store holds goods to the value of £1,000,000 and annual issues amount to £10,000,000 then it can be said that the rate of turnover of stock is 10:1, perhaps expressed simply as '10'. This is because the value of issues in a year is ten times the average value of the stock. From a financial point of view, the higher the rate the better. A high stockturn means that materials are not spending a long time in storage. Different figures will, of course, be achieved by different kinds of organisations. A retail dairy or newsagent may have stocks which turnover hundreds of times in a year. Perhaps materials which are turned over at this rate should not be regarded as stocks at all, as their time in storage is so short. A company involved in heavy engineering, undertaking work of a jobbing nature, will have large amounts of stock held on a 'just in case' basis, and will possibly achieve a rate of turnover of two or three times a year.

When calculating the rate of turnover it is sometimes difficult to get a representative value of the stock held, perhaps because of seasonal factors. It is common practice to place a value on the stock a few times each year, and to average this figure to deseasonalise the information.

Service level

The service level is an indication of the proportion of requests from users or customers which are fulfilled at first pick. A service level of 95% would mean that ninety-five out of every one hundred requests for material were met without delay.

Although the service level is a very useful and direct measure of performance, addressing as it does the basic responsibility of the stores function, it is rather difficult to apply in practice. It depends on a system for recording unsuccessful requests for material, and this in itself may be difficult to maintain. Recording the fact that nothing has happened is unlikely to be viewed as a priority by the store-keeper who is busy dealing with those requests he can do something about.

There is also the question of what constitutes a failure to provide service. Does the inability to supply something against a second request, made in the hope that stocks might have been replenished, constitute an additional failure to supply or not? A further point to be made in connection with service level is that items differ in oper-ational importance, or criticality, and it may well be appropriate on economic grounds not to attempt a very high level of service. The maxim 'If you never run out, you've got too much' might be remembered here, though, of course, this in no way applies to materials for planned production, or items where a stockout would give rise to major problems.

Although it can easily be seen that a high service level, and a high rate of turnover of stock are both desirable, it should be pointed out that it is not easy to attain both, in that one comes at the expense of the other. A high service level is only really attainable with high stocks, unless demand can be forecasted with ease. High stock levels, of course, make a high rate of turnover impossible to achieve. In reality, an appropriate balance or trade-off between these variables needs to be sought and maintained.

A simple performance index

An index of stores performance could be constructed by going through the following steps:

1 Decide which variables are to be taken into account.
2 Decide how each is to be measured.
3 Determine a relative weighting for each variable.
4 Calculate the index.

The idea can be illustrated by means of the following example:

Variables to be considered:
    Investment in stock
    Costs
    Performance level

We will assume that it has been agreed that each of these variables makes an equal (⅓) contribution to efficiency, though any figure could have been chosen.

The following methods are adopted for calculating the three indices

$$\text{Stockholding index} = \frac{\text{Value of stock one period ago}}{\text{Present stock value}}$$

$$\text{Cost index} = \frac{\text{Cost for present period}}{\text{Cost for previous period}}$$

$$\text{Service level} = \frac{\text{Rating for previous period}}{\text{Rating for present period}}$$

For last year and this year the following are the relevant figures:

	Last year (£)	This year (£)
Value of stock (average for year)	900,000	1,000,000
Costs for year	250,000	300,000
Percentage of requistions fulfilled at first pick	90	88

Therefore:

$$\text{Stockholding index} = \frac{900,000}{1,000,000} = \frac{9}{10} = .9$$

$$\text{Cost index} = \frac{250,000}{300,000} = .83$$

$$\text{Service index} = \frac{90}{88} = 1.02$$

$$\text{Overall index} = \frac{.9 = .83 + 1.02}{3} = .917 \text{ (a deterioration of 0.083)}$$

This is a rather crude example, and a performance index derived in this way will, of course, not indicate performance in absolute terms, but it will provide a guide to significant changes and possibly to trends. It is not suggested that the example would be of practical value as given; it is outlined merely to illustrate the principles involved.

Many firms use formulae which take several factors into account, with a weighting system built in to allow for the different levels of importance of factors. It might be found useful to chart these factors as a time series graph, so that any variable which seems to be getting out of line in its relationship to the others can be identified and the reasons sought.

The mission of the warehouse/stores is to ensure raw materials, components and products are:
(i) subject to appropriate procedures on receipt from internal and external suppliers (completion of delivery advice note, inspected, recorded, and stored);
(ii) stored safely and securely under appropriate conditions until required;
(iii) goods required by customers (whether internal or external) are accurately identified and made ready for collection when required.

Role	Customer	Customer requirements	Objective measurements	Useful tools
1. Receipt of goods from internal and external suppliers	1. Production	1. Goods should be received in good condition	1. Number/value of damaged goods received into stock	1. Goods inwards checking procedures 2. Ship to stock status for approved suppliers
2. Storage of goods	1. External customer 2. Production	1. Goods should be properly identified 2. Goods should be stored in the correct location 3. Goods should be stored securely 4. Goods should be protected from damage and deterioration	1. Number/value of items stolen, damaged or subject to deterioration ir storage 2. Time taken to pick stock items	1. Packaging and handling procedures 2. Stock management procedures
3. Checking and despatch of goods (i) raw materials and components (ii) finished goods (iii) replacement goods	1. External customer	1. The correct items are received undamaged and at the right time	1. Time to despatch goods after receipt of request 2. Number of errors in goocs despatched	1. Packaging and handling procedures 2. Despatch procedures
4. Receiving, checking and sorting returned goods for replacement or repair	1. External customer 2. Production 3. Service 4. Design/ engineering	1. All goods returned to be identified; replacements sent out and the investigating department informed	1. Time taken to send out replacement goods 2. Time taken to inform investigating department	1. Documentation procedures governing the receipt of returned goods

Fig. 11.4 Meeting customer requirements (Source: *Implementing Total Quality Management*, Pitman)

Other measurements

There are, of course, a fair number of variables that can be measured in assessing stores performance. Figure 11.4 is a rather neat guide to customer requirements and how they might be met.

REDUNDANT STOCK

Redundant stock arises in all organisations to some extent, and can be defined as 'all usable material stocked in excess of requirements'. It can arise as a result of over-ordering, in which case it is usually called excess or surplus stock. Other common causes are failure to relate stock levels to declining production of certain lines, and unexpected changes in the pattern of demand, a particular problem where 'fashion' is a consideration. Such stock, where the need against which it was purchased has ceased to exist, is often said to be 'obsolete'.

While it is unlikely that the problem of redundant stock can be eradicated completely, there are several practices which might be followed in order to minimise redundancy.

1 Ensure that stock levels are as low as is economically practicable on materials prone to obsolescence.
2 Ensure that stock controllers and buyers are fully informed of changing marketing policies, production programmes or design specifications.
3 Monitor changing patterns of consumption in order to detect obsolescence at an early stage.
4 Ensure that, where new materials or components replace existing ones, the old material is used up before the new is introduced.
5 Relate material acquisitions for production very closely to actual needs through the use of planning techniques such as MRP.

Disposal of redundant stock

If it is established that material held in stock is unlikely to be used, then the only sensible course of action is disposal. Naturally, the best possible return for unwanted material, either from sale or by finding an alternative use, will be sought. Notwithstanding this need to seek a payment of benefit from disposal, it should be remembered that giving material away might result in some intangible benefits such as increased goodwill. Simply dumping unwanted material will vacate storage accommodation, often a scarce resource and hence valuable.

Without going into any commercial detail there follows a list of the more common approaches to the disposal of unwanted stocks.

1 Circulate other potential users.
2 Negotiate with the supplier on a return price.
3 Advertise, inviting offers.
4 Sell by auction.
5 Sell to a merchant or dealer.
6 Sell to employees.
7 Give to a 'deserving cause'.
8 Recycle.
9 Dismantle for spares.
10 Dump.

CHAPTER 12

Health and safety

In common with most other industrial operations, safety is a very important matter in storekeeping, and all material must be stored so as to minimise the risk of injury to staff or damage to goods or equipment. Most accidents occur when movement is taking place, and all such activities should be very carefully undertaken. Even a simple, manned, lifting operation is potentially harmful, and strain will be likely unless the correct 'straight-back knees-bent' method is employed. It is disturbing to note that about 25 per cent of reported injuries in industry result from manual handling.

The UK Health and Safety at Work legislation of 1974 has, along with other earlier Factories Acts, made it very clear that the law sees safety as everybody's responsibility, not just the managers' or supervisors or operators'. Each individual is legally bound to take responsibility for his own safety and the safety of others around him or her.

Some important points for consideration when operating a storehouse and its associated equipment follow.

1 Training. Those employed in the store should be made aware of the major hazards to be encountered in the particular location or locations in which they are working. There should also be more general promotion of safety awareness, covering such topics as health and safety law, what to do in the event of an accident, and information on the incidence of accidents and their effects. Staff should also be instructed in the skills of manual handling.
2 Housekeeping. An untidy store is an unsafe store, and an organised approach with properly marked aisles, gangways and walkways kept clear of obstruction should be taken. Adequate supervision is necessary to prevent untidiness and carelessness.
3 Conditions need to be given careful consideration. An agreeable working temperature and good lighting are important considerations, and level and even floors ought to be provided.
4 Storage and handling equipment needs to be right for the job, and properly maintained. It must be operated within its designated rating and within the manufacturer's instructions and specifications.

Periodic checks by qualified personnel are desirable, particularly for high-risk items such as stepladders, or mechanical equipment which is subject to wear.

5 Safety equipment should be provided and its use insisted upon. In an industrial environment hard hats and protective footwear and gloves will, typically, be required.

6 Safety signs should be used to signal hazards. These come in a profusion of types and designs; examples include the black and yellow 'wasp' signs which mark obstructions, no smoking signs in risk areas, and signs indicating particular risks associated with individual items.

7 Equipment for use in the event of an accident, at the very least a suitable first aid kit, and possibly high-volume showers, antidotes, emetics or gas masks should be kept close to stocks of hazardous materials. Emergency communication channels should be established and kept clear.

8 Codes of practice are highly desirable, and should be placed in the possession of all stores personnel, as well as placed in a convenient position for reference in the store. Such a document might contain many pages of guidance, under such headings as how to handle materials, principles of storage and stacking, discipline and behaviour, protective clothing and its use, first aid, health and hygiene and so on. Stores regulations will reinforce the legal requirement that accidents must be reported to management.

Many organisations, including the Royal Society for the Prevention of Accidents, The Factories Inspectorate, suppliers of handling equipment and safety equipment, and vendors of hazardous materials will provide literature and guidance on safety. This should be taken advantage of.

EUROPEAN DIRECTIVES ON HEALTH AND SAFETY AT WORK

At the beginning of 1993 six related sets of regulations came into force, all of some significance for those concerned with warehouse management and operation. They cover:

- Health and Safety Management
- Work Equipment
- Personal Protective Equipment
- Display Screen Equipment
- Workplace (health, safety and welfare)

- Manual Handling

The regulations come into force for any new workplace taken into use for the first time on or after 1 January 1993, though the date for compliance for existing workplaces has been established as 1 January 1996. The new regulations replace, either entirely or in part, thirty-nine existing Acts. Large parts of the Factories Act 1961 and the Offices, Shops and Railway Premises Act 1963 will cease to apply.

The last regulation on the list of six, the one dealing with manual handling, is the one of the most obvious importance to materials management personnel, but a moment's thought will lead to the realisation that all six themes are of relevance when the breadth of stores work is considered. It is beyond the scope of this book to examine any of the regulations in detail, so it may be helpful to point out that the regulations, and associated guidance, are obtainable from HMSO, and through the book trade.

The salient details of the manual handling regulations are that all employers are required to look at their manual handling operations which involve a risk of injury and either to avoid manual handling altogether if this is reasonably practicable. If this is not the case, then to assess the operation and to take steps to reduce the risk of injury down to the lowest level reasonably practicable. The fundamental requirement is that employers should adopt a 'suitable and sufficient' assessment, meaning of course that the level of complexity and thoroughness of the assessment is dependent upon the level of risk.

The purely weight-based approach to the determination of risk, and the move to the adoption of ergonomic concepts, means that new factors need to be taken into account when making risk assessments. Included, for example, are considerations such as:

1 The nature of the task (is twisting, stooping, stretching, pushing, pulling involved?)
2 The load itself (is it heavy, bulky, hot, sharp?)
3 The work environment (are there space constraints, extremes of temperature, slippery or uneven surfaces?)
4 The individual's capability (is unusual strength or specialised training involved?)

In view of the fact that the new regulations are concerned with ergonomic principles, their implementation should not only result in reduced costs through a reduction of the incidence of injury, but also give rise to quicker and more efficient handling systems and practices.

Figure 12.1 is an assessment checklist published by the Health and Safety Executive.

MANUAL HANDLING OF LOADS
EXAMPLE OF AN ASSESSMENT CHECKLIST

Note: This checklist may be copied freely. It will remind you of the main points to think about while you:
- consider the risk of injury from manual handling operations
- identify steps that can remove or reduce the risk
- decide your priorities for action.

SUMMARY OF ASSESSMENT	Overall priority for remedial action: Nil / Low / Med / High*
Operations covered by this assessment:	Remedial action to be taken:............................
....	....
....	....
Locations:..	Date by which action is to be taken:..................
Personnel involved:	Date for reassessment: ....
Date of assessment:......................................	Assessor's name: .... Signature: ....

*circle as appropriate

Section A – Preliminary:

Q1 Do the operations involve a significant risk of injury?   Yes/No*
    If **'Yes'** go to Q2. If **'No'** the assessment need go no further.
    If in doubt answer **'Yes'**. You may find the guidelines in Appendix 1 helpful.

Q2 Can the operations be avoided / mechanised / automated at reasonable cost?   Yes/No*
    If **'No'** go to Q3. If **'Yes'** proceed and then check that the result is satisfactory.

Q3 Are the operations clearly within the guidelines in Appendix 1?   Yes/No*
    If **'No'** go to Section B. If **'Yes'** you may go straight to Section C if you wish.

SECTION B – More detailed assessment, where necessary:

Questions to consider: (If the answer to a question is 'Yes' place a tick against it and then consider the level of risk)	Yes	Level of risk: (Tick as appropriate) Low	Med	High	Possible remedial action: (Make rough notes in this column in preparation for completing Section D)
The tasks – do they involve: holding loads away from trunk? twisting? stooping? reaching upwards? large vertical movement? long carrying distances? strenuous pushing or pulling? unpredictable movement of loads? repetitive handling? insufficient rest or recovery? a workrate imposed by a process?					
The loads – are they: heavy? bulky/unwieldy? difficult to grasp? unstable/unpredictable? intrinsically harmful (eg sharp/hot?)					
The working environment – are there: constraints on posture? poor floors? variations in levels? hot/cold/humid conditions? strong air movements? poor lighting conditions?					
Individual capability – does the job: require unusual capability? hazard those with a health problem? hazard those who are pregnant? call for special information/training?					
Other factors – Is movement or posture hindered by clothing or personal protective equipment?					

When you have completed Section B go to Section C.

Fig. 12.1 An assessment checklist

Section C – Overall assessment of risk:
Q   What is your overall assessment of the risk of injury?   Insignificant / Low / Med / High*
     If not **'Insignificant'** go to Section D. If **'Insignificant'** the assessment need go no further.

Section D – Remedial action:
Q   What remedial steps should be taken, in order of priority?
     i ....
     ii ....
     iii ....
     iv ....
     v ....

And finally:
     - complete the SUMMARY above
     - compare it with your other manual handling assessments
     - decide your priorities for action
     - **TAKE ACTION . . . AND CHECK THAT IT HAS THE DESIRED EFFECT**

Fig. 12.1   continued

References and further information

The EC Directive on manual handling

Council Directive of 29 May 1990 on the minimum health and safety requirements for the manual handling of loads where there is a risk particularly of back injury to workers (fourth individual Directive within the meaning of Article 16(1) of Directive 89/391/EEC) (90/269/EEC) Official Journal of the European Communities, 21.6.90, Vol.33 No. L156 9–13

HSE publications (available from HMSO)

Troup, J.D.G. and Edwards, F.C *Manual handling – a review paper,* HMSO, ISBN 0 11 883778 8

HSE, *Human factors in industrial safety,* HS(G)48, HMSO, (1989) ISBN 0 11 885486 0

HSE, *Lighting at work,* HS(G)38, HMSO (1987) ISBN 0 11 883964 0

HSE, *Seating at work,* HS(G)57, HMSO (1991) ISBN 0 11 885431 0

HSE, *Watch your step – prevention of slipping, tripping and falling accidents at work,* HMSO (1985) ISBN 0 11 883782 6

HSE, *Work related upper limb disorders – a guide to prevention,* HS(G)60, HMSO (1990) ISBN 0 11 885565 4

HSE leaflets (available free from HSE public enquiry points)

HSE *Ergonomics at work,* IND(G)90(L) (1990)

MANUAL LIFTING

The TUC, in the interests of the safety of its membership has made the following recommendations in relation to manual handling:

1 Make a manual handling assessment of your workplace:
   What sort of loads are moved by whom, and how often?
   Through what height?
   Over what distance?
   Under what conditions?
   With what assistance?
   What weights are involved?
2 Look at accident and sickness records for signs of 'back trouble' and 'rheumatism'.
3 Identify workers who may be at special risk.
4 Circulate a questionnaire to members.
5 Make a short written report to your shop stewards' committee, union branch or safety committee. Post a copy on the notice board giving details of loads manually handled by your members. Make a plan of action. Counter the opposition to mobilise support.
6 Press your employer to agree a forward programme of action and to examine ways of eliminating manual handling altogether by mechanical handling or modifying systems of work to reduce the scale of manual handling – preferably at the design stage – but pay attention to mechanical hazards. Ask for information from manufacturers and suppliers of mechanical handling aids.
7 See that your employer matches the job to the workers. Make sure they protect those most at risk, including workers disabled by ill health, pregnant women, young workers etc. But guard against job discrimination or dismissal.
8 Agree appropriate weight ranges with your employer for particular manual handling tasks. Make a list of all relevent factors which justify reduction of the weight values set out in the table including:
   Nature of load
   its weight
   working conditions
   nature of lift
   frequency of handling
   skill, experience and any relevant personal factors.
9 Also agree a maximum weight per shift.
10 Where loads above agreed limits have to be handled, examine arrangements for:
    personnel selection

training workers in manual handling techniques (especially for
itinerant workers) and 'authorisation' of trainers
supervision of manual handling tasks
rest periods or job rotation
personnel protection
manning arrangements and provision for assistance with difficult
loads.

11 Also ensure:
heavy loads are stored at the correct height
the weight, contents and centre of gravity of heavy loads
(including those above agreed action levels) are marked
all work areas are well laid out and adequately lit
that all means of access and exits are clear and free from
obstruction
floors and walkways are clean and free from water or oil – insist
on non-slip surfaces where necessary
the use of ladders as a means of manoevring heavy loads from one
level to another is discouraged
make sure members understand the need for safe manual
handling techniques – examine the need for retraining
resurvey your workplace regularly to pinpoint manual handling
hazards and review accident and ill health records for signs of
manual handling injury.

Figure 12.2 'Weight ranges in lifting' whilst not following the ergonomics principles embodied in the EC Directive provides useful suggestions, though it does not have the force of the EC Directive.
Figure 12.3 gives guidance on how to manhandle materials.

THE CONTROL OF SUBSTANCES HAZARDOUS TO HEALTH REGULATIONS

These regulations, generally known as the COSHH regulations, were approved in 1988 and came into force on 1 October 1989. Approved codes of practice in relation to the regulations are prepared by the Health and Safety Commission, and are published by HMSO.

The COSHH Regulations are a legal framework for controlling the exposure of people to hazardous substances relating to work activities. One of the requirements is that employers should make an assessment of the health risks created by the work and of the measures that need to be taken, as a consequence, to protect people's health and meet the requirements of the rest of the COSHH Regulations. The duty to make an assessment applies in all sectors of the economy,

WEIGHT RANGES IN LIFTING: RECOMMENDED ACTION BY EMPLOYERS	
Range	*Action*
All weights	• All employees should be made aware of good practice relevant to their manual handling activities. • Employees who may be especially at risk should be identified along with their capacity for manual handling. • Reducing the scale of individual manual handling activities should be periodically considered.
Below 16 kg (35 lb)	• No additional action required.
From 16 kg (36 lb) to 34 kg (75 lb)	• Exclude people unable to lift safely such loads with mechanical aids.
From 34 kg (75 lb) to 55 kg (120 lb)	• Mechanical or team systems or handling aids should be introduced wherever reasonably practicable. • Special selection, training and supervision will be necessary for unaided lifting.
Above 55 kg	• Mechanical handling or team systems or handling aids should be introduced except only where the workpeople involved are assessed capable of the regular lifting of such loads. *Note.* There will be very few people in this category. Special selection, training and supervision will be necessary for unaided lifting

Fig. 12.2 Weight ranges in lifting
(Source: *Hazards at Work, TUC Guide to Health and Safety*)

whether it be manufacturing, agricultural or service activity, and wherever substances hazardous to health are used, processed, manufactured, given off or produced. Whilst the Regulations extend to all aspects of the use of substances hazardous to health, the storage and handling of substances is an aspect which must receive full consideration. Guidance from the Health and Safety Executive confirms that one of the reasons that the assessment duty is explicitly included in the COSHH Regulations to ensure that in the case of *all* work involving substances hazardous to health, whether in progress or yet to be started, the same, systematic approach is taken, identifying precautions which are correctly matched by the risks.

Substances hazardous to health include gases, vapours, liquids, fumes, dusts and solids and can be components of a mixture of materials. They can also be micro-organisms. Employers should find

STACKING
Relax knees
Move upwards with
swinging movement

PUSHING
Arms and back straight
Balance on front foot
Push off back foot

LEVERING
Use body weight to reduce effort
Place rear foot well back to
maintain balance

PULLING
Arms and back straight
Maintain balance on rear foot
Push off front foot

LIFTING
Relax knees
Keep arms and back straight
Feet correctly balanced
Push off back foot

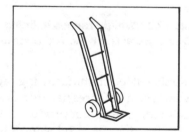

A HAND TROLLEY
Is an invaluable aid
to handling

Fig. 12.3 How to handle materials manually

out what substances are coming into the business and where they are
used, worked on, handled or stored. All should be accounted for.
Check stocklists.

Wastes and residues (amongst other classes of substance) should be considered, including substances used in, or arising from mainten-ance, cleaning, repair work, research or testing.

It may be that hazardous substances are being stored or handled without the employer being aware of this fact. The duty is, of course, to be fully aware, and one of the important sources of awareness is the information provided by suppliers. They are legally required to provide information if they are supplying hazardous substances, and should supply labels or data sheets. If you feel that a substance may be hazardous, and information is not supplied, then ask the supplier. Also contact the supplier if you are unable to understand what has been sent and seek clarification. There are a number of other ways of determining whether a substance is hazardous; guidance is included in the Health and Safety Executive guide 'COSHH Assessments '

Further information

Summaries and explanations are contained in the following leaflets, obtainable free from HSE Area Offices:

Introducing COSHH (a brief guide for all employers)
Introducing Assessment (a simplified guide for employers)
Hazard and Risk Explained

MECHANICAL LIFTING

Rider operator lift trucks – operator training

In the section of this text dealing with mechanical handling there is a note on good practice in the operation of counterbalanced fork-lift trucks. However, it is appropriate to deal more fully with the ap-proved code of practice on operator training published by the Health and Safety Commission because the code has a legal status. It applies to individuals whose new employment requires them to operate lift trucks. The Health and Safety at Work Act 1974 requires employers to protect employees by 'the provision of such information, instruc-tion, training and supervision as is necessary to ensure, so far as is reasonably practicable, the health and safety at work of his em-ployees'. Failure to comply with the provisions in the code is not in itself an offence, though failure may be taken by a court in criminal proceedings to judge that a person has contravened the Health and Safety at Work Act.

Approved Code of Practice: The basic training of operators of rider operated lift trucks

While it is not possible to reproduce the Health and Safety Commission's Approved Code of Practice, the salient features of this document are given below. Readers whose employment involves the operation of 'ride on' lift trucks or responsibility for the control or management of this type of equipment are strongly recommended to purchase the *Approved Code of Practice and Supplementary Guidance, Rider Operated Lift Trucks–Operator Training* ISBN 0 11 885459 3, available from HMSO bookshops or HMSO's accredited agents. This document is currently undergoing review and revision.

It is essential to note that this is only intended to give an appreciation of the nature and scope of the Code of Practice and should not be relied on as operational guidance in respect of operator training. Those concerned should acquire and use the Approved Code of Practice itself.

The Code of Practice is approved by the Health and Safety Commission with the consent of the Secretary of State and under Section 16 of the Health and Safety at Work Act of 1974. Representatives of the Confederation of British Industry, The Trades Union Congress, Local Authority Associations and independent experts were consulted in its preparation, which relates to the provision of training at basic level for new lift truck operators.

The code has no specific legal status and failure to comply with it is not itself an offence. However, any such failure might be taken by the court, if criminal proceedings should arise, as proof that the requirements of the Health and Safety at Work Act have not been complied with. The relevant parts of the Act are:

Section 2(1)   It shall be the duty of every employer to ensure, so far as is reasonably practicable, the health, safety and welfare at work of all his employees.

The duty referred to above includes:

Section 2(2)(c)   the provision of such information, instruction, training and supervision as is necessary to ensure, so far as is reasonably practicable, the health and safety at work of his employees.

The code is concerned with the basic training of all employees whose employment after 1 April 1989 includes the operation of lift trucks for the first time. The scope of the Health and Safety at Work Act is, however, much broader, requiring that all operators, whether existing or new, are adequately trained, and that sufficient refresher training is provided so as to maintain the necessary level of competence.

However, the code should be of use in determining the assessment of training needs of experienced operators, and includes guidance as to appropriate remedial training where deficiencies are found.

The code contains guidance, *inter alia*, on the following topics:

Types of vehicle covered by the code. Industrial counterbalance lift trucks; industrial reach trucks; rough terrain counterbalanced lift trucks; telescopic material handlers.

Types of vehicle not covered by the code. Other types of truck, including order picking trucks, straddle trucks, lateral stacking trucks, pallet stackers, pallet trucks, platform trucks, side loaders, straddle carriers, wheeled loaders, tractor mounted fork lifts or pedestrian operated trucks of any type, are not included. It should be noted that while the code does not extend to cover these types of equipment, it is the employer's general duty under the Health and Safety legislation to provide training to cover all types of equipment.

Instructors. Guidance is given to the effect that only instructors who are appropriately trained in respect of the equipment concerned should be employed. The employer should satisfy himself that any training given is in accordance with the code.

Training area and facilities. Training may take place at a suitable training centre or on an employer's own premises. Basic training should be given off the job, and the sessions should be dedicated to training only, not interspersed between completing operational needs. The trucks themselves should be in good order, and guidance is given as to the provision of a suitable manoeuvring area, and access to it. Appropriate conditions (terrain, ramps etc.) are mentioned, as is the provision of appropriate loads. Suitable classroom training accommodation should be provided, along with appropriate training aids such as projectors or models.

Training structure and content. The code indicates that the training should be essentially practical, and gives an indication of the length of time required, and the ratio of trainees to instructors. There is also guidance in relation to the structure and development of training programmes. Course content is not specified, but objectives which may be included in a basic course are appended.

Testing and records. The code requires that appropriate continuous assessment takes place, and that tests are set. There should be records of each trainee's progress and performance.

HUMAN FACTORS IN ACCIDENT PREVENTION

The following material has been adapted, with permission, from the course manual 'Managing Safely', published by University of Glamorgan Commercial Services.

Studies published by The Accident Prevention Advisory Unit of the Health and Safety Executive have indicated that some 90 per cent of fatal accidents were preventable and of these about 70 to 75 per cent were directly related to failures in management, rather than physical failures. To try to make these errors less likely or have less serious consequences, it is useful to consider the following three areas of influence – organisation, job and personal.

Organisation

The 'culture' of any organisation has a fundamental effect on health and safety.

Culture can be defined as a set of values which are common throughout an organisation, e.g. is it understood at all levels that health and safety is of equal priority to other management functions such as quality, progress, finance etc?

A positive safety culture is achieved by a number of actions including:

- commitment by the higher levels of management
- communication throughout the organisation
- control
- cooperation
- competence

The job

Work and the workplace is often planned to meet the needs of the process or product and problems arise because the personnel then have to try to adapt to the conditions they face. The correct approach is to design equipment, plant, tasks, layout and other aspects of the work environment while taking into account the mental and physical capabilities and limits of the work personnel. This is the *ergonomic* approach.

Major considerations include:

- Identification and analysis of critical tasks expected of individuals and consideration of likely errors
- Evaluation of operator decision making and the optimum balance between human and automatic actions
- Ergonomic principles applied to design of man/machine interfaces
- Procedures and operating instructions
- Working environment
- Tools and equipment
- Work patterns
- Communications

Personal factors

Individual managers or operatives will have habits, attitudes, skills, personality, knowledge, etc., which can affect health and safety in a positive or negative way.

It is important that the person is matched to the job. Considerations taking into account personal factors include:

- Detailed job description and specifications, including age, skill, physique, qualifications, and experience, etc.
- Training – induction and continuation
- Monitoring of personal performance
- Physical fitness

FIRE PRECAUTIONS

The minimum level of fire precautions in a storehouse should be that:

1 Smoking is prohibited and notices posted to this effect.
2 Fire prevention and fire fighting equipment is provided, maintained and inspected regularly. Various types of extinguishers, ladders, fire buckets (sand and water), stirrup-pumps, hoses, etc. should be provided as appropriate. In a large complex a fire engine or trailer pump may be required and sprinkler systems are sometimes called for.
3 Fire prevention and fire drill instructions are posted prominently.
4 Fire 'First Aid' training is provided for stores personnel. They should have knowledge of risks, precautions, fire fighting drills and practices.
5 Everyone should know precisely how to call out the Fire Brigade and the information they need so that as little time as possible is wasted.
6 Special flammable stores are stored separately, probably in buildings with particular design features.

There are also aspects of storehouse design which must be considered when taking fire risks into account. Some of these are mentioned in Chapter 10.

CHAPTER 13

Storage equipment

To cope with the enormous variety of materials held in storehouses of all kinds, an extensive range of storage equipment has been developed. It is proposed to consider here the more conventional types, but it must be understood that there are many special applications for which individual storage fixtures or containers can be and have been designed.

ADJUSTABLE STEEL SHELVING

In describing this equipment it will be helpful to quote a few limited extracts from the British Standard Specification BS826 (1978), amended 31 March 1986, for steel single tier bolted shelving (angle upright type) as follows:

BS826

Scope This British Standard relates to single tier bolted steel shelving not more than 3,075 mm high prepared as open type or closed type and installed in the form of bays or runs. The rigidity of the shelving depends on bracing or sheeting.

It specifies the material from which the shelving is to be manufactured, the finish, the method of construction for assembly purposes and those dimensions necessary for interchangeability.

The nomenclature used is defined and the safety of the finished assemblies is ensured by the provision of tests for safe working loads on the uprights.

Notes on erecting technique are contained in an appendix.

Definitions For the purpose of this British Standard the following definitions apply:

Bay. The unit of steel shelving, either single or double sided, open type or closed type.

Single sided bay. A number of shelves placed as required and supported by uprights, the whole being accessible from the front only.

Double sided bay. Two single sided bays joined back to back having a common back sheet or cross braces. The assembly thus provides two sets of shelving, each of which is accessible from its front only.

Run. A number of bays joined side to side, either single or double sided.

Level. The vertical space between any two adjacent shelves in he same bay.

Bin. A level fitted with a bin front (retaining lip).

Subdivision. The spaces resulting from the subdivision of a level by the insertion of shelf dividers.

Plain shelves. Shelves without reinforcement.

Single reinforced shelves. Shelves reinforced front and back.

Double reinforced shelves. Shelves reinforced front, back, sides and centre.

Ledge shelving. Shelving the upper shelves of which are of less depth than the lower.

Dimensions of assemblies *Single sided bays.* The overall dimensions of single-sided bays shall be in accordance with the values given in the following ranges.

(a) Range of nominal heights: 975, 1,875, 2,175, 2,475, 2,775 and 3,075 mm.

(b) Range of nominal lengths: 600, 900 and 1,200 mm.

(c) Range of nominal depth from front to back: 250, 300, 400, 500, 600 and 750 mm.

Double sided bays. The range of dimensions for double sided bays shall be identical with those for single sided bays except that the depths are combined.

Runs. The range of heights and depths for runs shall be identical with those given for bays.

The length of a run is the sum of the lengths of the individual bays of which it is composed.

Note The length of the openings between the front flanges of the angle uprights of a bay is the length of the bay less 80 mm.

The access height at the front of a level is the centre to centre dimension of the shelves less 30 mm. When bin fronts are fitted the height dimension is further reduced.

Access to subdivisions will be further restricted by the thickness of the divider.

Of course this British Standard Specification gives a good deal more information than the short extract above. It also covers components, materials and finish, construction, loading of shelves, safety limits and tests. It has several very useful appendices, one showing site requirements to be met and information to be supplied by the purchaser with the enquiry or order. There is also a complete range of drawings giving detailed dimensions (see Figs. 13.1, 13.2 and 13.3).

Open-type shelving

Shelves of this type may be used for many purposes, but they are most suitable for storing packaged items, e.g. small boxes of components,

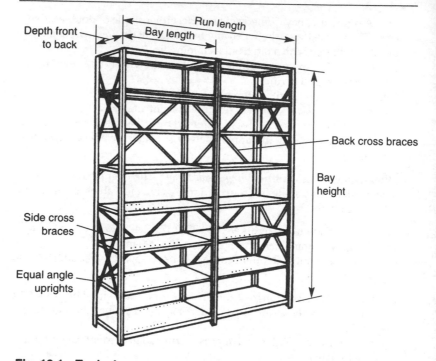

Fig. 13.1   Typical arrangement of a single-sided two-bay run of open-type shelving

screws, ball-bearings, tins of paint, files, drills, canisters or boxes of cleaning materials.

A variation of the standard model is the ledge type of open shelving which has a deeper section at the bottom, thus providing about waist level a ledge which can be used during the binning or selection of goods. The ledge-type fixture has the disadvantage of taking up more floor space to its total cubic-storage capacity than the standard type, which is the same depth from top to bottom.

Closed-type shelving

This is probably the most widely used form of storage fixture, and it can accommodate a very extensive range of stock. It is just as convenient for packaged goods as open shelving (but is more expensive), and it is most suitable for loose items such as nuts and bolts, hand tools, pipe fittings, machinery spares, small components, etc. It can be supplied with or without bin fronts, i.e. metal inserts which fit horizontally along the front of each compartment in order to retain loose items stored in the compartment.

Fig. 13.2 Typical arrangement of a single-sided two-bay run of closed-type shelving

For additional security or protection from dirt or damage for valuable tools or instruments, medical supplies, stationery, clothing, etc., lockable doors can be provided. In addition, for the proper segregation and protection of very small items, the compartments can be fitted with shelftrays. A ledge type of closed shelving is also available.

Arrangement of stacks

Individual bays of shelving can be bolted together to form a single-sided stack as long as is required, and a saving of material is made by using common-sheet sides between each bay. In a similar way, two ranges of bins can be set up back to back, with the main frames bolted together, to form a very strong, rigid structure.

Multi-tier binning

Any storage fixture above about 2.20 m in height will require the use of steps or ladders to reach the materials in the top compartments. This slows down the process of binning on receipt and selection for

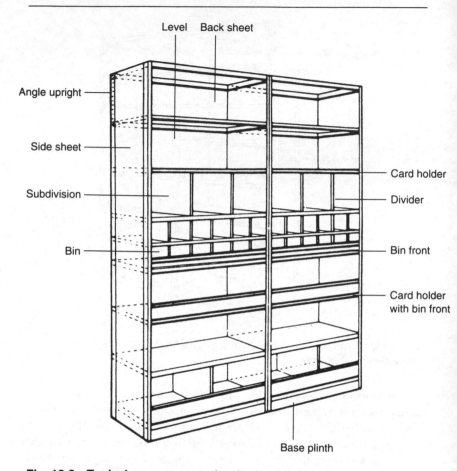

Level   Back sheet

Angle upright

Side sheet

Subdivision

Bin

Card holder

Divider

Bin front

Card holder with bin front

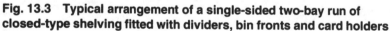

Base plinth

Fig. 13.3 Typical arrangement of a single-sided two-bay run of closed-type shelving fitted with dividers, bin fronts and card holders

issue, and the steps are always an impediment in narrow gangways. It is, however, possible to make the best use of the available space by having two or more tiers of bins, one on top of the other. This can be arranged quite economically because, within limits, the lower tier of the bins will support the upper tier. Thus the advantages of a multi-storey building can be obtained without going to the expense of having walls and other members strong enough to support floors above ground level. In a multi-tier binning arrangement, the gangways for the upper tiers can be provided by the use of chequer plate or metal gratings supported also on the bins beneath.

This type of storage is very common in modern practice, and its advantages are obvious. It has, however, two drawbacks: first, natural

A two-tier shelving system
(*Courtesy: Link 51 Ltd*)

lighting of the lower tiers is seriously impaired and artificial light may have to be provided, even in the daytime, and secondly, some kind of lift or hoist is needed to raise all the materials to the upper floors when received, and bring them down again as required for issue.

BINS

Metal or plastic bins are convenient for some stores, particularly loose components. They can be made in various sizes, provided with handles and label holders and fitted into shelves especially designed for the purpose. This type of equipment is particularly suitable for random storage. The trays in the shelves can be arranged either flat or sloping downwards towards the front so that their contents are more readily visible. Trays can be designed to stack inside each other when empty so as to take up less space. A popular type of bin is supplied as a flat paperboard profile which can be folded and slotted together to make a rigid bin.

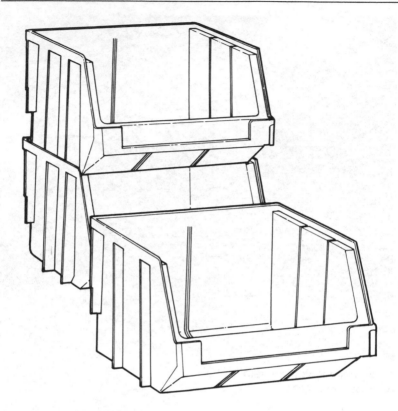

Fig. 13.4   A stacking plastic bin

PALLETS

A pallet is a piece of equipment especially designed to facilitate mechanical handling by fork-lift trucks, and may be used for both storage and transportation purposes. The flexibility and economy of this method of dealing with unit loads has great attractions and the employment of pallets in recent years has been steadily increasing. One important difference between pallets and other forms of storage equipment is that pallets are not only used within the organisation to which they belong, but are frequently provided to suppliers to make up deliveries into unit loads, and are also sent out carrying finished goods to customers. This practice is growing, and with it comes a need for a degree of standardisation so that pallets may be interchangeable within reasonable limits, and may be handled without difficulty by

Small parts storage using spigots and plastic bins
(*Courtesy: Link 51 Ltd*)

suppliers, manufacturers, customers and transport organisations all using similar mechanical equipment.

There is a British Standard specification in two parts for Pallets for Materials Handling for through transit:

BS2629   Part 1 – Dimensions, materials and markings.
          Part 2 – Recommendations for pallets for use in freight
          containers.

The following limited extracts are quoted from these two documents:

BS2629 Part 1

Scope The British Standard deals with the dimensions, designations, ratings, testing and marking of two-way and four-way flat pallets, post pallets and box pallets used for the unit-load method of materials handling for through transit purposes. It includes definitions relating to pallets of different types and to the component parts of pallets, and recommendations for the handling of pallets.

Terms and definitions *Note.* The following terms and definitions are applicable in this standard. Attention is drawn to BS3810, 'Glossary of terms and definitions used in materials handling', Part 1, which gives a more comprehensive list of terms and definitions used in connection with pallets, stillages, hand and powered trucks. The content of this appendix is substantially in agreement with ISO Recommendation No. 445, 'Vocabulary of terms relating to pallets'.

Pallets

Pallet. A load board with two decks separated by bearers, blocks or feet or a single deck supported by bearers, blocks or feet constructed with a view to transport and stacking, and with the overall height reduced to a minimum compatible with handling by fork-lift trucks and pallet trucks (see Figure 13.5).

Two-way entry pallet. A pallet whose bearers permit the entry of forks or fingers from two opposite directions only.

Four-way entry pallet. A pallet whose blocks permit the entry of forks or fingers from all four directions.

Full perimeter base pallet. A pallet usually of timber construction and four-way entry, having the bottom deck so arranged as to present a level bearing surface compatible with hand pallet truck usage.

Box pallet. A pallet with or without a lid, having a superstructure of at least three fixed, removable or collapsible, vertical sides, solid, slatted or mesh, which permits stacking. If the sides are mesh, the term cage pallet is sometimes used.

Post pallet. A pallet having a fixed or detachable superstructure of posts to permit stacking, with or without rails.

BS2629 Part 2

Scope This Part of the British Standard gives guidance on the most suitable plan sizes of pallets for use in general purpose freight containers of 2,435 mm × 2,435 mm (8 ft × 8 ft) external cross-section. Where the term pallet is used in this part of the standard, it should be construed as relating to returnable pallets conforming to Part 1 of this standard, non-returnable (i.e. expendable) pallets, or any other similar form of load handling device.

For full information on pallets the reader is advised to obtain copies of the British Standards concerned from the British Standards Institution.

Flat pallets in timber and steel

Wooden pallets have certain advantages over those made of steel:

Material which is stacked on a wooden pallet is much less likely to be dislodged when the pallet is lifted or moved.

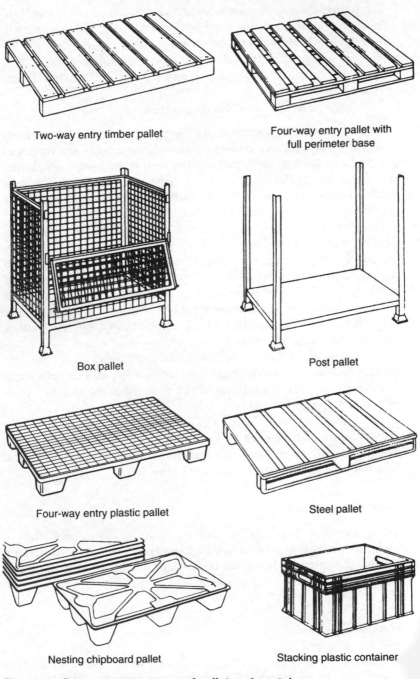

Two-way entry timber pallet

Four-way entry pallet with full perimeter base

Box pallet

Post pallet

Four-way entry plastic pallet

Steel pallet

Nesting chipboard pallet

Stacking plastic container

Fig. 13.5   Some common types of pallet and container

2 The pallets themselves are more secure when they are loaded into steel pallet racks, because they do not slip easily, and they are not so apt to slide off the forks of a truck.

3 There is less possibility of damage to materials or equipment.

4 They are cheaper to buy or make, and cheaper and easier to repair when damaged.

5 They require no painting and do not rust.

As a general rule, therefore, timber pallets are most extensively used, though specialised pallets are currently available in a variety of materials, including steel, various plastics, compressed fibreboard and chipboard. Materials are sometimes packed as unit loads in large cardboard containers, with timber battens stapled or glued to the base and forming a kind of 'built in' pallet.

Single decked pallets are, of course, not as strong as the double-decked variety but they are cheaper and, for this reason, are frequently employed in conjunction with pallet racking. Where flat-palletised loads are stacked one on top of another without the aid of racking, double-decked pallets are usually essential.

Flat pallets are most convenient for boxed or packaged goods, but may also be used for textiles, metal ingots, bricks, electric motors, switch-gear and many other items.

Box or cage pallets are most suitable for storing comparatively small, unpacked items which are held in quantity; for example, small castings or forgings, manufactured components of suitable size, plastic pressings, pipe-fittings.

Pallet collars. These enable loose parts to be loaded on to a pallet. They are not fixed to the pallet, but are attached when needed, and fold flat for easy transport when not in use.

Unit loads

The expression 'unit load' is used to describe the organisation of material into palletised batches, each loaded pallet roughly forming a cube shape and capable of being stacked. Unit loads are often designed so that they will fit neatly into a standard container.

RACKS

A rack is the generic name given to any kind of storage fixture which cannot be classified as shelving or binning. Racks for the

Pallet collar
(*Courtesy: Aston Timber Products Ltd*)

accommodation of palletised stores, tubes, bars, sheets, plates, tyres, cables and drums are the commonest types encountered in storehouses, but there are many racks designed for special purposes, e.g. shovels, 'V' belts, chains and a wide variety of heavy stores. A detailed examination of special types is beyond the scope of this boo and we shall, therefore, confine ourselves to the consideration of the more conventional forms.

Pallet racks

Wherever practicable, goods carried on flat pallets are stacked without the assistance of a storage fixture of any kind. This is quite easy with boxed items or items of regular shape which will not be damaged by the weight of loads placed on top of them, e.g. bricks, metal ingots, but the practice has its limitations. Palletised stores which are of irregular shape or which are liable to damage if stacked cannot be kept only on the floor; that would waste an enormous amount of storage space. Racks are therefore provided for goods of this nature. There are three main types of pallet racks: fixed, adjustable and drive-in.

Fixed pallet rack. A fixed pallet rack consists of a strong frame made of angle-iron, steel section or tube, with shelves of the same material or of solid steel plate.

Adjustable pallet rack. This is a similar structure, but so designed that the shelves may be set at any required height and moved easily when necessary. The reason for using adjustable racks is to save space; when storing palletised goods of assorted sizes and shapes, the rack opening can be arranged to the minimum necessary to accommodate each individual item.

Drive-in pallet racks. These do not have shelves upon which pallets are placed, but brackets at either side of the opening which are bridged by a pallet when in place. With pallets removed a forklift truck can enter the opening without restriction, and can access pallets held in a second row of racking immediately behind the first, thus enabling a much greater storage density (see Figs 13.6, 13.7 and 13.8).

Pallet racking safety considerations

Obviously the placing of heavy palletised loads in racks which support them at a great height above the storehouse floor, requires serious consideration of the safety aspects. Some of the major points to bear in mind when considering this type of storage installation are as follows:

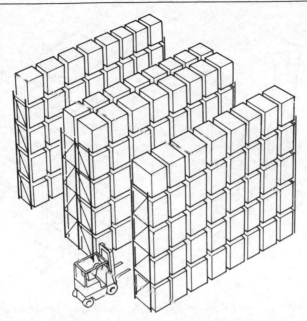

(a) Adjustable pallet racking – low storage density, high accessiblity

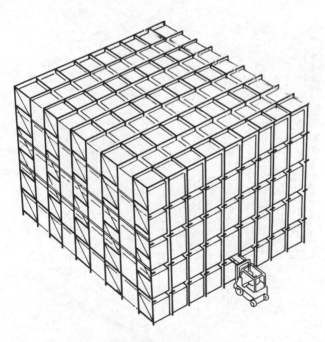

(b) Drive in racking – high storage density, accessibilty of inner pallets restricted

Fig. 13.6 The main types of racking used for unit loads

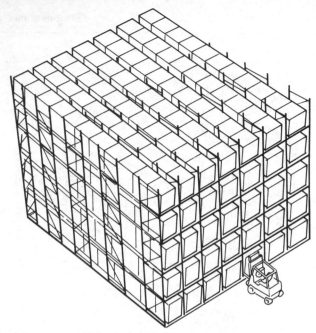

(c) Live storage – very high storage density. Can only be usd when a lane can be occupied by a single product

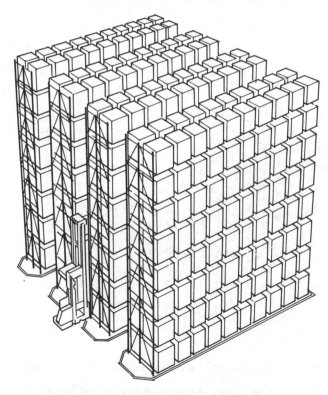

d) Narrow aisle racking – high storage density, good accessibility

Fig. 13.6   The main types of racking used for unit loads (cont'd)

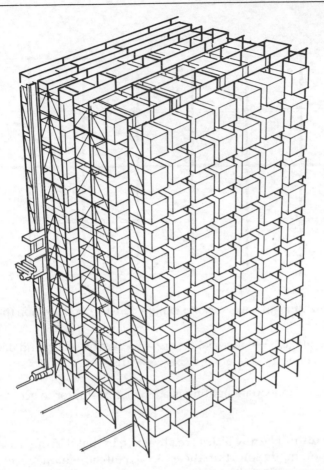

(e) Crane operated high-rise system – high storage density, good access to stocks

Fig. 13.6 The main types of racking used for unit loads (cont'd)

Loading. The racks must not be overloaded, and remember that the manufacturer's figures are for uniformly distributed loads.

Damage. Uprights are susceptible to damage, particularly the end frames of racking systems. They should be inspected regularly.

Floors. Floors should be flat. Racks impose very high point loads and can settle, causing dangerous leaning.

Pallet location. Pallets must be squarely located in racks; projecting corners are a hazard.

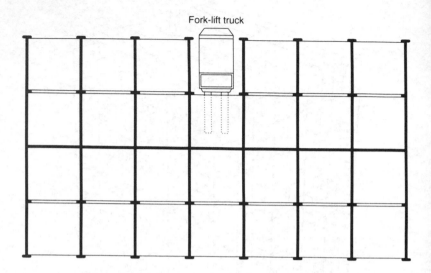

Fig. 13.7   Drive-in pallet racking in high density configuration (plan)

Pallet damage. Wooden pallets are subject to breakage and decay. If this goes unnoticed safety may be jeopardised.

Lighting. Inadequate lighting is a major contributor to accidents in storehouses.

Aisle width. Narrow aisles are attractive in that they increase storage accommodation, but the risk of collision damage may be increased as aisle width is reduced.

Pedestrian traffic. Pallet racking will be served by some kind of powered equipment. Every attempt should be made to avoid mixing pedestrian and truck traffic.

Training. Mention is made elsewhere in this book of the training needs of fork-lift truck operators. It is important that all stores personnel are aware of the safety implications of what they do, and that the condition and proper use of pallet racking is monitored.

Bar and tube racks

Bar and tube racks are normally of three main types: 'pigeonhole' racks, 'antler' racks and vertical racks.

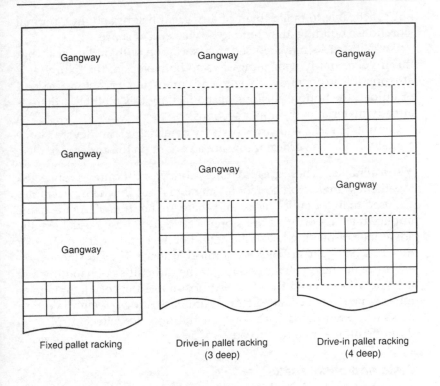

Fig. 13.8   Floor space utilisation of different types of pallet racking

Pigeon-hole racks. These are made of angle-iron and the bars or tubes are stored in them horizontally. They can be built as high as handling facilities allow, will hold large quantities of material and are, therefore, fairly economical of space. They have two main disadvantages. Firstly, it is not possible to load or unload them mechanically and manual labour must be used, and secondly, there must be sufficient clear space in front of the rack to allow the longest bars to be put in or taken out. These racks are best used for bulk stocks.

Antler racks. 'Antler' or 'Horn' racks consist of a series of vertical frames held together by horizontal members of angle-iron. The frames have 'horns' or lugs on which the material is carried horizontally. The main virtue of these fixtures is that the material is very easily accessible, and they are in common use in storehouses where small quantities of a large variety of bars and/or tubes are held, for example in toolrooms and maintenance shops. They can, however, be used for heavy loads and mechanical handling is fairly easy to apply, but it is not practicable to make them of any great height and, in a normal storehouse building, they tend to be wasteful of space.

Fork-lift trucks may be used in association with antler racks, but this involves fairly wide gangways on both sides of the fixture. It is also possible to operate with overhead cranes, but it is not easy to load or unload the bottom sections of the rack by this method if there is already material in the upper sections.

Cantilever racks with arms (usually detachable) cantilevered horizontally from the vertical frame are a variant on the antler rack idea.

Vertical racks. These are also made from vertical frames, connected together by angle-iron horizontal members, but much higher frames are used than for antler racks, and there are no 'horns'. As the name implies the bars or tubes are stored vertically. These racks have the advantage of making use of the height of the building if long bars or tubes are held, and are thus economical of space. They are inconvenient for really heavy items because of the difficulties of handling and the safety factor, and they are also unsuitable for very light bars or tubes which may become distorted under their own weight. Vertical racks are often fitted with trays on the floor to collect surplus oil draining off the material stored.

Plate and sheet racks

Large quantities of metal plate are best dealt with by simple floor storage and the same may apply to sheet, although sheet is often kept on pallets if the size is suitable. Sometimes, however, where stocks are not extensive, it may be desirable to have specially designed racks for these materials. Light plate or sheet can be stored horizontally or vertically in a rectangular angle-iron framework, but this arrangement allows manual handling only. Heavier items can be accommodated vertically in a rack made of two steel joists or channels along the floor with uprights of 'A' frames at intervals to act as spacers. One incidental advantage of this method is that, if steel plate is kept outside, vertical storage allows the rain to drain off quickly and minimises corrosion. Where mechanical handling is necessary for heavy plate, the best method is to use a crane with a special attachment known as a plate clamp, which can be fixed on the edge of the plate to allow it to be lifted.

Tyre racks

These are skeleton frameworks of angle-iron or tube so designed that tyres can be arranged upright, in rows, with each row of tyres resting on two or more horizontal tubes or bars.

Cable racks

These may be similar to tyre racks, with drums of cable sitting in troughs made by two long bars or tubes, or they can resemble ordinary racking, the drum of cable being moved by a fork-lift truck with a boom attachment passing through the boss of the reel.

Drum racks

Racks may be used for the storage of drums of oil or other liquids or powders in order to save floor space. They are of various styles and are usually made of a rigid framework of fairly heavy steel angle. If fork-lift trucks are used for handling the drums, the rack is very similar in appearance to a fixed pallet rack. If the lifting is done by crane or overhead-pulley block, the rack is designed so that loading is done from one end and unloading from the other, and the framework on which the drums are supported is arranged so that the drums run on 'guide rails' of angle-iron, and can be rolled along fairly easily. Where this arrangement is made, it is necessary to have a stop of some kind at the end of each line of drums to prevent them falling off accidentally. Drums are also commonly stored on end as palletised unit loads.

PORTABLE RECEPTACLES

The use of portable receptacles in storehouses has greatly increased in recent years, especially as mechanical handling in production shops has been extended. Mention has already been made of loose trays and pallets, but there are other variations, ranging from ordinary wooden crates to specially designed tote-boxes. Tote-boxes are usually made of sheet metal or plastic. They are arranged to hold a standard quantity of materials or components and often have special internal fittings. They vary in size and shape to match the particular materials and handling methods in use, and can be stacked on top of each other, full or empty. The use of tote-boxes in storehouses is very frequently associated with the standardisation of this equipment throughout the whole of the production shops.

MEASURING EQUIPMENT

All storehouses should have at their disposal sufficient equipment for checking receipts and issues by weight, by liquid measure and by size.

For the checking of large consignments of complete lorry or railway-wagon loads, weighbridges must be provided.

For consignments in the medium-weight range, up to two tonnes, platform scales are most suitable. These may be of the fixed type, where the platform is sunk into the floor to facilitate the handling of loads on and off trucks, trolleys or other forms of internal transport, or of an alternative style where the whole equipment is mounted on wheels and can be moved to any location where it is required. Both types can be fitted either with a steel yard or a dial to record the weight.

For smaller items, weighting up to about 6 kg, small scales of the balance type, fitted with a graduated dial, are commonly in use. A variation of this kind of equipment is the counting scale.

Liquids delivered in bulk into large tanks are measured by means of dipsticks graduated to suit the tanks to which they belong. Liquids in containers are usually checked either by weight or by visual inspection on receipt, e.g. by counting the number of drums of known capacity; liquid measures are used for issues, particularly in oil stores, and ¼-litre, ½-litre, one-litre and two-litre measures should be available with funnels for pouring liquids from one container to another. To avoid mixing, which might cause troublesome contamination, a range of measures and funnels for each particular class of liquid stored should be available.

For the measurement of dimensions, steel rules, folding boxwood rules and linen or steel tape measures are required. A common practice is to have a brass metre measure screwed to the issue counter. In addition to these more conventional types of measuring equipment, special instruments such as internal or external callipers, micrometers and various special gauges may be required.

LADDERS AND STEPS

Ideally, the use of ladders and steps should be avoided in storehouses but, in practice, the use of old or unsuitable buildings or binning very often makes ladders necessary. Various types are available, including ordinary ladders, shelf ladders, steps or travelling ladders. A travelling ladder usually runs on tracking fixed to the stack of shelving and, when not in use, can be placed vertically against the front of the storage fixture. Ladders, like fire extinguishers, should be inspected regularly and certified as fit for use.

CLEANING EQUIPMENT

It is important that sufficient equipment should be provided to ensure cleanliness in the storehouse and that an adequate supply of brushes, dusters, mops and buckets be made available, together with soaps, degreasing agents and polishes. In large storehouses, industrial vacuum cleaners may be used and, if so, it is necessary to provide electric sockets at appropriate intervals throughout the building.

GENERAL TOOLS

In the course of storage activities a good many tools and various other pieces of equipment may be necessary. In some larger storehouses special baling wire or banding machines are installed, and powered hacksaws, band-saws or circular saws are available for cutting metal to length before issue. If sheet or plate is an important item, powered or hand-operated guillotines are sometimes sited in the storehouse. Apart from any of these major items all storehouses require hammers, chisels, pliers, nail withdrawers, shears, screwdrivers, spanners, etc., to be used to connection with both receipt and issue.

LIVE STORAGE

Most storage equipment simply provides a static location for the housing and protection of stock, but in some cases it is found to be desirable to provide for the movement of materials held within the fixture. Equipment which enables this movement goes under the generic heading of 'live storage equipment', and is particularly useful where stock rotation is of great importance.

A simple example of live storage would be a chute, where boxes of material are placed at the top of the incline, whereupon they slide to the bottom of the chute to rest against an end stop. The picking point is at the bottom of the chute, so the material which has been on the chute for the longest will be taken first, and the principle of 'first in, first out' will be automatically followed. New material going into stock will be placed at the top of the chute, and will take its place at the end of the queue of items waiting to be issued. Stacks of material, where issues are drawn from the bottom and replenishment takes place at the top provide another illustration of the live storage principle,

A live storage installation
(*Courtesy: Stembeck Ltd*)

examples being the column of paper cups in a dispenser, or packets of cigarettes in a vending machine.

A development of the chute idea is the use of unpowered roller conveyors arranged in sets, with an arrangement of openings resembling bins at the ends of the conveyors, where incoming material is placed, and a similar set of openings at the tails of the conveyors provides the picking face. This system, apart from ensuring stock rotation, makes high density storage possible because the need for aisles or gangways is much reduced. The material comes to the operator rather than the operator needing to go to the material. The use of this type of live storage installation has the further advantage that, as a result of the fact that picking and replenishment take place in different locations, the movement of materials through the warehouse can take place in a continuous flow. When ordinary storage equipment is in use problems often arise as a result of issuing activities and replenishment work causing opposing flows and congestion. Quite large live storage equipment is available, enabling palletised unit loads to be stored and moved in just the same way as has been described.

Live storage of palletised loads
(Courtesy: Stembeck Ltd)

A high density mobile racking system
(*Courtesy: Barpro Storage Systems*)

Mobile binning

Where storage space is limited a variation on the live storage theme
which is sometimes used is mobile binning. The idea is that instead
of having fixed bins with gangways between each fixture, the bins are
mounted on rails or tracks. The bins are thus able to be placed close
to each other, and the floor space which would otherwise be needed
for gangways can be used for storage. When access to a particular bin
is needed the fixtures are parted at the appropriate point by sliding
them along the tracks. In the lighter type of installation simply pushing the fixtures is all that is necessary, though most arrangements of
this type have some kind of rack and pinion arrangement to make
movement easier.

Fig. 13.9 illustrates the principle of mobile binning.

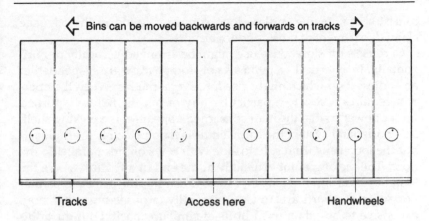

⟵ Bins can be moved backwards and forwards on tracks ⟶

Tracks   Access here   Handwheels

Fig. 13.9 The principle of mobile binning

Carousels

In recent years there has been widespread adoption of carousel systems, where bins or storage trays are located in some kind of rotating
storage device, so that material can be brought to the picker by
rotating the fixture. Examples of the carousel idea which will be
familiar to most are the rotating picture postcard rack found in many

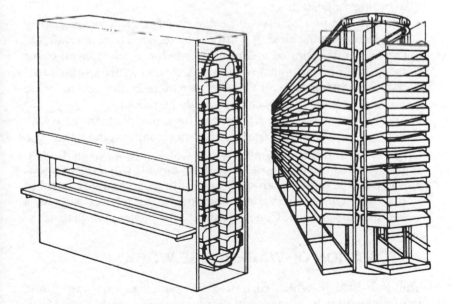

Fig. 13.10 A vertical and horizontal carousel

tourist shops, or the endless loop conveyor found in the baggage claim department of most modern airports.

Carousels for storehouse use might be arranged vertically or horizontally. In a vertical system rows of storage trays are suspended in an endless loop which might rise for several metres. When the operator requires access to a particular tray or bin the fixture is turned under power so that the item concerned appears at the picking shelf. In a horizontal system the same endless loop principle is employed but the loop runs from side to side with rows of bins parallel to the floor. The picking point is usually at the end of a fixture, where the loop passes around rollers. Fig. 13.10 illustrates the principle behind horizontal and vertical carousels. Naturally carousels are rather more expensive to buy than fixed units of similar capacity, but the additional cost might be outweighed by the following advantages:

1 The operator can remain in a fixed position, and have such equipment as scales, bags and desk equipment within arm's reach.
2 Supervision is much easier because the picker is in clear view all the time.
3 The productivity of operators will be increased, as they no longer have to bend and stretch while negotiating difficult gangways pushing a picking trolley.
4 The flow of material through the store will be smoother because picking and replenishment take place at different locations, thus avoiding congestion.
5 The idea of a picking list can be dispensed with. A visual display unit fixed near the picking point can be referred to continually.
6 Lighting and heating costs can be much reduced, since only the area near to the picking point needs to be provided with these facilities.
7 Because parts are brought to the user there is no need for wide aisles, so storage density can be greatly increased.
8 There is better use of vertical space. This is obviously the case with vertical carousels, but even with a horizontal system this also applies because bins or shelves can be accessed in one motion without the need for step ladders to be moved up and down aisles.
9 It is possible to place carousels under direct computer control so that, for example, the various components for a kit of parts for a complex assembly will be presented to the picker in sequence.

AUTOMATION OF WAREHOUSE WORK

This is a field in which current development is very rapid, and improvements in techniques and designs are being made almost from day to day. Most early applications of automation in the warehouse involved materials capable of being stored and handled in packages of regular shape and size. Goods in cartons such as biscuits, or boots and shoes in boxes are ideal for automation. Palletised unit loads also lend themselves to automatic storage. The more recent introduction of robotics into the warehouse has meant that it is now possible to automate warehouses containing a great variety of items of different shapes, weights and sizes.

The very high capital cost of an automated warehouse is unlikely to be justified unless the store has a very high throughput of materials or there are very acute problems associated with a shortage of storage space, in which case automation might provide a lower cost alternative to the erection of a new warehouse perhaps at a remote location. Storage densities where automated systems are employed are much greater than in a manually operated store; the actual increase in density will of course depend upon the system used. The continuing trend towards larger industrial and commercial distribution units suggests that automation in the warehouse will become much more common in the future.

It is not possible here to described all known automated methods of warehousing, because there are too many variations, and each installation has to be tailor-made both in size and system to suit the conditions of the particular job it has to do. However, there are some lines of approach which are reasonably identifiable.

One such general method involves the use of vertical pallet racks of conventional design with the goods stacked in the racks on pallets. In the gangway there runs, on a track, a power-operated fork mounted on a frame which extends from floor to ceiling. The fork can move up and down and can also advance into the racks to pick up a pallet and retract to withdraw it. This kind of 'stacker crane' installation could be operated with selectors of a type other than forks, e.g. suction apparatus working on compressed air, or hydraulic or mechanical grabs or rams. The main principle involved is that the goods are in fixed positions in static racks, and the selector mechanism moves about and can be 'programmed' to put in or take out items from given locations, the items then being transported to the assembly or dispatch point by powered conveyors or shuttle units. The usual arrangement is for the articles (normally in cartons) to be stored on sloping skate-roller racks in lines, one line to each stock item. The front carton of each line is held by a powered clamp. When an issue is to be made, the clamp is automatically released, and the goods roll forward on to a belt conveyor situated at right angles to the racks. The cartons so released are automatically counted and the clamp closes again when the programmed number has passed. Within the electronic and mechanical limitations of the plant, any number of items can be released simultaneously. The racks can be arranged above each other, each tier with its own belt conveyor in front of it. In this way, several hundreds of fast-moving stock lines can be handled at a very high rate of throughput. In a large installation, when the order is complete, it is automatically released from the assembly station and guided to the appropriate dispatch conveyor, which is usually a roller conveyor of telescopic construction so that it can be extended to deliver goods direct into the biggest road or rail vehicle normally employed.

Carousel units, already described, lend themselves very well to automation. A carousel is normally powered by an electric motor controlled by a manually operated switch which can cause the carousel to rotate in either direction and stop it when necessary, and it is obviously not very difficult to provide for computer control of the

An automated stacker crane installation
(*Courtesy: Siemag Ltd*)

switch so that picking instructions can be accompanied by the presentation of the appropriate bin or shelf to the operator. Some applications dispense with human involvement altogether, using robot interfaces which, under computer control, perform the insertion and extraction of parts. The next stage, in a fully automated system is for the parts to be dispatched to the appropriate location using a system of powered conveyors.

Of course, automation in a store does not necessarily imply *full* automation. Some systems combine picking by hand with the automatic movement of materials to their correct location. One approach is that an automatically controlled vehicle of some kind circulates in the warehouse, visiting various pick-up points where the people selecting issues can put their items on the vehicle, which moves off on its rounds and eventually takes its accumulated load to a predetermined dispatch area. There is one vehicle at least for each point of dispatch area. Similarly incoming consignments can be taken to their appointed storage location by working the system in reverse. This can be done in several ways.

1 By a towline conveyor installed in the floor and trucks fitted with a hook which automatically engages or disengages with the towline chain through a continuous slot in the floor.
2 By free-moving electric trucks controlled by a cable sunk under the floor. A variation of this is an optically guided electric truck which follows a white line taped or painted on the floor. If the machines are radio-controlled, they can be operated either manually or automatically.
3 By an overhead towline conveyor system to which either trucks or containers can be attached.
4 By powered roller or belt conveyors installed throughout the warehouse.

In a large organisation, especially one dealing with a considerable variety of sizes and weights of stores, several of these systems may be used at the same time, and integrated with one another.

Some other features of automated warehouses are as follows:

1 Automatic weighing of items on receipt or before issue.
2 Automatic switching of incoming cartons from one 'holding' conveyor (i.e. a conveyor on which goods are stocked) on to the next one available when the first one is full.
3 Automatic labelling of cartons.
4 Identification of packages by photoelectric cell instruments which sense bar codes on packages for different destinations and switch

them into the appropriate dispatch conveyors by means of sorting levers or 'arms'. The device can not only do this, but arrangements can be made for it to feed the information into a computer at the same time.

5 Control panels with a facsimile of the warehouse showing by coloured lights the position on each holding bank, receipt and issue dock and all intermediate conveyors.

6 Closed-circuit television by means of which the operator or operators controlling the whole system can see what is going on at various key points.

CHAPTER 14

Materials handling

Materials handling has been defined in many ways, but the activity is rather neatly summarised by the British Standards Institution as: 'Techniques employed to move, transport, store or distribute materials with or without the aid of mechanical appliances.' The scope of this chapter is rather narrower than the definition; the emphasis is on the movement of materials.

Handling materials, which is a major activity in storehouses and stockyards, is a costly operation and therefore the methods and equipment should be efficient. As in many other aspects of storekeeping, the approach depends on the nature of the business, the kind of stock carried and the size of the accommodation. In small storerooms dealing with comparatively light materials (e.g. a tool store) all the handling may, in fact, be done by hand. At the other end of the scale, in a large storehouse catering for a wide range of mixed goods with a weekly output measured in hundreds of tons, while there will be some manual handling, there will certainly be mechanical equipment for moving the heavy items and this equipment will probably be of more than one type. In such a store it is not unusual to find overhead cranes, fork-lift trucks and conveyors all in operation, with mobile road cranes and dumpers in the stockyard.

Materials handling is of major importance not only in the stores but also throughout the production processes. We must not lose sight of the fact that the handling facilities controlled by the stores department in a manufacturing concern may have to be correlated to the methods employed in the production shops. For the purposes of this chapter, however, materials handling will be considered from the stores angle only, that is, from the point of unloading goods on arrival to the point where they are issued for use.

BENEFITS OF PROPER MATERIALS HANDLING

Carefully planned and operated materials-handling policies can result in the following benefits:

1 Reduced handling costs
2 Greater economy in use of space (through higher storage density)
3 Reduced risk of damage to stocks
4 Reduced labour requirement
5 Less fatigue
6 Increased safety

Basic considerations

The variety of factors affecting the handling of materials makes it very difficult to enumerate all the basic principles. Each problem must be examined on its own merits according to the physical and financial circumstances prevailing in the organisation concerned. Subject to this proviso, the following points should be considered when examining any stores-handling problem:

1 The position of the storehouse
2 Handleability of the material
3 The case for manual handling
4 The method of packaging incoming material
5 Economy of movement
6 The selection of suitable machines
7 The storehouse layout
8 Training of operators

Position of storehouse

From the transport aspect, the nearer the storage area is to the point of use the less will be the expense of moving stores, and the shorter the time between dispatch and delivery. As far as materials handling is concerned, therefore, the storehouse should be as near as practicable to the place where the stores are consumed. It should be noted, however, that this is not the only consideration when storehouse location is being decided.

Handleability

When considering the way in which material is to be moved, stored and located it is important to consider its handleability. A common approach is to identify goods according to a four-way classification:

1 Easy manual handling. Small components or piece parts, individual garments or user packages of stationery would fall within this category.

2 Normal mechanical handling. Parts or materials of regular shape
   which can be moved easily either individually or as palletised unit
   loads. Pallets of canned foodstuffs, medium-sized iron castings or
   packaged washing machines would be representative.
3 Difficult items are those which pose particular handling problems
   because they are heavy, bulky, particularly susceptible to damage
   or of an awkward shape. A large gate valve, electric motor or lathe
   chuck would be regarded as a difficult item.
4 Bulk items. Liquids, granules or powders are sometimes stored in
   silos, hoppers or tanks and moved by conveyor or pipeline.

MANUAL HANDLING

This is the natural way to handle anything which is not too heavy,
and it should not be neglected or superseded without careful thought.
Much can be done by the use of sack barrows, selection trolleys and
manually operated stillage trucks. All these are cheap to buy and their
running costs are negligible. Stores which are not unduly heavy
should be handled manually unless it can be proved conclusively that
it is uneconomic. For the purpose of putting away or selecting small
items for issue from fixed binning, there is no reasonable alternative
to the use of hand-propelled trucks, unless the rate of movement is
exceptionally high.

Package sizes

This is a matter deserving the greatest attention when goods are
ordered from suppliers, for it is essential to start off on a sound basis
if handling is to be effective. One of the difficulties is to deal with large
numbers of loose items. As far as is practicable, suppliers should be
instructed to pack incoming goods in a convenient manner is such
quantities that they may be handled in store with the minimum of
effort. This is best illustrated by examples:

1 Electronic components, fasteners, small bearings etc., packed in
   cardboard boxes or cartons containing standard quantities. These
   boxes should not be broken open in the storehouse and the contents
   put into bins loose. If detailed issues are required, only one box
   need be opened at a time.
2 Bar or tube material should not ordered in excessively long lengths
   unless this is essential for production purposes. Small sizes should
   be wired together in batches so that they can be handled in bulk
   and not dealt with singly. It might be possible to relate lengths

to production application, so that waste arising from offcuts is minimised.

3 Small components not delivered loose, but packed in tote-boxes or other containers in specified quantities convenient for production batches.

4 Appropriate materials delivered on pallets in unit loads.

5 Oils and other liquids delivered in bulk from tanker vehicles into bulk-storage tanks whenever the consumption justifies this instead of using drums.

6 Items of intermediate size received in box pallets.

This principle is well worth pursuing, even to the extent of providing suppliers with specialised containers. Approaches such as those enumerated above are not only useful for handling purposes, but they also minimise damage to materials and facilitate the counting and checking of goods.

Packaging methods

There are of course many other different situations which demand special consideration. For example, on a building construction site, the available covered storage will probably be very limited. The emphasis therefore is likely to be on having the main construction materials packed and delivered in such a way that they can be left in the open for some time without deterioration. When the shell of the building is erected and has a roof on it, the building itself will probably be used to store the internal fittings such as sanitary ware, central heating equipment, internal woodwork, decorating materials and so on. At this stage the packaging need no longer be weatherproof. The main hazard then is accidental damage caused through handling, and such things as baths, wash-basins and so on must be protected by corrugated paper, polystyrene or some similar packaging material.

It is likely that packaging needs the most careful study where the warehouse is not serving a production unit, but is of the nature of a redistribution centre where goods are taken in in bulk and sent out to a number of subsidiary locations or customers. Instances of this kind are large food warehouses serving a chain of supermarkets, wholesale book warehouses dealing with numerous retail outlets or central army ordnance depots supplying a number of units in the field. The whole business of packing methods, unit loads and the associated transport problems should be scientifically studied from the beginning to the end of the chain from the initial orders on suppliers, through the receipt, storage and issue procedures, to where the items are finally used, or sold to the ultimate retail customer. Some of the matters to be considered are:

1 Legal regulations about perishable or potentially dangerous materials.
2 Fire hazards – some packaging materials are inflammable.
3 Transport regulations about the size and carrying capacity of road or rail vehicles.
4 Most suitable method of transport – sea, inland waterways, road, rail or air. The method of transport employed has a significant effect on the packing methods, package sizes and weights, palletisation or otherwise, and the bulk and strength of the packing.
5 Available handling methods at all stages. Loads coming into the warehouse must not be too heavy for the equipment there. Probably more importantly, loads going out to customers must be suitable for their unloading facilities. Packages must be easily loaded into and unloaded from the transport employed.
6 Cost. This is most important. First of all the packaging materials and methods must be adequate for the purpose. Then it has to be decided whether the packing is returnable and, if so, whether a charge is to be made. For returnable packages, the design and the materials must obviously be robust, because they will be used many times: strength and durability are the main requirements and the cost is a secondary consideration. For non-returnables, the problem is to design and make the packing as cheaply as is consistent with its ability to do its job.
7 Safety precautions. In the interests of hygiene certain materials must not be used for packing foodstuffs. Some goods have to be stored right side up, or in a cool place or in a warm place, etc. – the packaging must be designed and marked accordingly.
8 Labelling. There may be statutory requirements for labelling to show on the outside of the pack what the nature of the contents is. It may be necessary for identification in the warehouse or elsewhere. Sometimes it may be convenient and desirable for packages to carry advertising matter.
9 Where consignments are to be shipped overseas the business becomes even more complicated. The import, export and customs regulations of both the country of origin and the country of destination have to be met. Climatic conditions must be taken into account, and a full knowledge of the transportation and handling facilities at both ends is essential.

Economy of movement

All materials handling is based on the actions of lifting the goods, transporting them and laying them down again. Where these operations are performed by hand, no special problem arises. If the weight involved is so heavy that mechanical assistance is essential, unless the articles themselves or their containers are provided with hooks, lugs, brackets or other devices to permit slinging from overhead, it is necessary to have access to them from below if they are to be lifted. For this reason, heavy materials should never be placed directly on the floor. If they are not palletised, suitable blocks, rails or scantling should be placed for them to rest upon, so that the forks of lifting trucks can be inserted easily or slings can be fitted without difficulty.

Unless the whole storehouse procedure is carefully planned and properly supervised, there will inevitably be a certain amount of wasted effort. This can occur at various stages. At the time of receipt it is not uncommon to find materials unloaded from the carrier's vehicle and 'dumped' on the nearest available empty space, perhaps in an untidy manner; precise instructions about the immediate location of incoming consignments will prevent this. Another problem is inspection. Too slavish an adherence to the principle of inspection before storage may lead to heavy loads being placed in the inspection bay to await clearance before being removed to their ultimate location; double handling could be avoided by locating the goods in the storage area in the first place and notifying the inspector so that he or she can either examine them there or take samples. In recent years, the increased emphasis on quality assurance and the recognition that inspection is not an activity which adds value has reduced the extent to which incoming goods are inspected. Nevertheless, the practice is still essential in some cases, and ought to be undertaken in such a way that double handling is avoided. Bad planning easily results in overcrowding sections of the storehouse and major movements may have to be undertaken to rectify the position. Inadequate supervision can lead to confusion about proper locations, necessitating subsequent relocation, and bad timing of issues sometimes means that goods sent out have to be brought back into the storehouse because the user is not in a position to take delivery.

The flow of materials in the storehouse and stockyard should be carefully examined and planned to reduce to a minimum the frequency of movements and the distances through which the goods have to be moved.

MECHANICAL HANDLING

Four main purposes are to be served by the introduction of mechanical handling equipment:

1 To cater for loads too heavy to be handled manually
2 To save time
3 To save labour
4 To save space

Saving time

It is evident that machines can lift and transport sizeable loads much more quickly than is possible by manual labour. Apart from any question of expense, the time factor is frequently important, especially as regards issues to production. When stores in large quantities are to be loaded on to road or rail transport the work should be done quickly to avoid waiting time for the vehicles.

Saving labour

From the point of view of cost, this is the most important aspect of mechanical handling. Practically any piece of mechanised equipment will save some labour; the important thing to find out is whether the value of the labour so saved is more than the total cost of operating the equipment, i.e. in relation to:

Depreciation
Fuel or power
Spares and maintenance
Labour cost of drivers and slingers or other assistants

At the same time the cost of using any associated equipment (e.g. special containers) should also be taken into account.

Saving space

The most economical use of available space is an ever-present problem. For most materials, especially heavy items, stacks of maximum height can only be obtained by using machines. On the other hand, mechanised equipment requires wider gangways than manual methods.

ASSESSMENT OF HANDLING PROBLEMS FOR MECHANISATION

In recent years there has been remarkable progress in the field of mechanical handling equipment, and an enormous variety of general and special purpose machines is now available. Before making a choice of one or more types of equipment from the wide range on offer, it is advisable to make a detailed assessment of the problem; something on the following lines:

1 Ascertain the tonnage to be moved, now and in the future as far as can be foreseen.
2 Consider the types of vehicles making deliveries, how their loads are arranged and how they are to be unloaded.
3 Examine the nature and weight of all the packages and materials to be handled.
4 Assess the possibilities of using existing bins, racks and other storage equipment.
5 Consider the available storage space, and the height, length, width and layout of the buildings to be used.
6 Check the arrangements required for stores issues.
7 Ascertain the lifting power, speed, mobility, versatility, size, operating-space requirements, purchase price and running costs of the various types of handling equipment which may be thought suitable.
8 Assess the labour force required.
9 List any new storage equipment necessary to employ the machines efficiently (e.g. pallets, special containers, additional operating attachments).
10 Make a detailed assessment of both the capital and running costs of any proposed new scheme.

A careful examination of all these points will disclose what is physically practicable and, subsequently what is most profitable.

HAND-OPERATED EQUIPMENT

Hand trucks and sack barrows

The common wheelbarrow is ideal for carrying small quantities of sand, gravel and other loose materials, particularly in stockyards.

Sack barrows are naturally intended for bagged goods, and they are still widely employed in spite of the increasing trend towards mechanical handling of this type of store.

Selector trucks

Selector trucks are extensively used where incoming and/or outgoing consignments consist of numbers of varied items of reasonable size and weight held in fixed locations in different parts of the building; for example, machinery or transport spares. The operator can conveniently deal with a list of items by wheeling the truck round the various bins or racks, picking out the articles as he goes along and placing them on the truck until he has collected a complete consignment, when he takes the load to the issue counter. Mixed incoming consignments are put away in their appropriate locations by the reverse process. Selector trucks may be two-wheeled and there are several variations in size and shape. Supermarket trolleys are useful for this purpose.

Stillage trucks

These consist of wheeled platforms managed by a drawbar. As a rule they are fitted with a small hydraulic unit, actuated by 'pumping' the drawbar to raise or lower the platform a few inches. In operation, the truck platform, in the lowered position, is run in between the legs of a stillage; the platform is elevated, thus lifting the stillage clear of the floor, and the truck, complete with load, is wheeled away.

Pallet trucks

These are very similar to stillage trucks, except that they are fitted with forks instead of a rectangular platform and are, of course, designed to handle pallets and not stillages.

Hand stackers

A hand stacker consists of a vertical framework of angle-iron carrying a platform which can be raised or lowered for stacking or unstacking. It is based on the windlass principle, or alternatively the lift is hydraulically actuated.

Pulley blocks

This is a geared pulley system fixed to an overhead beam and fitted with a lifting hook at the end of a chain. A separate endless chain is used to operate the mechanism. Blocks are not fast in operation, but are suitable where the need for a heavy lift is only occasional.

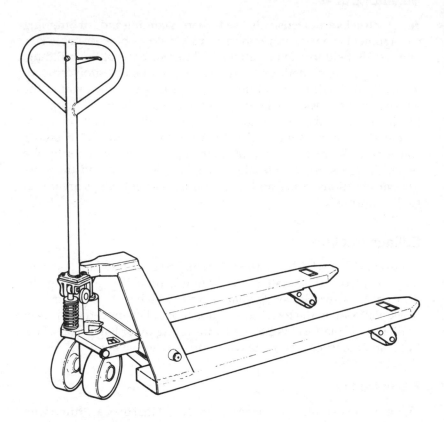

Fig. 14.1   A pallet truck

Appropriately designed models can cope with loads even up to 20 tonnes, but the heavier the load, the slower the lift.

Monorails

A monorail is a single 'I' section rail fixed overhead and bearing small wheeled trolleys which run on the rail. From the trolleys, loads can be suspended and then moved by hand along the rail to their appropriate destination. Monorails are often used in conjunction with pulley blocks for handling heavy loads out of or into vehicles in receipt or dispatch bays.

Chutes

A chute is a wooden or metal trough inclined at such an angle that articles will slide down when placed upon it. Chutes are used for transporting stores from upper to lower floors, but they are convenient only for loose materials, robust packages or other goods not liable to damage.

Roller conveyers

These are made of a metal framework bearing horizontal rollers spaced at intervals, and the goods to be conveyed are pushed along the top of the rollers. Conveyers will transport materials between floors in the same way as chutes, and can also be used for horizontal movement at or above floor level. They can be built up in portable sections and rearranged as required. Roller conveyers are generally used for fairly heavy packaged goods.

In many storehouses, a large proportion of the items in stock are binned or racked by hand or with manually operated trucks or trolleys. Shelves and racks should be arranged back to back as far as possible to save space and travelling time, and gangways need be

Powered belt and roller conveyors
(Courtesy: Lansing Linde Ltd)

wide enough only for pedestrians with small trucks. The minimum width can be 75 cm, but in most cases one metre will be found more comfortable for walkways between rows of bins; the main gangways down the middle of the building, and perhaps also at the sides, should be wide enough to allow two people with trucks to pass each other and to accommodate a motorised vehicle if one is required from time to time.

POWER-DRIVEN EQUIPMENT

No attempt can be made here to classify and describe exhaustively all the available types of power-operated materials-handling equipment, or to examine the many variations of each type. For present purposes, materials handling is being considered in relation to storehouse and stockyard work only, and the following paragraphs seek merely to give an indication of some of the equipment most frequently encountered in stores work.

Fork-lift trucks

The most important type of mechanical handling equipment encountered where lifting and stacking operations are to be performed is the fork-lift truck; there is today an enormous range of types and sizes of such vehicles available, ranging from pedestrian-operated stacker trucks to giant machines capable of handling containers weighing 40 tonnes. The more important types are described in the following paragraphs:

Counterbalance trucks. This is the most populous branch of the fork-lift truck family, including most of the general purpose trucks and many special purpose ones too. The load is carried on forks projecting forward of the front wheels and counterbalanced (hence the name) by built-in weight located above and behind the rear wheels. The forks are movable vertically, but cannot be moved in the fore and aft plane, any such movement being provided by manoeuvring the truck itself. (See Fig. 14.2)

Reach trucks. In this type of vehicle the forks can be accommodated within the wheelbase of the truck while goods are in transit, and projected by moving the mast and forks forward when a pallet or other load is to be lifted. The advantages of this type of truck are that there is no need for heavy counterbalancing, so the mass and length

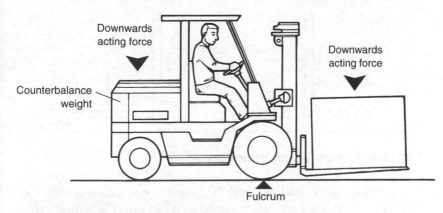

Fig. 14.2 Principle of the counterbalance fork-lift truck

A general purpose LPG powered counterbalance fork-lift truck on stockyard operations
(*Courtesy: Lansing Linde Ltd*)

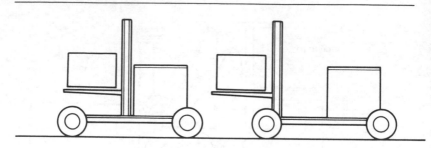

Fig. 14.3 Principle of reach truck operation

of the truck can be reduced, and, because the truck travels with the forks drawn back within the wheelbase, it can turn more easily in a confined space. The gangway requirement for a 2-tonne machine would be approximately 2.3 metres as opposed to about 4 metres for a counterbalance truck. (See Fig. 14.3.)

Side-loading trucks. These trucks are a variation on the reach truck theme, but the mast and forks can be projected from the side of the vehicle rather than on a fore and aft basis. These trucks are particularly useful where lengths of material such as piping or timber are stored alongside aisles, and can operate in a gangway only 750 mm wider than the truck itself. It is possible to acquire side-loading reach trucks equipped so that all wheels can be turned through 90°, enabling four-way travel and further increasing the versatility.

Turret trucks. These are fitted with a rotating mast (or sometimes a rotating head) to enable the truck to traverse an aisle and then rotate the forks through 90° from the direction of travel for the placing or extraction of a load. These trucks are employed in locations where space is very restricted, and consequently tend to be designed to cope with high stacking heights. This in turn leads to stability problems, and turret trucks require very smooth floors, and some kind of track or guidance system.

Fork-lift truck attachments. There is a wide range of equipment available for general purpose fork-lift trucks, each type of attachment making the vehicle more appropriate for handling a particular kind of load while detracting from its general usefulness. Examples included clamp jaws, for handling drums; crane beam and hook, useful for slinging irregular loads or raising and lowering material in a restricted space; and booms which can be inserted through the centre of coils of material so they can be handled without damage.

Side-loading reach truck handling sheet-material in cantilever racks
(*Courtesy: Lansing Linde Ltd*)

Fork-lift trucks are, of course, associated with the increasing use of pallets. They are not suitable for transporting goods for long distances or for really heavy materials.

Where the system of handling is by fork-lift, gangways must be wide enough to allow the trucks to manoeuvre, and pallet racks or stacks should be of the maximum height at which the forks can operate. To save space, pallet racks ought to be arranged back to back in pairs and, where circumstances are suitable, block stacking of crates, box pallets or post pallets should be practised.

A point worthy of special mention in connection with fork-lift trucks is that, if full advantage is to be taken of the versatility of the truck and it is to be used for the unloading and loading of vehicles as well as for transport and stacking, it is desirable to provide a raised loading dock in the receipt and dispatch areas of the storehouse. The dock should be at a height to correspond with the normal height of the platforms of the road or rail vehicles which deliver or collect goods so that the truck can be driven on to the vehicle using a suitable and safe bridging arrangement to pick up or deposit palletised stores. Such an arrangement avoids a great deal of unnecessary lifting and lowering.

An order picker
(Courtesy: Transhift Material Handling Ltd)

Order pickers

In organisations where mixed loads have to be taken and collated from bulk store, order picking machines are commonly employed. A variety of types are available, such as those with front or side lifting forks, machines which use a special latch on stillage, or those with a cage arrangement around the pallet so that the operator can walk out on to the pallet to pick bulky items. An order picker differs from a fork-lift truck in that the operator rises so he can hand-pick goods from storage.

Platform trucks

These are of two types: fixed-platform and platform-lift trucks. The lifting-platform variety is based on the same principle as a 'low lift' fork-lift machine, but instead of forks it has a platform which can run under a suitable container or stillage and lift the load clear of the floor. Both types of platform trucks are best used where stores have to be carried fairly long distances.

Tractors

Tractors of various sizes are found in storehouses and stockyards, employed in conjunction with trailers containing the stores to be moved. The use of two or more trailers per tractor in suitable circumstances is economical, because the tractor can be transporting one or more trailers while others are being loaded or unloaded, thus getting the maximum loading facilities and the maximum work from one powered unit. This kind of vehicle is, like platform trucks, most suitable for long hauls. Some tractors can be fitted with various attachments for particular jobs, such as forks for handling pallets or buckets for sand and gravel. Tractors can also be useful for shunting railway wagons, or pulling narrow-gauge rail trolleys.

Cranes

Overhead electric cranes. Weights of stores to be handled seldom exceed 10 tonnes at a time and this is well within the capacity of overhead cranes. There are special cases where bigger machines are used, but 5-tonne and 10-tonne overhead-electric travelling cranes are the sizes most commonly to be found engaged on stores work. There are two main types: floor-controlled and cab-controlled. In the first case there is a control panel attached to a cable leading from the crane 'bridge' overhead; the operator holds this panel in his hand to control the machine and walks up and down underneath it as it travels to and fro along its rails, which are supported on the columns of the building. In the second case, the crane is managed from above by an operator sitting in a cab mounted in the crane bridge. Floor control is best where use of the crane is spasmodic, as the operator concerned can easily move off to do other jobs when he is not required for the crane. Cab control is quicker to operate and more satisfactory when the machine is in continuous use, but it is more expensive.

Overhead cranes are very satisfactory for heavy lifts, particularly when loading or unloading road vehicles or railway wagons with 'box' bodies. They can serve the whole area enclosed between the rails supporting the crane bridge as far as the rails extend and only a few gangways, wide enough to allow the slingers access, are required. There is a 'dead area' all along both sides of the building under the crane rail which cannot be served by the crane, but this can usually be occupied by stacked or palletised goods. The method of storage under the overhead crane itself depends on the nature of the material and the maximum height of the crane hook. Circumstances vary greatly but, as far as is possible, items should be stacked one on top of another, either with or without the assistance of box pallets, cradles

A semi-goliath crane in use in a steel stockholders
(*Courtesy: John Smith Cranes*)

or other devices. Overhead cranes can be employed for outside work, but a special supporting structure has to be set up to carry the rails and the crane itself and the capital cost is heavy. Therefore they are best employed in stockyards only where substantial tonnages are involved and the throughput is high.

Goliath cranes. A Goliath crane is a special version of the overhead travelling crane. Instead of erecting an overhead gantry track all along the travelling distance, the crane is mounted on legs fitted with wheels, and the whole structure moves along railway lines set in the ground.

Stacker cranes. In large storehouses economic considerations may lead to the adoption of stacker cranes, which perform similar lifting and transport actions as a fork-lift truck. They operate from an overhead fixed track set above the aisles. Suspended from this track runs a carriage with a driver's cab below which is a post reaching practically to ground level. Forks travel up and down this post and also rotate about it. Pallets can thus be raised or lowered and inserted and withdrawn from the racks. The aisle width can be reduced to the space required for the manoeuvre of the post and forks. Disadvantages are high installation costs and inflexibility (it being restricted to the fixed routes of the track).

Mobile jib cranes (road). Machines of this nature are not particularly suitable for inside work because they are mounted on wide-wheeled chassis which require wide gangways and the long jibs need high doorways for clearance, but they are very useful in a stockyard. They can be designed for much heavier lifts, but the commonest types in use for stores work are from 2 to 6 tonnes, with jibs up to about 12 metres or so, which can be lifted or lowered to increase or decrease the reach of the crane. When the superstructure of the machine complete with jib is capable of turning round on the chassis, the equipment is described as a 'slewing' crane. Practically all mobile road cranes are of the slewing type.

In common with overhead cranes, jib cranes have the advantage of being able to unload box wagons. In addition, being self-propelled and completely mobile, they can go anywhere and, by virtue of the length of the jib, can arrange materials in solid stacks which are both wide and high. Because of 'outreach' (the farther out, the less weight the crane can lift) heavy material should be kept at the front of the stack.

A high rise installation serviced by stacker cranes
(*Courtesy: Mannesmann Demag Ltd*)

Locomotive cranes. These are rail-mounted, self-propelled jib cranes somewhat similar to the mobile road crane. They are, of course, suitable only for use in stockyards served by railway lines.

Other cranes. There are other types of crane to be found in stockyards, such as tower-mounted, hammerhead and derrick cranes of various kinds, and cab-controlled monorail cranes.

Crane accessories. Cranes are normally fitted with hooks, which are used to lift loads either with or without the assistance of slings made of wire or fibre rope, or chains. They can also have various attachments for particular jobs, such as grabs or buckets for loose materials such as coal, sand or gravel, magnets for iron, steel or scrap, and crane forks for handling palletised goods.

Powered conveyers

There are four main types of powered conveyer employed in storehouses: roller, belt, overhead towline and sub-floor towline.

Roller conveyers. These consist of a metal structure carrying horizontal rollers spaced at suitable intervals. The rollers are revolved by means of a chain or belt drive from an electric motor, and the goods to be transported slide along the surface of the rollers.

Belt conveyers. These are made of endless lengths of rubber, canvas, PVC or other appropriate material. At one end, known as the 'head', the belt passes round the outside of the drum driven by an electric motor, suitably geared. At the other end, known as the 'tail', the belt passes round another drum, which is free to revolve and not power-driven. Between the head and the tail, the belt is stretched tightly and supported by idler rollers spaced at intervals along its length. Material handled is carried on top of the belt. Slat, plate, bar and chain conveyers are variations of this based on the same principle.

Overhead towline conveyers. These consist of a power-driven chain running on rollers or pulleys attached to some overhead structure, usually fixed to the roof of a building. At intervals along the chain, containers or hooks of suitable design are attached and these carry the materials, or even pull selector trucks.

Sub-floor towline conveyers. These are somewhat similar to the overhead type, except that they have the chain drive underneath trays or other receptacles carrying the stores.

The use of conveyers in storehouses is widespread. They are usually associated with a fixed-location system of storage or with tote-boxes, and are most satisfactory where large numbers of comparatively small items have to be transported quickly and regularly or where loose materials are handled in bulk. They are convenient for the marshalling on a regular, routine basis of large consignments of assorted detail stores such as are required in army base stores or mass-production assembly shops. Very frequently they are installed in storehouses as an extension of a system in the production shops.

It will be realised that conveyer layouts are not necessarily limited to one single conveyer; a main conveyer may be fed at right-angles from either or both sides by subsidiary conveyers in the same way as a river is fed by its tributary streams. For example, where a storehouse is laid out on the basis of handling by belt conveyers, the whole of the binning or racking is located in such a way as to follow the conveyer pattern. This is usually has a main conveyer straight through the building from the receipt bay to the issue bay, served from the sides by a series of subsidiary conveyers at right-angles to it and running between rows of back-to-back shelves or racks. These conveyers are normally supported on the floor and operate at about waist-height. Arrangements vary in different organisations, but the main conveyer is commonly of the power-driven moving belt or plate type. The subsidiary conveyers are, as a rule, smaller; in some cases they also are power-driven, but the roller-type gravity conveyer is frequently used for this purpose. Incidentally, it will be readily understood that, if conveyers are arranged as described above, there will be no access down the middle of the building for either people or vehicles. A gangway must therefore be provided at one or both sides of the storehouse to allow for through traffic by pedestrians or trucks.

Automated guided vehicles

Trucks with no driver, but guided automatically, are now fairly frequently encountered in the storehouse environment. The first systems used for pallet transportation were developed in Sweden in the early 1970s, though widespread adoption of AGVs (as these trucks are usually called) did not take place until the late 1970s. It is the developments in computer technology which have made it possible for these vehicles to compete with and replace normally driven trucks (see Figure 14.4).

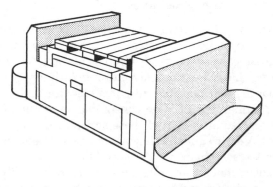

Fig. 14.4   An automatically guided vehicle (AGV)

Automated guided vehicles have a growing role in the automated warehouse environment, where they offer certain advantages over conveyer or monorail systems for the movement of materials. These advantages include freedom of routeing, flexible capacity (vehicles can be put into or removed from service) and the fact that if one AGV develops a fault it does not stop the whole system. Guidance may be by radio control, sub-floor wiring, or optically read lines of tape or paint.

Robots

Many handling operations associated with storage and distribution are fairly repetitive, yet need to be undertaken with some precision. They are not very different in fact from the assembly tasks and machine loading and unloading operations in which robots are already fairly widely employed. It has been suggested that there will be rapid growth in the use of robots in storage, packing and handling activities. The advantages are obvious, in that the work can be done more consistently, at a faster rate, with no fatigue or boredom related problems, and of course with no labour costs. Frequently an analysis of the cost of acquiring and operating a robot as compared with labour costs is the sole criterion for making the investment decision, but 'incidental' benefits arising from their adoption are discovered later, such as improved quality, less damage to materials in handling and smoother flows leading to lower inventories. Robots are proving valuable in reducing the effects of skill or labour shortage, and bring benefits in avoiding the need for difficult manual handling tasks and the associated risk of accident or injury.

Palletising is an activity which has been found to be very appropriate for the employment of robots. Robots differ from earlier crude palletising machines in that they can be programmed to palletise different package sizes, insert slip sheets and position the completed unit loads. Robot palletisers have been combined in some case with pallet wrappers.

The organisations which are marketing robots for handling purposes stress that potential users should give thought to designing their systems and procedures for automation. It is seldom the case that robots can be used to displace manpower without some radical changes to the organisation and flows of work.

Miscellaneous handling equipment

Electro magnets. Magnets are normally used with cranes and can lift or lay articles without slings or grabs with the minimum of risk or damage, and can stack very neatly. They are particularly useful for dealing with unsorted loose ferrous metal items of irregular shape and size, such as small forgings or steel scrap. If the generator is on the crane, the chassis must be a special purpose-built job, but alternatively batteries can be incorporated in the magnet itself, which can then be used by a general purpose crane.

Vacuum lifting devices.   These are also associated with cranes, but they can be provided as special attachments to fork-lift trucks. The power is provided by an air compressor, and the device works by attaching a suction pad to the goods. This arrangement is best suited to the handling of bulky but comparatively light articles in large cartons.

Scissor lifts.   These are rigid, power-operated platforms for raising goods or containers from ground level to be put into or taken out of vehicles at places where there is no built-in loading dock. The mechanism is usually sunk below the floor and operates on the scissor principle as the name suggests. They are frequently seen at airports loading and unloading aircraft.

Pneumatic and hydraulic equipment.   In special circumstances, particularly for the movement of bulk materials, pneumatic or hydraulic systems may be employed. Such arrangements are exceptional and the methods are especially designed for each installation.

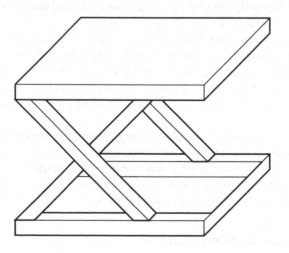

Fig. 14.5   A scissor lift

Lifts and hoists. The operation of lifts is too well known to need description here. Electrically driven hoists or lifts are frequently provided in storehouses for conveying goods between floors.

Training of operators

To get the best service from any machine, and to minimise damage to equipment, buildings and materials, the drivers and others concerned with the operation of any mechanical handling facilities must be both efficient and careful. Therefore they should be adequately trained and instructed in their duties and in the need for safety precautions at all times. Equipment is expensive, and time taken to instruct operators properly will be well repaid in improved performance. To get the best out of a typewriter, we do not employ a 'one-finger' amateur, but a trained touch-typist; the same argument applies to materials-handling machines. In this connection, it is worthy of note that instructional handbooks are often available, e.g. the *Operator's Safety Code* for industrial power trucks published by the Industrial Truck Manufacturers' Association.

Proper training is essential for anybody who uses any handling equipment, whether hand-operated or power-driven. It is not practicable here to discuss at length overhead cranes, jib cranes, sack barrows, conveyers and all the other apparatus which may be employed in a warehouse. However, to give the student some idea of what is involved, the following brief notes about fork-lift trucks may be helpful as an example.

First of all, the machine itself has to be considered. There are international standards for the stability of fork-lift trucks and all reputable manufacturers abide by these standards or exceed them. Appropriate safety features are provided on the machine such as overhead guards, leg guards and load guards to protect the operator. In most instances the truck has two separate braking systems – electrical and mechanical. Nevertheless, these machines are potentially dangerous. Serious or fatal accidents can easily happen if the driver is not expert at his job.

It is not wise to be casual about training. Operators should not be taught the business simply by learning how to do it from a workmate on the same job. A proper training instructor should be available. This person should of course have practical experience and be able to operate the truck himself. But also he should have training skills and theoretical as well as practical knowledge. Many people are taught to drive a car by a friend or relative who already has a driving licence and no other qualification. It is much better to be taught by a professional driving instructor. He knows not only how to drive, but how to teach – and teach in such a way that the pupil avoids bad habits and develops a basically safe technique permanently. The same principle applies to fork-lift trucks, but with greater force, because they move around in confined spaces and carry heavy loads which are lifted and lowered and otherwise manoeuvred.

Before training, potential operators should be selected by a preliminary test. What is required is manual skill. This cannot be assessed by an interview, however long, and can only be judged by a practical test. It takes less than an hour to give someone elementary instruction and demonstration in how to use the controls and how to transport an empty pallet. Then he can be given a ten-minute test on his own to see how much he has learned. From the number of errors he makes, his suitability can be determined. Unless his performance is above average, it is best not to choose him for further training.

When suitable people have been thus selected, they should have a carefully designed training course covering at least these main points:

1 Knowledge of safe loads and operating methods.
2 Manual dexterity and coordination.
3 Readiness to recognise and correct mistakes.
4 Remembering the proper sequence for every operation.
5 Ability to judge the height and position of forks and the relation between the steering lock and the movement of the other parts of the machine, particularly the forks, the top, and the back end.
6 Accuracy, especially in picking up a load squarely.
7 Understanding the theory of handling the truck and its safe operating limits.

At the conclusion of this training course he should have a practical and a theoretical test. If successful, it is a good idea to give him a certificate showing the date of test and what kind of trucks he is qualified to operate. In the course of time it may be desirable for qualified operators to be tested again at intervals of say three to four years.

Some firms give each one of their qualified truck drivers a reminder card, which he should always keep by him. We are indebted to Fork Truck Training Ltd of Osborn Way, Hook, Hampshire, UK for most of the above information and for permission to reproduce the contents of their fork-lift truck operator's card, which reads as follows:

Safety is one of the most important aspects of your training programme. For this reason we have collected together in this reminder the most important safety rules you have been taught. Never forget that a safety minded operator protects both himself and others and eliminates the risk of damage to the truck and its load.

Learn these rules thoroughly.

- **ALWAYS** Endeavour to work safely and efficiently.
- **ALWAYS** Carry out a pre-shift check and report all faults.
- **ALWAYS** Raise the forks or load handling attachment clear of the ground before travelling.
- **ALWAYS** Look in the direction of travel 'before' and whilst travelling.
- **ALWAYS** Pick up and transport loads correctly.
- **ALWAYS** Travel at a speed consistent with ground and load conditions.
- **ALWAYS** Operate all controls smoothly.
- **ALWAYS** Slow down when cornering, especially when unladen.
- **ALWAYS** Watch out for overhead obstructions, other mobile equipment and pedestrians.
- **ALWAYS** Report any accident or damage immediately.
- **ALWAYS** Keep your truck clean and wheels free from string, swarf, plastic wrapping etc.

- **NEVER** Use a faulty truck or misuse the machine.
- **NEVER** Lift loads which exceed the truck's maximum rated capacity.
- **NEVER** Carry passengers or lift anyone unless an approved personnel cage is fitted.
- **NEVER** Travel forks leading with a bulky load obstructing your vision (travel forks trailing).
- **NEVER** Drive directly up to anyone who is standing in front of a wall, bench, stack or other fixed object.
- **NEVER** Allow anyone to walk under raised forks or load.
- **NEVER** Travel with the forks/load above the recommended travel position.
- **NEVER** Forget the rear end swing of the truck when cornering.
- **NEVER** Drive over bridge plates or dock levellers until you have checked their capacity and security.
- **NEVER** Park your truck where it will create an obstruction or hazard.

FINALLY – NEVER ALLOW UNAUTHORISED PERSONNEL TO USE THE MACHINE.

Try the test in Fig. 14.6, which has been set so that warehouse managers can gauge the efficiency and safety of their operators.

According to Fork Truck Training's instructor and supervisor Roy Barton, a competent operator should be capable of completing the trial in under three minutes, error free. Any operator taking longer than three minutes has an unacceptable skill rating. The longest time allowance is eight minutes.

Roy Barton comments that 'An operator who can get round the course cleanly in three minutes or under is a skilled professional.

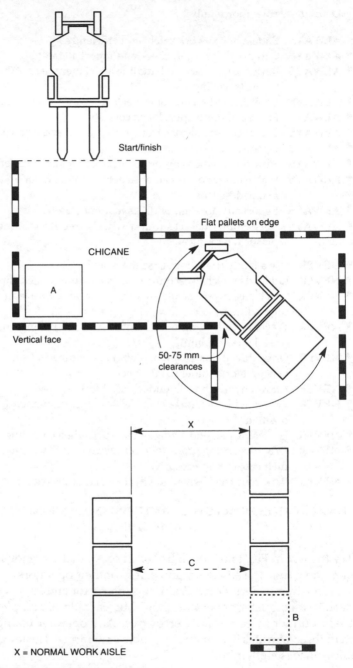

Start/finish

Flat pallets on edge

CHICANE

A

Vertical face

50-75 mm
clearances

X

C

B

X = NORMAL WORK AISLE

Fig. 14.6   Fork-lift truck operator test
(*Courtesy: Fork Truck Training Ltd*)

Anyone requiring longer than eight minutes is costing your company a fortune.'

1 Drive forward from start line.
2 Pick up loaded pallet at A.
3 Manoeuvre through the chicane – load leading.
4 Stack the load in a location at B.
5 Reverse truck to C, forks trailing.
6 Drive forward and pick up loaded pallet.
7 Reverse back through chicane, load trailing.
8 Deposit load at A.
9 Return truck to start line and park it.

Care of lifting tackle

To avoid accidents, care must be exercised in the use and treatment of lifting machines and gear of all kinds, and details of statutory requirements in this respect are to be found in the Factories Act and legislation on health and safety. It is neither practicable nor desirable here to enumerate all the official regulations, but the following points give some general indication of the precautions necessary:

1 Every lifting machine should be marked with an individual ident-ification number and the safe working load. Machines should be tested before being put into service, and at regular intervals thereafter.
2 Cranes with movable jibs must be provided with an automatic load-radius indicator clearly visible to the driver and, in some cases, have to be fitted with warning bells which ring when the load is exceeded.
3 Where the use of a goods lift is prohibited for carrying persons, there must be a notice on the lift to that effect.
4 Controls, handwheels, etc., on lifting equipment are to be provided with name plates indicating their function.
5 Chain and rope slings, hooks, shackles, etc., must be stamped or labelled with an identification number and the safe working load. All are required to be inspected and tested at specified intervals and, for some tackle, regular annealing is essential. Items which fail on test are to be scrapped.
6 Registers of all lifting tackle should be kept and entered up with particulars of inspections and tests.
7 When not in use, portable and transportable lifting appliances should be kept in a weatherproof store under the control of an appropriate storekeeper. Suitable facilities are required for hanging

all items of tackle and the location for each article should be labelled. Issues for use must be made only by the storekeeper.

Systems approach

This is a phrase used to describe a method of material handling based on the idea of making sure that the warehouse building, and all the packages, storage fixtures, mechanical handling equipment and inward and outward transport are 'integrated'.

Each individual application has to be dealt with on its own merits because the circumstances of different organisations vary so much. Subject to this qualification, the general approach is to determine the best type and size of unit load for incoming materials. This will indicate the nature of the transport to be used. The transport in turn will influence the design of receipt docks for unloading. At this point the unit load again becomes the controlling factor. It will dictate the type of handling equipment to be used within the warehouse – cranes, fork-lift trucks, conveyors or whatever else is most convenient. The design and layout of the storage fixtures must be suitable for the handling equipment.

From this point, the process goes into reverse, and the handling equipment, picking procedures, dispatch dock design and the type of vehicle used for outgoing materials will be dictated ultimately by the unit load which is considered to be appropriate for issues to customers.

Of course the warehouse building should be designed to accommodate most economically the particular storage fixtures, handling methods and receipt and dispatch docks which have been chosen as most suitable.

Brief notes on a specific simplified example may be helpful. Let us suppose we have a large central warehouse serving a chain of grocery supermarkets. The nature of the goods received, i.e. jars of jam, coffee, etc., tins of biscuits, boxes of cereals and so on are such that the best type of incoming unit load is on an ordinary flat wooden four-way entry pallet. The nature of the goods themselves demands that the incoming transport shall be fully enclosed vans. The size of loads from suppliers varies and the vans may be of 3-tonne, 5-tonne, 10-tonne or even 20-tonne capacity. Therefore the receipt dock must be able to accommodate the largest van. As the vans are closed, only a short canopy is needed at the dock to protect the back end of the vehicle from the weather when the doors are opened. There is no need to have an extensive canopy to keep the rain or snow off the whole vehicle. Because the vans vary in size and height of platform, the doors of the receipt dock are fitted with adjustable metal platforms which can be raised or lowered to form a short 'bridge' between the floor of the warehouse and the floor of the delivery vehicle. Here note that the whole of the warehouse floor is above ground level because of the handling methods. Because pallets are used, the handling equipment inside the warehouse consists of electric fork-lift trucks to unload incoming goods and deposit them in the marshalling area. Pallet transporters are used to take the goods from there to the storage area. Again because the unit load is on a pallet, the storage fixtures are open steel pallet racks, five pallet spaces in height. To make use of this height, high-lift reach-type fork trucks are used to put away and take out pallets which are stored above ground level. So that this particular type of truck can operate, the gangways are 2.5 metres wide.

From here on the outgoing unit load is the governing factor. Because of the mixed nature of the goods to be sent to the various retail supermarkets, box pallets are used for dispatch, so the order picking is done by an electric pallet transporter carrying a box pallet and the picking is done manually. Consignments for each retail outlet are marshalled near the dispatch dock which is similar to the receipt dock. Because of varying volumes of complete loads, outgoing vehicles are of different size and will accommodate variously 12, 15, 18 or 20 box pallets. Fork-lift trucks are employed to load the outgoing vehicles, which again must be of the closed van type.

THE RELATIONSHIP OF MATERIALS HANDLING TO TRANSPORT

If readers wish to study the question of transport in any depth, they are advised to study one of the many excellent textbooks on that specialised and complicated subject.

However, as transportation methods have a bearing on storage and material handling and are linked within the logistics concept, a few general comments may be helpful.

The most important considerations are cost, time and reliability.

Air transport

This remains the major growth area of freight transport. The development of very high-powered aero engines and large, freight-carrying aircraft has reduced the cost, but it is still relatively expensive. Goods terminals have been set up at most major airports, appropriate containers have been designed, and mechanised loading and unloading equipment has reached a high level of efficiency. Air transport has of course the great advantage of speedy delivery, and customs clearance at air terminals is also usually very prompt. It is obvious that the quickest way of sending goods for long distances, overseas, or over undeveloped terrain with poor surface communications is by air. Helicopters are widely employed for the movement of military materials, and in locations where facilities for fixed wing aircraft are not yet developed or are impracticable, such as offshore oil platforms, or work in mountainous regions. It is of course usually necessary to take the loads to and from the airport by other means – usually by road – and so the packages, unit loads, or containers must be designed to harmonise with both forms of transportation. Air transport is most suitable for perishable items and expensive materials. Damage in transit is minimal if the packing is good. At the same time, air freight is extremely fast and very reliable. The rapid growth of this method seems likely to continue.

Road transport

In countries with a good road system vast quantities of goods are carried by road. It is usually more convenient than rail, cheaper than air, and can deliver from door to door without any intermediate handling. Commercial road vehicles are available in many shapes and sizes. They can be open or closed, with flat beds or drop sides. They may be refrigerated or otherwise specially designed for particular materials like oil, chemicals, timber, motor cars, sheet glass, food, etc. It is usually much easier to have specialised road haulage than any other type of transport. It is obviously most suited to inland journeys, but is frequently used even where short sea-ferry journeys are involved, for example, between the UK and continental Europe.

Rail transport

The main disadvantage of the rail method is that unless there are railway sidings at the premises of the consignor and also the consignee, transhipment from rail to road is unavoidable. This increases costs, causes delays, and is liable to result in more damage to the goods in transit. Where sidings do exist, however, the railways may well be cheaper and/or quicker than any other methods. Railways are most suitable for heavy or bulky materials, and for intercity travel over long distances, including overseas if only short sea-ferry trips are involved. The railways also have custom-built trucks for perishable and other special loads. They have the advantage of being able to handle very large consignments, are less liable to delay by bad weather, and the speed of trains is increasing. The Channel tunnel has obvious implications for the increased use of this mode.

Inland waterway transport

This is obviously limited to circumstances where navigable rivers or canals are available. The vessels used are much smaller and slower than seagoing ships, but the cost is usually very low. Inland waterways are suitable for bulk loads like coal, sand, gravel, etc., but can of course be used for other cargoes. Much more use of this mode is made on the European mainland than in Britain.

Trailer mounted container, ramp, 'ride on' pallet transporter and palletised equipment
(Courtesy: Lansing Linde Ltd)

Sea transport

The principal disadvantage of ships is obvious – they can only travel on water and they are slow by comparison with other forms of transport. They also have a problem similar to that of the railways – unless both the consignor and the consignee are on the docks, trans-shipment to some other mode of transport is unavoidable. The large bulk of international trade is still seaborne, and ships are becoming larger, faster and more efficiently designed for their cargoes. For example, there are great tanker fleets to move oil around the world, and the old methods of loading and unloading by derrick crane have been widely superseded by more modern methods. More and more ships are designed with opening sterns or sterns that permit them to be loaded and unloaded by fork-lift trucks, or by roll-on, roll-off methods where the cargo is suitable, e.g., cars and tractors. Much freight is carried by container ships today. These vessels are designed to carry large rectangular containers of a standard size designed to

A standard container being handled by a counterbalanced fork-lift truck
(*Courtesy: Lansing Linde Ltd*)

make the maximum use of cargo space. When fully loaded, containers may weigh anything up to 30 tonnes. The ships are often very large indeed. They may require deep-water docks and purpose-built cranes to load and unload. These docks with the associated special cranes are usually described as container ports. Containers can be taken off the ships and put on either road, rail or coastal transport, and are thus very flexible. They are designed according to international standards for size and construction. They must be very strong and have to be carefully sealed in transit, not only for security but also to meet customs regulations.

The principle of using containers is not confined to shipping. They are also employed in suitable circumstances for inland transport by road and rail. As already mentioned, containers are used in air transport, but of course they are smaller and lighter than the seagoing type and are not always adapted for onward transport by surface means. Air transport containers are often specially shaped to fit the aircraft cargo space. They are therefore difficult to move by other forms of transport.

CHAPTER 15

Procedures manuals

THE NEED FOR PROCEDURES MANUALS

To operate any storehouse, some discipline and routine is inevitable and instructions must be given about procedures. Verbal instructions have obvious limitations and a certain amount of written guidance is a necessity. The bigger the organisation, the more important and numerous written procedures are likely to be and, at some stage, it becomes desirable to revise, extend, standardise and arrange all the existing instructions to produce one comprehensive document, which is called a stores manual. The document is usually printed and issued in the form of a book. It is also common practice for all stores forms to be reviewed, redesigned and standardised, and for specimen forms to be produced either as a part of the manual or as an appendix.

PROCEDURES

Procedures are instructions and rules on how the work of the stores function, or indeed any other function, is to be carried out. Procedures must:

be written;
be based on standard methods of work;
be in a logical sequence:
how to do it;
what to do;
what documents, tools, etc. are required

From procedures, i.e. working instructions, job specifications can be developed. Work measurement and method study also have a role in the compilation, revision and updating of procedures and are considered at the end of this chapter.

The stores procedure manual is like a rule book and might include, for example:

General introduction
Method of stock checking

How to deal with stock losses
How receipts will be controlled
How inspection will be undertaken
How rejected material will be controlled
How issues will be controlled
Special and attractive stocks
How to control and deal with unwanted materials and scrap
Stock control by quantity
Stock recording
Procedures in sub-stores
Control of stocks by value

ADVANTAGES AND DISADVANTAGES OF A MANUAL

The principal advantages and disadvantages of a stores manual are listed below. As a general rule, the need for a manual increases with the size and complexity of the organisation involved, and the advantages are therefore more marked in a large concern.

Advantages

1 Provides in readily accessible form a complete record of all standing instructions.
2 Facilitates the maximum standardisation of procedures and paperwork. This is of major importance, because the standards adopted are those considered to be most satisfactory and economical for the organisation concerned. There is also an incidental saving on the cost of printing forms, which may be considerable.
3 By reasons of standardisation, staff can be trained more quickly and efficiently, they become accustomed to a common procedure and are therefore more easily interchangeable. It is also a simple matter to define the duties of each member of the staff, and this assists supervision.
4 If all storehouses are operating on the same methods, their efficiencies can more easily be compared.
5 If the contents of the manual are agreed in principle with other departments concerned, e.g. production, finance and audit, their procedures can also be designed to fit in with the provisions of the stores manual. This ensures that a satisfactory service is provided and that the arrangements for internal checks are adequate.

Disadvantages

1 A detailed manual tends to limit local initiative unless proper arrangements are made to consider new ideas and to keep up to date.
2 Where there are a number of out-stations, it may be that complete standardisation of procedures is not entirely beneficial to all the units. It is difficult for local staff to appreciate the advantage to the organisation as a whole when, in the interests of standardisation, they are required to change some of their methods for new procedures which are more expensive or even less efficient in the particular circumstances. This can usually be overcome by arranging 'dispensations' to units where such a situation arises, allowing them to depart from the manual instructions within limits in the interests of local efficiency.

PREPARATION OF THE MANUAL

The following paragraphs outline a typical procedure for preparing and distributing a stores manual.

Stores directive

If there is not already a written directive with the full authority of the management covering stores policy and organisation, a suitable document is prepared and issued as the first step, stating clearly the responsibility and authority of the stores department on such matters as:

General policy on stock investment
Control of storehouses and stockyards
Authority for provisioning and stock control
Responsibility for stock checking and review of obsolete and redundant stock
Custody of stock record and stores accounts
Authorisation of issues
Centralisation of storage where considered desirable
Limitation of stockholding points
Standardisation of procedures and forms
Staff gradings and complements

The directive therefore defines the limits within which the stores procedure operates, and conveys authority to the stores department to act within these limits. It may be regarded as the stores 'charter' and is indispensable if policy is to be effectively enforced.

Previous instructions

All existing written instructions and forms are collected and carefully examined. Those which are out of date or have been superseded are eliminated. The remainder are sorted into groups according to their subject matter, e.g. stock checking, issue procedure, provisioning, etc.

Existing practices and systems

Visits are made to all stockholding points to check that current practices and systems are in accordance with present instructions and, where this is not so, to note the differences and the reasons for them. At the same time a record is made of all procedures, forms, books and other documents already in operation on matters not covered by the instructions currently in force.

CONTENTS OF THE MANUAL

At this stage, in the light of the content of the stores directive and the material accumulated relevant to the present position, the scope of the manual is decided and chapter headings listed in logical order. As far as is practicable, these chapters are self-contained and arranged in such a way that they can be issued as separate documents for the use of individual members of the staff whose duties do not require them to have a complete copy of the whole book. For instance a unit storekeeper does not necessarily need information on the detailed procedure to be observed in the stock-control section or in the stores accounts. A specimen list of chapter headings is given below:

Chapters

1 General Instructions
2 Procedure at Unit Stores
3 Procedure at Central Stores
4 Stock Recording
5 Stores Accounting
6 Stock Control by Quantity
7 Stock Control by Value
8 Stock Checking

 9 Standard Pricing
10 General Stock
11 Capital Stock
12 Fixed Assets Withdrawn from Use
13 Obsolete and Redundant Items
14 Reclaimed Material
15 Scrap
16 Packages
17 Stationery Stock

Appendix

   I Stores Vocabulary – Classification and Section Headings
  II Target Stock Levels
 III Summary of Duties of Stores Personnel
 IV Schedule of Returns
  V Periods of Retention of Documents
 VI Flow Charts
VII Specimen Forms

When the chapter headings have been decided, the next step is to list under each chapter the individual items of procedure to be described and the standard forms appropriate to these procedures; for example:

Chapter 2. Procedure at Unit Stores

Categories of stocks

Demands on central stores	– Form PS205
	– Demand on central stores
Purchase requisition action	– Form PS221
	Purchase requisition
Unit stock recording	– Form PS200
	Unit stock record
Receipts – general	
Receipts from trade suppliers	– Form PS201
	Goods inwards book
	Form PS202
	Goods received note
	Form PS203
	Shortage/damage report
Receipts from central stores	– Form PS205
	Demand on central stores
Receipts from other unit stores	– Form PS206
	Transfer form

Returns to store	– Form PS212
	Return to store note
Issues – general	
Issues to consumption	– Form PS208
Transfers to central stores or	
other units stores	Issue note
Sales to employees	

Finally, the first draft of the full script is prepared. At this stage, important points to be watched are as follows:

1 The language used is clear and free from the possibility of misinterpretation, the style being appropriate to the persons who are expected to read it.
2 As far as possible, operations to be performed are described in chronological sequence.
3 Technical terms are defined.
4 The manual says who is responsible for every operation.
5 Chapters are numbered and each paragraph in a chapter also has a number, a new series of numbers being used for the paragraphs in each separate chapter, e.g.
   Chapter 1 paras. 1–75
   Chapter 2 paras. 1–118
   Chapter 3 paras. 1–99.
   This ensures that additional paragraphs can be added to each chapter without too much disturbance of the sequence.
6 Descriptions of persons, procedures and forms are accurate and consistent. For instance it is confusing to refer to the same person as 'storekeeper in charge', 'storekeeper' or 'storeman' in different places. Similarly, a 'provision demand' must not be alternatively described as an 'order request' or 'supply requisition'.
7 When a form is mentioned, its number is always quoted as well as its name.
8 If the original drafts of various chapters are prepared by different people, they are submitted for editing by one person.

Flow charts

Flow charts (which are often included in manuals) are diagrams showing the route travelled by a particular form and its copies, and the operations performed en route (see Fig. 15.1). This briefly illustrates the major points of procedure and is useful in several ways:

1 At the time when a manual is being compiled, the preparation of charts quickly shows up any flaws in the procedure as drafted.

Form PS 212
Return to Store Note

User Department	Storehouse	Stock Control Section	Stores Accounts
1. Raise PS 212 in 3 copies (para. 277)			
2. Return material with No. 1 and 2 copies to storehouse ⟶ ⟶	4. Receive material and No. 1 and 2 copies		
3. Retain No. 3 copy	5. Action No. 1 and 2 copies (paras. 278–80)		
	6. Refer No. 1 copy to stock-control section if necessary, to obtain instructions ⟶ ⟶	7. Receive No. 1 copy	
		8. Insert instructions for dealing with material on No. 1 copy and return No. 1 copy to storehouse (para. 280)	
	9. Receive No. 1 copy ⟵ ⟵ ⟵		
	10. Deal with material as instructed		
	11. Post No. 1 copy to stock record (para. 282)		
	12. Pass No. 1 copy to stores-accounts section ⟶ ⟶ ⟶		15. Receive No. 1 copy
	13. Return No. 2 copy to originator as receipt ⟶		16. Analyse to cost code and classification Post from summary to classification control account (para. 586)
14. Receive No. 2 copy and file ⟵ ⟵			17. File No. 1 copy

Fig. 15.1 A specimen flow chart

2 Charts show the source and destination of documents at a glance and give a much clearer picture than can be obtained by reading the text of the manual itself.
3 Flow charts are useful for the purposes of instruction and, when fixed on the wall above a desk, provide a ready means of reference.

Algorithms

Materials work involves many different but interrelated procedures of a clerical or semi-clerical nature, and it can be helpful when learning an existing procedure, or devising a new one, to represent the procedure in some kind of diagrammatic form. This might be done by means of a flow chart showing the movement of various documents, or by mapping the movement of personnel, but one of the simplest and most widely used conventions for the representation of procedures is the algorithm.

It is possible to depict almost any procedure as an algorithm, using only four symbols.

1 A circle, indicating either the start or finish of the algorithm; the circle will usually contain either the word 'start' or 'end' so there can be no confusion.
2 A rectangle, which will contain an 'action statement' explaining what happens at that point in the diagram. Such statements as 'hand requisition to issuing staff', or 'place material in appropriate bin' are examples of action statements.
3 A diamond, which indicates a decision point or branch in the diagram. Examples of sentences which would appear in diamonds are:

'Is the invoice value greater than £100?' or
'Is the item marked with its correct code number?'

The question will always be answerable 'yes' or 'no', and therefore there will be a branch in the diagram wherever a diamond occurs, one fork to be followed if 'yes' is the answer to the question in the diamond, the other if 'no' is the answer.
4 Arrows, more correctly called flow lines, which connect the other elements of the algorithm and show the sequence of actions and decisions. Arrowheads are usually placed where a flow line enters an algorithm element and where a flow line changes direction.

The following stock checking procedure is represented by the algorithm forming Figure 15.2.

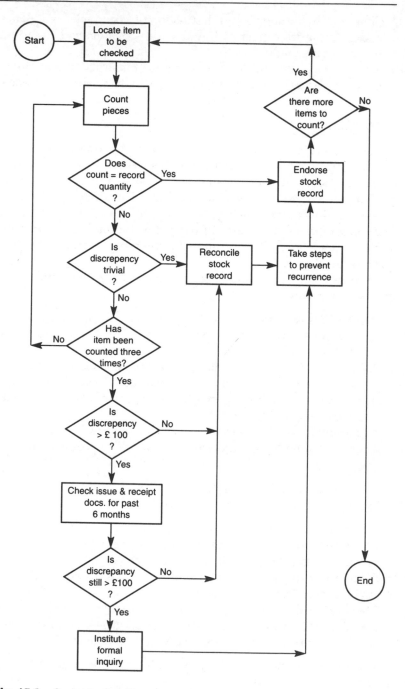

Fig. 15.2 A stock checking procedure

1 Select next item to be counted.
2 Count the item.
3 Check count against record.
4 If there is no discrepancy, endorse record and select next item.
5 If there is only a trivial discrepancy reconcile the record, endorse record and select next item.
6 If the discrepancy is not trivial, count the item twice more, checking each time to see if the discrepancy is found.
7 If the discrepancy is still more than £100 after three counts, then check records for past six months; if not, reconcile and endorse record.
8 If discrepancy after checking six months' records is less than £100 then reconcile and endorse record and go to next item.
9 Institute formal inquiry if discrepancy of more than £100 remains.
10 Take steps to prevent recurrence of any discrepancies found.

Duty sheets

A stores manual will say that certain duties are to be done at stated times by specified persons. The details are fully described in the body of the document but it is often convenient to summarise such duties and list them on a separate 'duty sheet' as an appendix, e.g.:

Duty Sheet for Stock Control Officer

Duty	Manual Paragraph Reference
Fix maximum stocks for unit stores	102
Examine return-to-store notes and give disposal instructions	183
Sign issue orders	194
Authorise issues on loan	197
Review outstanding loan issues	199
Notify unit storekeepers of stock and consumption monthly	216
Examine value of outstanding orders monthly	263
Approve purchase requisitions raised by unit storekeepers	315
Make test checks on the accuracy of stock-record posting	346
Approve central store provision demands	410
Approve sales of material to contractors	427

Returns and reports

The manual gives full details, including forms, for all regular returns or reports made by stores staff either internally within the stores department or externally to other departments or to general management.

There is a summary in the manual listing all such reports and returns, showing who is responsible for preparing them, where they are to be sent and the dates at which they are to be submitted. The manual does not deal with returns and reports of a temporary or non-repetitive nature.

Consultation with users and other departments

When the first draft manual is complete, with specimen forms, flow charts and lists of returns and reports, several copies are made. These are circulated to the heads of user departments (production, maintenance, toolroom, etc.) and other interested departments such as finance and audit. Individual consultations with each of these departments are then arranged to discuss any suggestions they have concerning the effect of the manual provisions on their own responsibilities and procedure, and ultimately to obtain general agreement.

Consultation with out-stations

Where there are a number of separate operating units, copies of the draft manual are sent to unit managers inviting general agreement, details of suggestions for improvement or serious objections.

PUBLICATION AND DISTRIBUTION

After receipt and consideration of all representations from other departments and out-stations, the final draft of the stores manual is prepared and printed.

Technical advice is sought on the most suitable paper and print, and in view of the use for which the document is intended, a strong and serviceable binder is provided. As a general rule it is desirable to issue the book in loose-leaf form to allow for the insertion of additions or amendments from time to time.

Copies of the manual are issued to those concerned by title and not by name, e.g. to the 'Storekeeper in charge of the Steel Store', and not to 'Mr. J. Smith'. Full copies of the text are supplied only where necessary, but all supervisors whose duties are substantially affected at least have a copy of the sections appropriate to their work. Receipts are obtained for all copies issued, and a permanent record is kept showing the original distribution.

Authority

The manual is issued with the authority of the board of directors or general manager, or equivalent.

IMPLEMENTATION OF THE MANUAL

Training courses

The use of a manual implies that all the recipients will read it. So that it shall be fully understood, it will be found helpful to arrange a short course of lectures or demonstrations by qualified officers.

Programme

To ensure that the provisions of the manual are observed as soon as possible, especially where major procedural changes are involved, a programme for its implementation by stages ought to be agreed, showing the dates by which each major section of procedure will be in force in each storehouse or section of the office. Regular reports should be called for, and progress supervised until implementation is complete. During this period, amendments to procedure should be avoided.

Dispensations

It sometimes happens that the circumstances in a particular storehouse or out-station are so unusual that it is not advisable to employ some of the standard procedures, and the supervisor in charge is given a dispensation, that is an authority in writing not to conform to the manual to the extent agreed. Dispensations obviously need to be very strictly limited; otherwise much of the advantage of a standard system is lost.

Amendments and additions

Manuals should not be amended unless it is unavoidable, but in practice some amendments and additions are necessary from time to time to keep pace with changing conditions. The extent to which users and other departments are consulted about these changes depends upon the importance of the subject matter. All amendments and additions should be published on the same kind of paper and in the same typeface as the original book, and the same arrangements made for distribution. There should be a recognised procedure whereby anyone whose work is affected by the instructions may make suggestions for beneficial amendments, additions or deletions, in such a way that his proposals are commented on by his supervisor and any other interested parties and then passed on to the person responsible for editing the manual.

Of course there is no reason why the manual should not be published electronically. As it becomes common place for staff to have a networked PC or workstation at their desk then it becomes feasible to 'call up' the latest edition of a procedure.

Authority. The authority and responsibility for approving amendments, additions and dispensations should be vested in one senior officer, who should sign all the appropriate documents and also be responsible for consulting other departments and obtaining their agreement as necessary.

Instructions on matters not included in the manual

A stores manual, as a rule, covers only standing procedures and there is still a need for some other form of stores instructions for everyday use on matters which cannot await the preparation of manual amendments or which are of a temporary or trivial nature. All such instructions, before issue, should be scrutinised by the manual editor:

1 To make sure that they do not conflict with the provisions of the manual.
2 To note those which are of sufficient importance to be included in the manual in due course.

The preparation and printing of manual amendments is normally a fairly slow operation. For this reason the majority of stores instructions are issued separately as the need arises and, where necessary, incorporated in the manual at a later date.

WORK STUDY

Work study is employed to ensure the best possible use of human and material resources in carrying out a specified activity. Work study finds several potential applications in the storehouse or stockyard environment, for example it might be used to improve the layout of the receiving or dispatch areas, to select an appropriate picking procedure or to devise an efficient stock location system.

The application of work study techniques requires little capital outlay and has been found by many organisations to be a very cost-effective activity, the main advantages being:

1 It is systematic, thus ensuring that facts about an operation are gathered and taken into account.
2 It is an effective means of setting standards of performance, thus enabling proper planning and control to take place.
3 The savings resulting from properly applied work study begin immediately.
4 The savings are not 'one off' benefits, but go on for as long as the operation continues in the revised form.
5 Work study is a very versatile approach; it can be applied in warehouses, factories, offices, distribution activities – almost anywhere.

Basic work study procedure

Work study embraces *method study*, which is the systematic recording, analysis and critical examination of existing and proposed ways of doing work and the development and application of easier and more effective methods. It also encompasses *work measurement* which is the application of techniques designed to establish the work content of a specified task by determining the time required for carrying it out at a defined standard of performance by a qualified worker.

In a complete work study exercise, there are eight basic steps:

1 Select   – the job or process to be studied.
2 Record   – by using a suitable recording technique.
3 Examine   – the facts, consider each operation critically.
4 Develop   – alternative methods of fulfilling the function.
5 Measure   – the quantity of work involved.
6 Define   – the new method and related time, show savings.
7 Install   – demonstrate the advantages of the new method to management and staff and install the new method with joint cooperation.
8 Maintain – set up control procedures to continually monitor performance.

Critical examination. Each stage in any operation carried out by the worker or each of the items involved is critically examined. There are various operations recording techniques available to the work study practitioner. The most familiar problem is known as the six step pattern:

1 What is actually done, is it necessary?
2 Why is the activity necessary?
3 Where is it being done, is it suitable?
4 When is it done, need it be done then?
5 Who is doing it, could it be done better by someone else?
6 How is it being done, could it be done better?

Glossary of abbreviations

ACDS	Anti-corrosion dessicant system
AGV	Automatically guided vehicle
AID	Aeronautical Inspection Directorate
ANS	American national standard
ANSI	American National Standards Institute
API	American Petroleum Institute
AVDP	Avoirdupois
AWB	Air way bill
AWG	American wire gauge
BA	British Association (thread)
BEAMA	British Electrical and Allied Manufacturers Association
BG	Birmingham gauge
BHP	Brake horsepower
BL	Bale; barrel
BOM	Bill of Materials
BPICS	British Production and Inventory Control Society
BRG	Bearing
BS	British standard
BSF	British standard fine (thread)
BSI	British Standards Institution
BSP	British standard pipe (thread)
BSW	British standard Whitworth (thread)
BWG	Birmingham wire gauge
CAD	Computer aided design
CAM	Computer aided manufacture
CC	Cubic centimetres; centrifugal casting
CD Rom	Compact disc read only memory
CEN	European Committee for Standardisation
CIE	Company (French)
CIF	Cost insurance and freight
CIPS	Chartered Institute of Purchasing and Supply
C and I	Cost and insurance
COD	Cash on delivery
COSHH	Control of Subtances Hazardous to Health
CP	Charter party

CPA	Contract price adjustment; critical path analysis
CTS	Crates
DC	Direct current
DEG	Degree
DIA	Diameter
DIN	Deutsches Institut für Normung (Germany)
DISCH	Discharge
DRG	Drawing
DWT	Deadweight tonnage
EA	Each
EC	European Community
EDI	Electronic data interchange
E & OE	Errors and omissions excepted
EOQ	Economic order quantity
EPOS	Electronic point of sale
EQT	Equipment
ETA	Estimated time of arrival
FAQ	Fair average quality
FAS	Free alongside ship
FIFO	First in, first out
FIG	Figure
FLT	Fork–lift truck
FO	Firm offer
FOB	Free on board
FOC	Free of charge
FRT	Freight
FT	Foot; feet
GR	Grade; gross
GRWT	Gross weight
GRN	Goods received note
GRV	Goods received voucher
HEX	Hexagon
HMC	Her Majesty's Customs
HRC	Hardness, Rockwell C-scale
HTS	High tensile strength
ID	Inside diameter
IL	Institute of Logistics
IM or IMP	Imperial
INSTR	Instrument
ISWG	Imperial standard wire gauge

JIS	Japanese industrial standard
JIT	Just in time
KG, KILO,	
KILOG,	Kilogramme
KILOGRAM	
LB	Pound
LH	Left hand
LIFO	Last in, first out
LO/LO	Lift on, lift off
LPG	Liquefied petroleum gas
MAX	Maximum
MESC	Materials and Equipment Standard Code
MHE	Mechanical handling equipment
MIN	Minimum
MISC	Miscellaneous
MPS	Master production schedule
MRO	Maintenance repair and operating
MRP	Material(s) requirements planning
NA	Not applicable
NBS	National Bureau of Standards (US)
NC	American national coarse (thread)
NF	Norme française
NOM	Nominal
NOS	Numbers
NPL	National Physical Laboratory
NT	Net
OD	Outside diameter
OR	Owner's risk
OS	Oversize
OZ	Ounce
PA	Per annum
PC	Personal computer
PO	Post Office
POB	Post Office box
POD	Place of delivery
PRESS	Pressure
PPM	Parts per million
QUAL	Quality
QTY	Quantity

RECD	Received
RH	Right hand
RORO	Roll on, roll off
RPM	Revolutions per minute
SAE	Society of Automotive Engineers; stamped addressed envelope
SG	Specific gravity
SPEC	Specification
SQ	Square
SS	Stainless steel
STD	Standard
STK	Stock
SWG	Standard wire gauge
SWL	Safe working load
SWP	Safe working pressure
TBG	Tubing
TEMP	Temperature
THD	Thread; threaded
TIR	Transport International Routier
TPI	Threads per inch
TQM	Total Quality Management
TS	Tensile strength
UL	Unit load
ULW	Unladen Weight
UNC	Unified coarse (thread)
UNF	Unified fine (thread)
US	Undersize; Unserviceable
USS	United States standard
VA	Value analysis
VAR	Various
VE	Value engineering
WG	Wire gauge
WP	Working pressure
WT	Weight
WW	Whitworth (thread)
YS	Yield strength

INDEX

L982980